JESUS IS THE WAY

CHRIST • CHURCH • SACRAMENT

The Third Volume of a Dominican Series
of Theology Textbooks
for Youth

IN CONFORMITY
WITH THE *CATECHISM*
OF THE CATHOLIC CHURCH

Published by
The Priory Press
7200 Division Street
River Forest, Illinois 60305

"The Ad Hoc Committee to Oversee the Use of the Catechism, National Conference of Catholic Bishops, has found this catechetical series, copyright 2000, to be in conformity with the *Catechism of the Catholic Church.*"

Staff and Contributors

General Editor	Dr. Gerald Lordan, Ph.D., Director of Institutional Advancement, Fenwick High School, Oak Park, Illinois
Manuscript Editor	Mrs. Mary Lou Lammers, mother, teacher, paralegal
Art and Design	Mr. John Sarsfield, M.Ed., M.A. Art Institute
Sponsor	Fr. William J. Bernacki, O.P., M.Ed., past President-Principal, Fenwick High School

THE AUTHORS OF THIS VOLUME

Priory Press is especially grateful to the first general editor of the Dominican Series, Fr. richard Butler, O.P., Ph.D., who with Fr. Damian Fandal, O.P., S.T.D., originally authored Jesus is the Way. Fr. Robert B. riley, O.P., nationally know for his lectures and retreats and was on staff of Priory Press as well as Fr. Norman Fenton, O.P. Much of this volume bears their wise input. However, new materials have been added from the *Catechism of the Catholic Church* and from recent papal documents to enhance and bring its contents into the new millennium.

We are especially greatful to Mr. Bartholomew J. Juncer, MRE (Religious Education), MA (High School Administration), Priory Press Advisor for Catechetical Update and Revision.

Library of Congress Control Number 2001094127
Copyright © 2000 AD
All Rights Reserved
ISBN Number 1931161038
Printed in the United States of America

Imprimi Potest:	Very Reverend Donald J. Goergen, O.P. Prior Provincial
Nihil Obstat:	Reverend Zachary Hayes, O.F.M. Censor Deputatus
Imprimatur: **May 19, 1986**	Most Reverend James P. Roache Vicar General, Archdiocese of Chicago

Fourth Printing, First Catechetical Update and Revision
December 8, 2000   Feast of the Immaculate Conception of our Blessed Lady.

Acknowledgements

We are grateful to:

Very Reverend Donald J. Goergen, O.P., Prior Provincial, for his encouragement.

Fr. John Marr, O.P., S.T.D., first official reader and Fr. Victor LaMotte, O.P. for his spiritual insights.

Ms. Priscilla Borsch, for her technical assistance and typing.

Mr. Tom Sommers and Mr. Dan Sommers, for their printing advice and expertise.

Mrs. Mary Henson for her computer technology.

Mr. Matt Kipp, for his preparation of the index.

For those who hunger for truth in the culture of life.

Sacred Scripture quotations are taken from the Revised Standard Version except quotations from the New American Bible which are designated as (NAB).

CONTENTS

PREFACE

THE NATURE AND DIVISION OF THEOLOGY

The time has come to reflect again on the precise meaning of *theology*. Most schools speak of "courses in religion" and students often refer to "taking religion."

Religion courses can be varied and extended in content: ethics or morality, the history of the Church, comparative religion, liturgy, social justice, the sacraments, Church law, Bible teaching, et cetera. In other words, various aspects of religious doctrine are chosen, sometimes to favor popular interests: the diabolic, death and dying, atheism in our time, charismatic experiences. Such courses teach something about their subjects, but they are not organized and lack a systematic order and a logical sequence. Theology is a different kind of study, as we will see.

The word "religion" may be deceiving. Objectively it refers to some body of doctrine with some rites and rituals to which some persons adhere. This notion could apply to a great many sects, and it does. An old joke goes: "If you want work, go to California and start a new religion."

Subjectively we mean the following of a particular body of believers. That in itself is often distorted because many persons do not practice their faith.

Simply going to a church of some denomination does not make a person "religious." It may attract people with no real faith that is virtuous, but true faith is a habit of living a virtuous life. Many go to church through a sense of duty or obligation or for some social benefits. Their religion then is shallow, perhaps hypocrisy. The Church, it has been said, is the bark of Peter. You cannot survive the storms of life with one foot on the ship and the other on the ground. The non-practicing Catholic is even a contributing cause of atheism according to the bishops assembled for Vatican II.

What is the relation between "religion" and "theology"?

What is theology? Theology comes from two Greek words: *theos,* meaning God, and *logos,* meaning word. Words express ideas. When ideas are properly organized and presented in a logical way, we have what we call a science. Literally, then, theology means the study of God. Consider other "ologies": biology, sociology, psychology, anthropology.

All of the natural sciences are logically organized and begin with nature itself. From observations and experience, the human mind is able to deduce certain conclusions. Such sciences begin with reasonable principles, such as *every effect must have a cause.* The study of God is different only because it begins with God as he has revealed himself; hence this study goes from cause to effect as the principle and is guided by revelation. Theology therefore uses both induction and deduction. Its principal function is to draw out and expand the elements of truth found in the deposit of faith. Theology is not merely a body of knowledge but wisdom, a survey of all things, because theology is about God and his creation, especially human beings.

The sources of theology are Sacred Scripture, clarified by sacred tradition, and presented in each age by the Magisterium (the official teaching of the Church). Sacred Scripture is the Bible, the work of God himself as transmitted by his chosen ones to all of us. Sacred tradition (from the Latin *tradere*, to hand over or hand down) refers to the transmission of the deposit of faith from the apostles to our own time. To avoid any errors in interpretation, Christ handed over to the apostles and their successors an infallible teaching and governing authority. ("Infallible" simply means "without error.") When the Church exercises that authority through our Pope and our bishops, we know with certainty, guided by the Holy Spirit, the official teaching of the Church. Then we can be sure of the content of our faith. Theologians amplify these sources but should not contradict them. If they do so, they are heretics.

Theology is divided into three parts according to the area of revelation it covers. The first part explains God and his creation and his call to us to our salvation and everlasting life (covered in this series by *God Calls You*). The second part of theology is on our relation to God, how we respond to his call through our behavior by the practice of faith, a life of grace and of virtue. (*Responding to God* is the title of this second section of our series on theology.)

The third and the final part of theology concentrates on Christ, God made man. We consider the mystery of Jesus, his person, his personality, his mission, and redemption. Then we examine his Church, its nature, its history, its God-given mission, and also the mystery of our supernatural life above and beyond our natural life. This is the life of grace which comes to us in special ways through our Lord, Jesus Christ. Hence we entitle this book very simply *Jesus is the Way*.

THE MYSTERY OF CHRIST

Now when Jesus came into the district of Caesarea Philippi, he asked his disciples, "Who do men say that the Son of man is?" And they said, "Some say John the Baptist, others say Elijah, and others Jeremiah or one of the prophets." He said to them, "But who do you say that I am?" Simon Peter replied, "You are the Christ, the Son of the Living God." And Jesus answered him, "Blessed are you, Simon Bar-Jonah! For flesh and blood has not revealed this to you, but my Father who is in heaven. And I tell you, you are Peter, and on this rock I will build my Church, and the powers of death shall not prevail against it. I will give you the keys of the kingdom of heaven, and whatever you bind on earth shall be bound in heaven, and whatever you loose on earth shall be loosed in heaven." Then he strictly charged the disciples to tell no one that he was the Christ.

— Mt. 16: 13-20

Chapter 1

THE PERSON OF JESUS CHRIST

The most important question   Ever since he appeared among us we have all been faced with the crucial question: Who is Jesus Christ? Another prophet, as the Muslims say? Another man, but of heroic proportions, like Ghandi and Dr. Albert Schweitzer, as the Unitarians today might respond? A man, surely, but with more of the so-called "divine spark" in him than most of us, as the modern agnostic might admit?

Jesus pressed this pivotal question on his apostles; he also forces it on us in our own time. We cannot avoid his insistent question now when he asks us: "But who do you say that I am?" Simon Peter, always impulsive and blunt, did not hesitate to reply: "You are the Christ, the Son of the living God." Consequently Jesus declared that he would build his Church on him, with all the responsibilities that charge entails. If we can make that same profession of faith, we too incur responsibilities, continuing his Church with a firm commitment to the moral ramifications of a Christian life. For we truly are "the Church," continuing the tradition of Christian faith in our time. This lays a heavy burden on us, but we cannot avoid our obligations or shirk our responsibilities. We are either in the bark of Peter or out of it. If we try to straddle our position, half in and half out, we are doomed to drown in the murky sea of noncommittal indifference.

We are studying Catholic theology. We must explore the sources of the Church's fundamental teaching about Christ, through the revelations of Sacred Scripture, and the orthodox tradition of the Church through the ages, and the Magisterium, the definite official teaching of the Church in our time.

The fundamental teaching of the Church   The Church's principal teaching about Christ is his *Incarnation,* that the Second Person of the Blessed Trinity, God himself, assumed, at a predetermined moment in history, a true human nature. Christ is God and Christ is man, and there is but one Christ. As St. John, in the prologue to his gospel, put it very simply, "The Word was made flesh and dwelt among us." The term "word" is from the Greek (logos) which means word or idea or a mental concept, used to indicate the Second Person of the Trinity.

More formally, we can say that Jesus Christ is: *One person, the Son of God, with two complete natures, a divine and a human, each truly distinct from the other and yet most intimately united in, and according to, that divine person.*

The two essential mysteries of our faith are the Trinity, three persons in the one divine nature, and the Incarnation, two natures in one person. A mystery of faith is not a contradiction, but a truth we cannot comprehend because of our limited experience. I am one person with one nature, a human one, and all human beings that I know are such.

A person is a subject, one who is, while nature is the principle of activity which enables a person to do what he is capable of doing. We may say that a certain athletic star is "superhuman," but we mean that he possesses unusual ability and that he performs to the utmost of his ability. Characters such as "Superman" are products of our imagination. For no human being can fly without mechanical assistance. We may say romantically that some person we know is "divine"; but we fully realize that we are using that adjective in an exaggerated way, employing what we call hyperbole.

Hence, three persons in one nature, or one person having two natures, is incomprehensible to me and therefore it is a mystery, something that is altogether beyond my experience.

In the union of body and soul (a human nature), there emerges a human person. Not so with Christ. His human nature does not give rise to a human person. The only person involved is the Word, the Second Person of the Trinity. To the person of the Word belongs the divine nature. The person of the Word assumed a human nature. In the Incarnation, the divine nature and a human nature are joined in the *person of the Word*. The Greek word for person is "hypostasis"; thus the term *Hypostatic Union* to designate the union of the two natures in Christ.

The two natures reside in the one person, the Son of God. I am a person and I have a human nature. The Son of God is a divine person who, in the Incarnation, assumed a human nature. So, Jesus Christ is one person who, because of his divine nature, is God, and who, because of his human nature, is man. Jesus Christ is both God and man, or the God-man, or the man-God.

The union of the two natures in Christ is not superficial, but deep; not vague, but definite; not commonplace, but unique. Conceivably, the divine and human natures could have been placed in contact with each other in an accidental union, comparable to the union between a man and his hat. The divine plan was that God would unite a human nature to himself so intimately that there would be a genuine, authentic unity, not two things in casual contact. Nor would there be a blending of divinity and humanity, so that what resulted would be something that was neither God nor man. Christ was both God and man, and each perfectly.

It is possible to conceive various ways in which God could have joined a human nature to himself; but of them all, the most wonderful, the most intimate union possible, was the union that was actually established by God. We have some understanding of the intimacy that exists between our own person and nature. In Christ, the human person which is the normal complement is "supplanted" by the person of the Son of God the Father. To imagine a closer union is not possible.

That is precisely why we refer to the Incarnation and the Trinity as mysteries of faith. We *believe* in these incomprehensible mysteries because we accept God's revelation of them.

THE DIVINITY OF CHRIST

Theology's principal source is Sacred Scripture. The evidence of the divinity of Christ is manifest in both Sacred Scripture and the tradition of the Church, which is proposed to us through the Magisterium, the official teaching of the Church.

The Old Testament alone is not an adequate source Why? It offers little more than foreshadowings of the full revelation to come through Jesus Christ. Such advance indications as given were vague and sometimes symbolic, recognized more now by hindsight than they were recognized and accepted by the Jews generally. Through the prophets that appeared in salvation history, they looked forward to a Messiah. ("Messiah" is a Hebrew word for "anointed one," which is translated into Greek as *christos*; hence the English word "Christ." The name "Jesus" is a form of Joshua, a name frequently given to newborn Jewish boys during the time of Jesus.)

Some Jews knew, especially from the prophet Isaiah, that the coming of the Messiah would be extraordinary. Isaiah declares that the Savior will not have a human father (7:14) and that his name will be Emmanuel, meaning "God with us" (from the passages 7:14 and 8:8). These hints about the extraordinary nature of the Messiah are amplified in a later passage: "For a child is born to us, a son is given us; / upon his shoulder dominion rests. / They name him Wonder-Counselor, God-Hero / Father-Forever, Prince of Peace." (Is. 9:5 NAB). All of these titles have the authentic ring of divinity about them, especially "Strong God" which in Hebrew is *el gibbor*, a title exclusively reserved for *Yahweh*, the one true God. Two additional passages from the Book of Psalms (2:7 and 109:1-3) reenforce this striking superiority of the Messiah. The author of the Epistle to the Hebrews (1:5) teaches that the verse Ps. 2:7 speaks of a divine sonship by nature, and in this is the superiority of the Messiah found.

But the actual Incarnation, God becoming man, was beyond the expectations of the Jews. In fact, because of political oppression, their anticipation turned to a desire for a political Messiah who would liberate them from their bondage. That is why even the chosen apostles of Jesus, despite his fuller revelation to them, still thought and talked about his promised kingdom as a temporal one. Hence, their fear and dismay at the time of Christ's suffering and crucifixion and their hesitation in accepting his resurrection. While the Old Testament provides only shadowy clues about the divinity of Christ, the New Testament abounds in evidence that may be disbelieved but cannot be discredited, especially in the light of what happened to Jesus according to historical witnesses.

An act of faith is necessary to accept this evidence and act accordingly. But there is no doubt of the credibility of this essential revelation of Jesus Christ. The approach to Christian faith is to understand and then take the necessary step of faith. Understanding, one of the gifts of the Holy Spirit which we receive in baptism, is given to us without any effort on our part. But with maturity that supernatural wisdom should be, if possible, reinforced by our own exploration of the content of our faith. That is why we study theology.

The evangelists, authors of the New Testament, clearly indicate the belief of the faithful in the divinity of Christ St. Matthew offers a complete catechesis (originally an oral instruction) given principally by St. Peter. He himself was an apostle of Jesus, well versed in what the Lord said and did, and was a witness to the divine prophecies and miracles, especially the resurrection of Jesus. Mark accents the divinity of Christ, relating many incidents which lead to the inescapable conclusion that Christ was the Son of God. St. Luke, an evangelist and first-hand witness, a medical man of Greek origin, accompanied St. Paul on his second and third apostolic missions, and recorded his own personal experience in his oral catechesis as well as the thoughts of Paul. The apostle John professedly wrote his gospel to establish the divinity of the Messiah, and in the prologue of that gospel he gave us the most profound understanding of this great mystery.

> In the beginning was the Word, and the Word was with God, and the Word was God. He was in the beginning with God; all things were made through him, and without him was not anything made that was made. In him was life, and the life was the light of men. The light shines in the darkness, and the darkness has not overcome it.
>
> There was a man sent from God, whose name was John. He came for testimony, to bear witness to the light, that all might believe through him. He was not the light, but came to bear witness to the light.
>
> The true light that enlightens every man was coming into the world. He was in the world, and the world was made through him, yet the world knew him not. He came to his own . . .
>
> Jn. 1:1-11

(This prologue should be read in its entirety. All scriptural references should be read by the student.)

Christ claimed for himself certain attributes which are proper to God alone:

1. He claimed for himself *divine power*. By his own power he worked miracles and in return required an act of faith, e.g., the curing of the blind man (Matt. 9:18). "Power went forth from him and healed all" (Lk. 6:19). He perceived this power going forth from him (Lk. 8:46). He worked miracles in God's name (Lk. 10:17) and he bestowed a share in it on his disciples (Lk. 10:9, 10:17, Mk. 16:17, Matt. 10:8).

2. He claims for himself *supreme moral authority*. He declares this power equal to that of God. He communicates his commands with the same authority as God did in giving the commandments to Moses when he declares the indissolubility of marriage (Mk. 10:7-9). He proclaims himself Lord of the Sabbath (Mk. 2:23-28).

3. He claims *absolute authority*. He forgives sins, which only God can do (Mk. 2:5-12, Lk. 7:47-50), and he assumes the supreme power of moral judgment, likewise proper only to God (Matt. 24:30-31, Mk. 13:26, Lk. 21:27, 36). For him, one should be willing to leave all things (Matt. 10:37-40, Mk. 10:29-30, Lk. 12:26); and those who wish to be saved should take up their own crosses and follow him (Matt. 19:29, Mk. 8:34-35, Lk. 22:29-30).

4. He says he is *the very Son of God*. Three times Jesus proclaimed his divine filiation in words which cannot be otherwise interpreted: before his disciples on the occasion of Peter's confession of faith (Matt. 16:13-20, Mk. 8:27-50, Lk. 9:15-22); before the people when he explains the allegory of the wicked vine-dresser, applying it to himself so clearly that the chief priests and the Pharisees perfectly understood him (Matt. 21:33-44, Mk. 12:1-12, Lk. 20:9-19); and before the judges of the Sanhedrin (Matt. 26:63-66, Mk. 14:61-64, Lk. 22:66-71).

Before the Sanhedrin he is asked a double question. First, is he the Christ, the Messiah promised by the prophets? When he answers affirmatively, applying to himself the words of the Messianic psalm (109:1), they put a second, even more crucial question to him: Is he, then, the Son of God? "You have said it," Jesus replied. The high priest then, we are told, tore his garments in disgust, shouting that Jesus had blasphemed, and, without hearing more, he demanded his death—all certain signs of recognition of the fact that Jesus had solemnly affirmed his divine sonship.

To declare himself Messiah or even Son of God in a metaphorical sense would have been no blasphemy, nor would death have been the penalty for such a declaration. The chief priests understood his claims very literally: "We have a law, and by that law, he ought to die, because he has made himself the Son of God" (Jn. 19:7). *It was precisely because Jesus claimed divinity that he was put to death.* Jesus made his claims clearly and unequivocally.

5. He explicitly proclaimed *his divine nature.* When his disciples returned from their first mission, highly enthusiastic about their effectiveness, he reminded them: "All things have been delivered to me by my Father; and no one knows who the Son is except the Father, or who the Father is except the Son and anyone to whom the Son chooses to reveal him" (Lk. 10:22).

When he questions the Pharisees concerning the Messiah and his origin, they say that he was the son of David. Jesus pursues his argument: "How is it then that David, inspired by the Spirit, said:

'The Lord said to my Lord,
Sit at my right hand,
Till I put thy enemies under thy feet?'
If David thus calls him Lord, how is he his son?"
(Mt. 22:43-45; the reference Jesus quotes is from Psalm 110:1)

14

Similar accounts of this exchange are given by Mark 12:35-37 and by Luke 20:41-44.

Of all the evangelists, the apostle John most clearly and insistently proclaims the divinity of Christ. He emphasizes in every possible way the transcendence and divinity of Jesus. The very purpose of his gospel, he says, is "that you may believe that Jesus is the Christ, the Son of God, and that believing you may have life in his name" (20:31).

He shows Jesus asserting his divinity before the Jews:

"Truly, truly, I say to you before Abraham was, I am" (8:58).

". . . the Father is in me and I in the Father" (10:38).

Before the disciples at the Last Supper, he says:

"I am the way, and the truth, and the life; no one comes to the Father, but by me" (14:6).

"Philip said to him, 'Lord, show us the Father, and we shall be satisfied.' Jesus said to him, 'Have I been with you so long, and yet you do not know me, Philip? He who has seen me has seen the Father; how can you say, 'Show us the Father?' Do you not believe that I am in the Father and the Father in me?" (14:8-10)

Not only directly but indirectly through his miracles, Jesus manifests his divine power and by his prophecies he shows his divine knowledge.

The testimony of miracles The miracles attributed to Jesus are many and indicate a power over nature that belongs to God alone. He heals the sick, enables the blind to see and the lame to walk. He not only works physical miracles but spiritual ones as well, converting sinners and even forgiving sins. He absolves from sin, reconciling the sinner to God, as he did with the woman taken in adultery. This manifest power of absolution shocks the indignant Jews who were hostile to him.

And getting into a boat he crossed over and came to his own city. And behold, they brought to him a paralytic, lying on his bed; and when Jesus saw their faith he said to the paralytic, "Take heart, my son; your sins are forgiven." And behold, some of the scribes said to themselves, "This man is blaspheming." But Jesus, knowing their thoughts, said, "Why do you think evil in your hearts? For which is easier to say, 'Your sins are forgiven,' or to say, 'Rise and walk?' But that you may know that the Son of man has authority on earth to forgive sins"–he then said to the paralytic–"Rise, take up your bed and go home." And he rose and went home.

–Mt. 9:1-7

The greatest of his miracles was the raising of the dead to life, as he did for his friend, Lazarus, and the only son of the widow of Naim, and the daughter of Jairus, a ruler of the synagogue. Above all, by his own power, he raises himself from the dead. His resurrection is the keystone of our faith and the foundation of our hope that he will raise us up also from death to everlasting life.

. . . If Christ has not been raised, then our preaching is in vain and your faith is in vain. We are even found to be misrepresenting God, because we testified of God that he raised Christ, whom he did not raise if it is true that the dead are not raised. For if the dead are not raised, then Christ has not been raised. If Christ has not been raised, your faith is futile and you are still in your sins. Then those who have fallen asleep in Christ have perished. If for this life only we have hoped in Christ, we are of all men most to be pitied.

–I Cor. 15:14-19

The testimony of prophecy   To foretell the free actions of others is a prescience possessed by God alone. We may guess what people may do based on their past behavior; but we cannot know precisely and accurately if we attempt any predictions of the future. We are guessing. Fortune tellers are also only guessing about the future, and so are contemporary professed prophets. Only God can predict human events in the future. He has shared some of his foreknowledge with chosen persons who figured in the old covenant of God with man. God become man in Jesus Christ revealed with accuracy certain future events to his disciples: the fall of Jerusalem and the destruction of the temple, signs of the end of the world, the defection of Judas, the denials of Peter and, in detail, his own personal fate.

From that time Jesus began to show his disciples that he must go to Jerusalem and suffer many things from the elders and the chief priests and scribes, and be killed, and on the third day be raised.

–Mt. 16:21

. . . for he was teaching his disciples, saying to them, "The Son of man will be delivered into the hands of men, and they will kill him; and when he is killed, after three days he will rise." But they did not understand the saying, and they were afraid to ask him.

–Mk. 9:31-32

"The Son of man must suffer many things, and be rejected by the elders and chief priests and scribes, and be killed, and on the third day be raised."

–Lk. 9:22

The testimony of internal evidence and history

Every historian of that time and at the present time agrees that Jesus Christ was an extraordinary person who accomplished an unusual amount of achievements and impressions during his brief lifetime. All may not accept his divinity, which requires both faith and grace, but none deny his astounding effect on all mankind throughout the course of history. Not only were his thoughts lofty and his expressions accurate, but the truth and beauty he contributed to men of every age have inspired heroic virtue in many of his followers. Especially significant is the perpetuity of the Church founded by Christ, despite persecutions and divisions and scandals. To follow Christ has never been easy in any century; yet his Church endures as an historical sign of the divine guidance of its founder.

Reflecting on the trials and tribulations of the Church throughout history, John Henry Cardinal Newman perceived the assurance of Christ that he would be with his Church all days, a promise that no mere human being could ever make:

In truth, the whole course of Christianity from the first, when we come to examine it, is but one series of troubles and disorders. Every century is like every other and to those who live in it seems worse than all times before it.

17

The Church is ever ailing, and lingers on in weakness, always bearing about in the body the dying of the Lord Jesus, that the life also of Jesus might be made manifest in her body. Religion seems ever expiring, schisms dominant, the light of truth dim, its adherents scattered. The cause of Christ is ever in its last agony, as though it were but a question of time whether it fails finally this day or another.

–From the first volume of his *Via Media*

The testimony of the apostles We must bear in mind that the apostles Jesus chose were not among the wisest and most courageous men of his day. Most of them were simple peasants, many of them fishermen. Even after they had witnessed the wonders that Christ worked, after his miracles and prophecies, after he had intimately explained himself and his mission, after all his extraordinary deeds and words– all of them, except John, fled from the ignominy and the scandal of the cross. Frightened, they huddled together in an upper room, hiding from their enemies among the Jews and the Romans. Only *after* their witness to his resurrection and their reception of the Holy Spirit did they go fearlessly to preach and to be persecuted and to face an inevitable death, usually of a cruel nature. Why? Why did they so change and readily give themselves up to martyrdom unless they were at last fully convinced of the divinity of Jesus and the glory of the kingdom of heaven that he preached? They were not fanatics or blind zealots; they were not that type of men. It was the power of the Resurrection and the enlightenment of the Holy Spirit which opened their minds and hearts to the truth that Jesus is Christ the Lord.

St. John Chrysostom, a bishop and doctor of the Church in the fourth century, thus commented in one of his homilies on the conversion of the apostles after the resurrection of Jesus:

The cross, preached by ignorant men, persuaded the world, not of unimportant matters, but of God and true religion, of the evangelical way of life and future judgment. It turned the uneducated rustic into a true philosopher. Here the folly of God was wiser than men, the weakness of God stronger than men.

Stronger in what way? In that it pervaded the world and took men by storm; in that although countless men tried to eradicate the very name of the crucified, the opposite happened–his name flourished. Living men warred against a dead man and were impotent.

Paul says therefore: "The weakness of God is stronger than men." That the apostolic preaching was divine is thereby made clear. How could twelve men–and ignorant ones at that–have devised such an immense undertaking? How could men who perhaps never saw the city or its forum set out to besiege the universe? The evangelist who writes of these men shows them to us as fearful men of no great talent; he does not hide their defects–one of the best arguments for his truthfulness. What does he say of them? That when Christ was arrested, the leader among them denied him and the others fled.

How, then, did the apostles challenge the whole world if, as you claim, Jesus did not rise from the dead and speak to them and encourage them? Why, even while he was alive and with them, they could not stand up to the Jews! Had he failed to rise, would they not have said: "He could not save himself. How can he protect us? In his own lifetime he conquered no one. Are we to persuade the whole world in the power of his name?" No, it is evident that had the apostles not seen him risen and been given proof of his power, they would not have ventured on so risky an undertaking.

–Homilies on First Corinthians

So it is with us today. Only when we understand and accept the fact of Jesus' Resurrection from the dead are we able to acknowledge the he is the Messiah. By the enlightenment and grace of the Holy Spirit we are able to believe and proclaim, "Jesus Christ is Lord." This is the essence of our faith.

THE HUMANITY OF CHRIST

What do human beings do?　　They live and die, suffer and cry, eat and sleep, rejoice and are saddened, grow weary and sometimes discouraged, show love and anger, express admiration for some and scorn for others, are compassionate and patient; they are tempted and they pray; they enjoy family life and the satisfaction of labor; at times they feel lonely and abandoned.

So many things can be said of human nature, and they are all experienced by Jesus Christ. As St. Paul says, "He was like us in all things but sin."

The humanity of Jesus is abundantly attested to by the gospels. Mary conceives (although by the direct action of God rather than by man) and she bears a son, flesh of her flesh, fruit of her womb. The holy family returns to Nazareth from Bethlehem, and there the carpenter's son advanced in wisdom and age and grace before God and men. Simeon holds the child in his arms, the sinful woman dries the feet of Jesus and kisses them, John reclines on his breast. Wonderment is his, and anger, and pity, and sorrow. He is wearied by his journeyings, he sleeps, he needs food and drink. On the cross he suffers in body and spirit and is crucified. Then, his pierced body is laid in the sepulchre.

After his predicted resurrection from the dead, solidly attested to by many witnesses, he says to the disciples who thought they saw a spirit: "Why are you so troubled, and why do questions rise in your hearts? See my hands and my feet, that it is I myself; handle me, and see; for a spirit has not flesh and bones as you see that I have" (Lk. 24:38-39). To prove his point, he asks for something to eat.

In almost all of his appearances to his apostles, he shares with them something to eat, a human action to offset the sudden manner of showing himself in their midst.

Yet some in the early years of Christianity still thought that his body might have been an illusion, a mere appearance. The first heresy was Docetism (from the Greek *dokein,* meaning "appearance"). The first heresies in the early centuries of the Church centered on the mysteries of the Trinity and the Incarnation.

Few people in our time doubt the humanity of Jesus Christ, if they accept him as an historical figure at all. But many deny his divinity. Hence, his crucial question: "Who do *you* say that I am?"

Why did Christ become a man?   When we accept and believe the truth of Christ's full and complete humanity, the question we may ask ourselves is, "Why?" Why would the Second Person of the Blessed Trinity willingly choose to become a man?

During the Offertory of each celebration of the Mass, the priest pours a few drops of water into the wine. While doing so he prays:

> By the mystery of this water and wine, may we come to share in the divinity of Christ, Who humbled Himself to share in our humanity.

This brief prayer succinctly answers the question of why God became man. He humbled himself to partake in our humanity that we may share in his divinity. As St. Athanasius put it, "The Son of God became man so that we might become God." He does not mean that we will become gods unto ourselves, but that we will become sharers in God's divine nature by God's own desire and authority. As God and man become united in the Person of Jesus Christ, he opens the way for each individual human person to become united to him. Thus, we say, "Jesus is the Way."

Furthermore, by being a man like us, Jesus teaches us by example how to live a perfectly human life. He shows us how to live, love, suffer, and die with grace. He teaches us to pray, to worship and to obey his Father as we were created to do. He demonstrates by his very humanity how we can know, love and serve God in this life that we may be one with him in the life to come. He did not have to do this, but *chose* to do so. . .for *our* sake.

What greater love can we conceive than God himself freely taking on our nature, with all its sufferings, that we may share more fully in his divine nature?

Thinking it over • • •

1. How does Christ respond to Peter's answer to his key question of his identity?

2. What are the two essential mysteries of our Christian faith?

3. State precisely what the Incarnation means.

4. Why do we call them "mysteries," and not contradictions?

5. How would you distinguish a person from a nature?

6. What is meant by the phrase "hypostatic union"?

7. Which of the prophets describes the Messiah in divine terms?

8. What was St. John's stated reason for the writing of his gospel?

9. Precisely why was Jesus put to death?

10. Besides selected scriptural passages, what other evidence do we have of the divinity of Jesus Christ?

11. How does Jesus show his humanity when he appears to his apostles after his resurrection?

12. On what do the first heresies of the early Church focus?

Chapter 2

THE PERSONALITY OF CHRIST

Person and personality   The *person* is the subsistent "I" of the individual human being, which remains the same. I, for example, am today the same person I was when I was born. Oh, I have changed in my personality and my character, but my unique self is the same. In every created human being God infuses a distinct and individual soul into a particular disposed body. The body develops continuously from conception to birth and then throughout human life. When I die, I still go on, although incomplete until my resurrected body, made perfect by glorification, is reunited with my soul. My developing spiritual and physical qualities and defects during my lifetime alter my personality, but, strictly speaking, they do not change my person. When someone says, "He is a different person," what is meant is that his personality, which includes his character, is different.

Turning to Christ, we must bear in mind that Jesus is *one person,* the second person of the Blessed Trinity. He is *not* a human person, but he does have a human nature that is subject to some change and development during his lifetime. He does grow up and, as we will see, he does acquire knowledge in the same way we do.

Factors which influence human personality

Character, by the way, is an important part of one's personality. Character (which *is* subject to change and development) is the sum total of our virtues and vices, our good and bad habits of behaving.

Christ differs from us in his human nature in many ways. His nature is perfect and so is his character—all virtues and no vices. Many of our vices arise from our principal natural defect—original sin and its remnants in our weakened nature. But Jesus did not have the infection of original sin, and by his redemptive gift he preserved his mother Mary from its effects.

Personality, as we have said, is the total expression of our individual nature. Many factors influence its development, such as:

heredity: The unique composition and constitution of our genes, which are altogether unique because they bear the stamp of our forebears. We inherit our physical appearance, for example, and, to some extent, our psychological attitudes. (We do *not* inherit our moral dispositions and inclinations.) Each of us is responsible for his own character and behavior.

environment: This includes the people (especially family) and places (home, school, church) and the time and historical setting of our lives. We are born into this family in these circumstances in this place and at this time in history.

education: We learn in many different ways; not just by going to school. Our parents are our primary teachers. Both church and school merely help the parents in their awesome task to fulfill this responsibility. The whole of life, in fact, is a continuing process of education.

experience: No two people share the very same experiences in life, at least not in the same way. Furthermore, what happens to us is not as important as how we react to those happenings. The conclusive fact is that the personal history of every individual is different from that of every other.

NATURAL HUMAN DEFECTS

When we speak of Christ's perfect human nature, we must not eliminate the inevitable limitations and requirements of such a nature. We may falsely think of them as defects in an accusative sense. They are

ordinary restrictions that are
nature. Jesus did get hungry an
fer and die for our redemption.
human infirmities he clearly sh(
true human nature. We do not ha
not suffer and die, or which do not
feel heat and cold, or become w
Christ were to assume a body en
privileges, we might have doubted (
man. Secondly, by patiently bearing
Jesus gave us a wonderful example
bearing infirmities with patience. He
by our infirmities we can share in
sacrifice. He had no spiritual defects
without sin ("Which of you convicts
Jn. 8:46). Furthermore, he had special
mind and will.

Since Christ was human, he had (
emotions become bad only when they a
trol. So Jesus could be sad, even to the
ing. (Three instances are recorded in (
He shared the joy of wedding guests. (His
was done to increase that joy.) He certa(
anger, not only to the money-changers in
but to his adversaries, the Pharisees. He
called the scribes and Pharisees hypocrite
Perhaps his harshest statement to them v
them, ". . . white-washed tombs, which outv
pear beautiful, but within they are full of de
bones and all uncleanness. So you also outw
pear righteous to men, but within you ar
hypocrisy and iniquity" (Mt. 23: 27-28).

PHYSICAL APPEARANCE

There were no photographs in the time of
The closest we could come would be an imag
served, at least vaguely, such as that left o
Shroud of Turin. But we have no need of a shar

was probably average in height and build.
presume that he was bearded, the custom
men in that region at that time. (Among some
and Africans a beard is a symbol of wisdom.)
s not of "superman" proportions, not an eccen-
nius with the "weirdo" look, not effeminate in
nd manner (as some sentimental "religious" art
depict him). He was an ordinary manly type of
n such as one would expect to meet in a small
e in Palestine. We have no record of any
rks made about his physical characteristics—a
which should be a strong clue that his body was
extraordinary in any way.

KNOWLEDGE AND FREEDOM OF CHRIST

Our greatest gifts, derived from our creation in
image of God and our adoption by God through
grace of his redemption, are the knowledge and
freedom of choice we possess. Jesus shared in our
man nature. He too had both knowledge and lib-
y—infinitely more than we do, not only because of
e perfection of his human nature but because he
so had divine knowledge.

inds of knowledge in Christ   The *beatific vision*
as already his, so that he saw the essence of God
nd hence knew all there is to be known about crea-
ires without any limitation of time. He lived, by his
ivine nature, in the eternal *now*. Rarely, and only
when he wanted to manifest his divinity, did he use
his divine knowledge.

He possessed *infused knowledge,* as we do through
our life in grace, but his was more intense and more
comprehensive. He had immediate and intuitive
knowledge of all the realities of the created world.
Perhaps it was this kind of knowledge that he used
in reading the minds and hearts of those around him.

Finally, he also had the *acquired knowledge* that human nature achieves through education and instruction. After his parents found him in the temple, we are told he went home with them and he "advanced in wisdom and age." In those days, sons always learned the trade of their fathers. We can safely assume that Jesus learned the art of carpentry from his foster father, St. Joseph. Manifesting nothing extraordinary in his young days in Nazareth, he was called by his neighbors "the son of the carpenter."

The freedom of Christ   By his divine nature Jesus knew all things; but he also had a human nature capable of human knowledge. His human knowledge was enlightened by his constant beatific vision, by the infused gifts of understanding, knowledge and wisdom.

With knowledge goes choice. Besides his divine will, Jesus also enjoyed the human liberty which is part of human nature. The object of knowledge is truth; the object of the will is what is, or appears to be, good. The divine will can seek only itself because God alone is the ultimate Good. With respect to created goods, the will remains free: it can choose or reject them, move toward or away from them. We may make mistakes in our choices. Jesus, as God and man, does not.

The impeccability of Christ   Impeccability is the incapacity to sin, a prerogative of Christ. It is a typically modern error to equate freedom with the ability to sin. Nothing could be more absurd. The will is oriented only to that which seems good for us. To choose evil, to sin, is to elect that which at least appears as good. Basically, then, sin involves a wrong choice, and it is a sign of deficiency rather than of perfection: the sinner does not use his natural liberty as he should; he abuses it because his free will is too imperfect and therefore selects what is only apparently good. This being clear, it is obvious that Christ's impeccability in no way impairs his sovereign human freedom.

The harmony of wills in Christ   "My food is to do the will of him who sent me" (Jn. 4:34). So does Christ express the fact of the absolute accord between his human will and his divine will. Endowed with all the supernatural moral virtues in an ineffable degree, he could will only what God wishes and as God wills it. His human will, fixed irrevocably in God, is nevertheless sovereignly independent with regard to created objects; it makes its own decisions. But these choices are always exclusively for God, in perfect conformity with the divine wishes made known to him from on high, without the slightest deviation from the straight way plotted by God's eternal decrees. His is the perfect obedience unto death of which St. Paul speaks, obedience unto death, and yet the obedience of a man.

In the garden of Gethsemane, for example, his will and his sense appetite naturally recoiled from the prospect before him, the agony of his passion and death. But this shrinking of his sensibility, and the horror spontaneously arising in his will, occasion no conflict within him. For love of his Father and for us, he freely wills, with no compulsion whatever, to drink of this dreadful cup to its last dregs. His natural reaction of fear, of horror, of sorrow is not suppressed; "but Christ's human will follows his divine and omnipotent will, not reluctantly and with resistance, but in full compliance with it." Hence, the divine and human wills in Christ act in harmony. They are not turned off and on like water faucets. As with his divine and human knowledge, Jesus ordinarily used his sharpened human knowledge and perfect human will, only rarely exercising his divine will directly when he chose to manifest his divinity.

JESUS AS THE WAY

We go back to God through his Son, our Lord Jesus Christ. For it is through the redemptive sacrifice of Christ on the cross that we are reunited with God the Father. There is no other way. As Jesus said to Thomas, "I am the way, and the truth, and the life; no one comes to the Father, but by me" (Jn. 14:6). Jesus is also the way as a perfect exemplar of the virtues which we struggle to achieve and maintain.

Personal impressions　　From their contact with the gospel accounts of his life, everybody has definite impressions of the personality of Jesus Christ, an image of the kind of person he was as he lived among us and shared our human nature. Every member of a class could (and should) write about their impressions of Jesus. Though similar, none of them would be quite the same. Each of us sees different aspects of his personality; sometimes there is a perspective that others missed. That is because there is a rich treasure of personality traits in Jesus, with many facets, so that we can never exhaust our knowledge of them. Every Christian knows Jesus through his prayer life as well as by his reading of the gospel accounts of his life. Jesus is not just an object of study, but an experience of God in our lives. Some features of his personality impress us strongly as we meditate upon our Lord.

The power of his personality　　There is a definite power of attraction in a holy person. Jesus is the source of all holiness, and so there emanates from him an irresistible drawing of those who follow him. He is a magnetic person who draws thousands to him — not by haranguing as dictators do to sway crowds, but by gently teaching and healing. He simply went about doing good for people. His impact upon his chosen ones, the apostles, is striking. In calling them, Peter and Andrew leave their fishing nets, their way of making a living. Peter even leaves his wife. James and John were brothers who worked with their father in a family fishing business. They leave their nets and their father. He simply says "follow me" and they do.

29

Matthew, sitting in his tax collector's booth immediately answers the summons of Jesus. By answering that call, Matthew unhesitatingly left a lucrative, though despised, profession. Jesus looks at them and calls them to follow him and they do.

Some people who have followed Christ closely, those who are saints, are blessed with an appealing charismatic grace which flows from them and draws others to them, people who see in them a source of holiness that they long for in their own lives. Thus people flocked to a simple parish priest who lived in France during the last century, the saintly Curé of Ars. In recent years, Padre Pio attracted thousands to his monastery when he celebrated his Mass. In our own time, great crowds assemble to see our Holy Father, Pope John Paul II, and they reach out to touch him or just touch his garments. An incident is narrated by a professional observer who was present at a small gathering in India when Mother Teresa was there to speak. He describes the peace and adulation of the audience, and after the meeting was over, an old native, a shriveled man, stooped and bent by his years, made his way to her and lifted her hand to his lips—an ancient sign of reverence.

Children are attracted to him   Children seem to have a sensitivity to the sincerity of others, especially adults. Their knowledge seems to be intuitive. They are immediately drawn to some people and withdraw from others. They can sense whether someone really cares for them or not. According to the gospel accounts, Jesus was frequently with children. In fact, he uses them as models for adults and is strong in his condemnation of those who would scandalize them or lead them into sin. He says we must turn (*convert*) and become like them—not in their natural defects of immaturity, but in their unspoiled qualities such as: simplicity and humility and their quickness to forgive. They have not yet reached the age of corruption when they become complex and sometimes resentful.

> At that time the disciples came to Jesus saying, "Who is the greatest in the kingdom of heaven?" And calling to him a child, he put him in the midst of them, and said, "Truly, I say to you, unless you turn and become like children, you will never enter the kingdom of heaven. Whoever humbles himself like this child, he is the greatest in the kingdom of heaven.
>
> "Whoever receives one such child in my name receives me; but whoever causes one of these little ones who believes in me to sin, it would be better for him to have a great millstone fastened round his neck and to be drowned in the depth of the sea."
>
> —Mt. 18:1-6

Jesus goes on to say, "Woe to the world for temptations to sin! For it is necessary that temptations come, but woe to the man by whom the temptation comes . . . see that you do not despise one of those little ones; for I tell you that in heaven their angels always behold the face of my Father who is in heaven." (Mt. 18:7-11)

This is a strong condemnation for those who deliberately corrupt the young, a common commercial practice in our time.

The persistence and demands of Jesus in his call   If we are to follow him, Jesus insists that we leave everything else behind us. There can be no distractions, no diversions, no hesitations. Luke and Matthew include this passage:

> To another he said, "Follow me." But he said "Lord, let me first go and bury my father." But he said to him, "Leave the dead to bury their own dead, but as for you, go and proclaim the kingdom of God." Another said, "I will follow you, Lord, but let me first say farewell to those at my home." Jesus said to him, "No one who puts his hand to the plow and looks back is fit for the kingdom of God."
>
> —Lk. 9:59-62

Strong words, but they must be understood clearly. The young man who wanted to follow Jesus but said he first wanted to go and bury his father simply meant that, in accordance with Jewish law, he should delay any radical plans until his father did die. With the second man, Jesus is pointing out that in every happening there is a crucial moment; if that moment is missed, what we want to do most likely will not be done. Sacrifices usually have to be made to achieve a valuable goal. (Consider the many years of hard work and arduous study required of those preparing for professions.)

Following Jesus is a lifelong commitment that requires constant discipline and dedication. Jesus promised great rewards to those who left home and family for his sake not only in the life to come but in this life as well. But to follow him all the way demands total detachment and selflessness. "None of you," Jesus said, "can be my disciple if he does not renounce all his possessions." The rich young man who rejected the invitation of Jesus to follow him did so, we are told, because he had "many possessions."

Compassion and forgiveness Compassion means to share someone's sorrow as if it were one's own. Throughout his life Jesus showed compassion to the sick, the suffering, the poor, the hungry, the needy. Throughout his public life he showed his compassion in extraordinary ways, often involving his miraculous intervention even raising the daughter of Jairus, and the son of the widow of Naim, and Lazarus, from death to life. He had shared their loss. He joins the family of Lazarus in their grief and intervenes with nature itself to show that he is the resurrection.

Forgiveness flows from compassion. Jesus was always ready to forgive as long as the offender expressed sorrow for sin and faith in his healing power. There was no condition to his forgiveness except the injunction, "Go and sin no more." (Jn. 8:11)

To the ignorant he was patient and taught them in the simplest manner possible, by little stories called parables. To those stubbornly opposed to him, he tolerated their questions and responded wisely. To the malicious, such as the arrogant Pharisees, he reserved his harshest epithets, calling them vipers and hypocrites. But to those who sinned out of weakness, caught in the desires of the flesh, he offered immediate forgiveness if they were properly disposed. He forgave the woman taken in adultery, Mary Magdalene, prostitutes who repented, and the Samaritan woman at the well who had married five times and then lived with a man not her husband (Jn. 4:5-30).

The love of Jesus   Predominant among all the qualities of the personality of Jesus is his love for all mankind. This love that he shares with us he wants us to share with one another. St. John sums up the distinctly Christian character of love:

> Beloved, let us love one another; for love is of God and he who loves is born of God and knows God. He who does not love does not know God; for God is love. In this the love of God was made manifest among us, that God sent his only son into the world, so that we might live through him. In this is love, not that we loved God but that he loved us and sent his son to be the expiation of our sins. Beloved, if God so loved us, we also ought to love one another. No man has ever seen God. If we love one another, God abides in us and his love is perfected in us.

–I Jn. 4:7-12

His principal commandment is the precept of love: love of God and of others as ourselves. He said bluntly, "This is my commandment: Love one another as I have loved you." (Jn. 15-12)

The love which Jesus speaks of is not a mushy sentiment or a physical attraction. True love is based on sacrifice. "There is no greater love," he says, "than this: / to lay down one's life for one's friends." (Jn. 15:13 NAB) He insists that we follow his example. "This is my commandment: / love one another / as I have loved you" (Jn. 15:12 NAB).

We have examples in our lives of how love always involves sacrifice. Two friends cannot keep their friendship unless each one makes some sacrifice of personal preference for the sake of another. A marriage cannot survive if one or both partners hold on to selfishness and will not make any sacrifices. Parents cannot raise a family successfully unless they are willing to make daily sacrifices. The same can be said of children in relation to their parents. Broken marriages almost inevitably result from some violation of the couples' vows to sacrifice for each other.

Our love for God is shown by the sacrifice of our own selfishness in following his commandments. This is not an emotional kind of love, but a love of preference, choosing God over sin. All sin is based on self-gratification. The final words of Jesus at the Last Supper were simple and challenging.

Jesus said to his disciples: "As the Father has loved me, / so I have loved you. / Live on in my love. / You will live in my love / if you keep my commandments" (Jn. 15:9-10 NAB). The test of our love for God is simply stated, "If you love me, you will keep my commandments." (Jn. 14:15)

Our problem very often is that we do not match our moral behavior with our professed belief in Jesus. We may say that we love him, but talk is cheap and undemanding. Faith is expressed in action. As St. John writes, "Little children, / let us love in deed and in truth, / and not merely talk about it" (I Jn. 3:18 NAB). Otherwise we are hypocrites, deserving the scorn Jesus showed to the Pharisees.

Prayer, by itself, is not sufficient. Some may boast that they never miss Mass on Sunday and that they pray daily. But this is not enough. Jesus said: "Not everyone who says to me, `Lord, Lord,' shall enter the kingdom of heaven, but he who does the will of my Father in heaven" (Mt. 7:21).

Again, a stinging condemnation by Jesus Christ; to those who are pharisaical, not practicing what they profess, Jesus quotes Isaiah, saying, "This people honors me with their lips, / but their heart is far from me" (Mt. 15:8).

Thinking it over • • •

1. What is the difference between "person" and "personality"?

2. What is the relation of character to personality?

3. Jesus does get tired and hungry and thirsty. He cries and suffers and dies. Are these defects in his human nature?

4. Indicate from the gospel accounts that Jesus was, on occasion, emotional.

5. What are the three kinds of knowledge in Christ?

6. What is the relation of freedom to sin?

7. What is meant by the impeccability of Christ?

8. In two senses, Jesus is "The Way." What are they?

9. Why do we say that Jesus had a magnetic personality?

10. What are some of the good, natural qualities of children?

11. What is meant by "compassion"?

12. What is the most predominant quality of the personality of Jesus?

13. In our Christian lives, why is prayer alone not sufficient for our salvation?

Chapter 3

THE PREACHING OF THE KINGDOM

The object of the "good news" preached by Jesus is the kingdom of God. St. Matthew, in his gospel, prefers the phrase "the kingdom of heaven," but they are the same realities. The basic meaning of these phrases is the reign of Christ, but the idea of reign grows into the idea of realm. Does Jesus refer to a present or a future reality? Certainly it is a present reality, because when asked by the Pharisees when the kingdom of God was coming, Jesus answered, "The kingdom of God is in the midst of you" (Lk. 17:20). Thus Jesus identifies the kingdom with himself, a present reality but unrecognized by many. The kingdom is also identified with the Church that he founds.

How to be admitted   Admission to the kingdom demands that one become as a child (Mt. 18:3, Mk. 10:15, Lk. 18:17), exhibit righteousness (Mt. 5:20), do the will of the father (Mt. 17:21), and abandon one's wealth (Mt. 19:23, Mk. 10:23, Lk. 18:24). For the sake of the kingdom, men accept celibacy (Mt. 19:12). The kingdom belongs to the poor and the lowly and those who suffer for righteousness (Mt. 5:3, 19:14, Mk. 10:14, Lk. 6:20). These texts do not define the kingdom purely as a moral idea, but show that the reign of God is in complete opposition to merely human values and to sinful desires. The accomplishment of the reign of God demands a moral revolution in those who submit themselves to the reign and is itself the means by which the moral revolution is achieved (John L. McKenzie's *Dictionary of the Bible,* pp. 480-481).

Yet the kingdom of God is also presented as a future reality, a fulfillment of what Jesus began on earth. This double aspect of the kingdom as present reality and future reality is apparent in the parables describing the kingdom. Before considering these parables, it is necessary again to emphasize the identification of the kingdom with Jesus and also with the Church which continues the preaching of the kingdom and nourishes its members with the life of grace. Grace, as St. Paul says, is the seed of glory. Hence, the Christian is already a member of the kingdom of God but the full potential is not realized until the member is united with God in heaven.

The parables of Jesus   Jesus frequently taught in parables, short stories that were little more than expanded similes. This was a common form of rabbinical teaching. In fact, in all cultures throughout history, the illiterate have been instructed by storytellers. Unlike an allegory or a prolonged metaphor, every detail of a parable does not have some special meaning or significance.

There is a central truth in each of the parables, but the story itself is clothed with familiar details. These are taken from the experience of daily life, especially in agrarian settings and the common pursuits at that time in Israel: the planting of seed, the grazing of flocks, the catching of fish. Some images are used as common themes: sons or servants or slaves represented Israel; a king or a father referred to God; a feast indicated the joys of the Messianic age; and a harvest the last judgment. As we shall see, many of the parables are about the kingdom of God.

Are parables easy or difficult to understand?
In a sense, parables are easy to understand, even by children. But to grasp fully the basic truth contained in the story, certain dispositions are required, primarily an openness to understanding through personal faith. Jesus is explicit about this:

Then the disciples came and said to him, "Why do you speak to them in parables?" And he answered them, "To you it has been given to know the secrets of the kingdom of heaven, but to them it has not been given. For to him who has will more be given, and he will have abundance; but from him who has not, even what he has will be taken away. This is why I speak to them in parables, because seeing they do not see, and hearing they do not hear, nor do they understand. With them, indeed, is fulfilled the prophecy of Isaiah which says:

> 'You shall indeed hear but never understand, / and you shall indeed see but never perceive. / For this people's heart has grown dull, / and their ears are heavy of hearing, / and their eyes have closed, / lest they should perceive with their eyes, / and hear with their ears, / and understand with their heart, / and turn to me to heal them.'

—Mt. 13:10-15

(For parallel gospel passages, see Mk. 4:10-12; Lk. 8:9-10.)

There is one more added reason why Jesus spoke in parables, a reason which he indicates himself. Human nature is limited and cannot face the bluntness of incontrovertible truth. As the poet T. S. Eliot reminded us, "Humankind cannot bear very much reality." In his final discourse to his apostles, Jesus tells them that he has been "speaking in figures" but, he adds, "The hour is coming when I shall no longer speak to you in figures but tell you plainly of the Father" (Jn. 16:25). There is a ponderous weight to profound truth, too hard for us to hear plainly. As he said, "I have yet many things to tell you, but you cannot bear them now" (Jn. 16:12).

The parable is extended in meaning when it covers many forms of illustration of an instruction. Some may be simple sayings, metaphors, allegories, songs, as well as the brief story form of the parable. There are few parables in the Old Testament, mostly in the Book of Isaiah. Aristotle mentions the parable as a literary form in his *Rhetoric*.

There are approximately 35 parables that Jesus told, according to the evangelists. Many of them, though not all, refer to the kingdom of God. St.

39

Matthew is the principal teller of such little stories, many of them as brief as expanded similes. You should read the whole of the thirteenth chapter of St. Matthew, because it contains no less than seven parables of the kingdom.

Among these parables in Matthew 13:44-45 are two simple but pungent extended similes. The kingdom is compared to a treasure hidden in a field and to a fine pearl. In both cases, someone discovers something of great value which can be obtained only at a high price. The finders, the field worker and the merchant sell all that they have so as to obtain the valuable object which they have discovered. So it is, obviously, with the kingdom of heaven. Nothing is comparable in value to our union with Christ: now through the Church with its word and sacrament, and eventually through the everlasting joy of our ultimate union with God in heaven.

But we enter the kingdom and at last possess it only at a great cost, the spending of ourselves in commitment to Christ and the emptying of ourselves (the sacrifice of our selfishness) in order to "put on Christ," as St. Paul says, so that "it is no longer I who live but Christ who lives in me."

Fr. Wilfred J. Harrington, O.P., in his commentary on *The Parables Told By Jesus,* applies this exceptional value of the kingdom to the parables themselves; for they are, as he says, "windows into the kingdom."

Further, he points out their value in making the kingdom immediate to us through their illustrations taken from daily life. They proclaim general truths through their very human and familiar details. Beyond that, they have both a personal and universal relevance, transcending a specific time and a particular place.

Thus the parables are not merely stories that are pleasant or intriguing to read, but, more pertinently, they are authentic witnesses to the teaching of Christ. There is a cost to understanding the parables, the cost of discipleship, because we have to be pure of heart to see God as he reveals himself to us through these little stories. Only Christians of deep faith and personal commitment perceive the profound truths of these parables. There is joy in these perceptions because they open up new realms of thought and extend our experience. The parables of Jesus, as well as the beatitudes, provide us with new vistas—of God, of ourselves, of all people—that are clear and unblurred by any distortions of contemporary culture.

The simple parable of the sower and the seed is explained by Jesus himself:

a. he is the sower
b. the field is the world
c. the good seed refers to the sons of the kingdom
d. the weeds are sons of the evil one
e. the enemy who sows is the devil
f. the harvest is the end of the world
g. the reapers are angels.　　　　　　　—Mt. 13:36-43

This is one of the few parables in which every item has meaning and significance. Further, this passage records the rare event of Jesus explaining these details. Notice, however, that he does this for his disciples, not for all his listeners. The story of the sower and the seed is actually two parallel stories. The other five parables in Matthew 13 are more directly related to the kingdom. The "seed parables" focus on the problems of the citizens of the kingdom.

Jesus came among us to save us from our sins through his sacrificial act of redemption. He also came to "preach the good news of the kingdom." He came not only to reunite us to God, but also to give us life, through grace and glory, so that we can share in his life. Hence, he repeats descriptions of that kingdom which is at the center of Christian life. What is that kingdom like, as recorded by St. Matthew?

41

The kingdom of heaven is like   This is the usual introduction to a parable about the kingdom. Matthew refers to five comparisons that are direct references: a mustard seed, leaven for bread, a hidden treasure, a valuable pearl, a net filled with fish. The previous parable about the destiny of seeds is told to a large crowd in public, whereas the more intimate parables of the kingdom are given "in a house" and they are obviously intended for the disciples.

THE MUSTARD SEED

All of these kingdom parables are obviously meant to show us the high priority value of the kingdom. First, he stresses the amazing growth of the kingdom within us, from grace to glory. The image of the mustard seed is also applied to faith (Mt. 17-20).

The mustard seed actually was not the smallest of seeds (that of the cypress seed, for instance, is still smaller), but the Jews frequently used this comparison to emphasize the smallness of anything. The growth of the mustard seed was unpredictable. A writer visiting Palestine reported seeing one that was "more than twelve feet high." They are so broad and bushy that many birds are found on them. They settle on the tree to pick at its little black seeds. The kingdom, too, starts out very small (a little measure of grace), but no one can predict how big it will become. Surely, many saints were unrecognized as such by their parents during the formative years. His disciples must have wondered about Jesus. Could their little band, so few in numbers and weak in status, endure and at last change the world? That is precisely what did happen.

THE LEAVEN

Jesus used familiar events in all of his parables, including occupations engaged in by his listeners:

fishermen, farmers, field diggers, pearl divers. But here he touches on an everyday occupation of the women of his time—the baking of bread. Leaven was a bit of dough kept over from a previous baking which had fermented in the keeping. Jesus could have taken this illustration from his early life in Nazareth, watching his mother, Mary, baking bread every day.

William Barclay, the Scot scripture scholar from Glasgow, says in his commentary on this passage:

> The whole point of the parable lies in one thing—*the transforming power of the leaven.* Leaven changed the character of a whole baking. Unleavened bread is like a water biscuit: hard, dry, unappetizing, and uninteresting [such as matzos used by the modern Jew in ceremonial eating]. Bread baked with leaven is soft and porous and spongy, tasty and good to eat. The introduction of the leaven causes a transformation in the dough; and the coming of the kingdom caused a transformation in life.

He goes on to describe the Christian transformation as it affects both the individual and society:

The transformation of the individual Christian transformation begins in the individual. Every person, in some way and at some time in his life, has an encounter with Christ, an experience which changes his life and sets him in one direction or another. A direction may be radically altered, turning the sinner into a saint. The change may be gradual, not sudden or dramatic. Every Christian should be developing in his life of grace, growing in virtue and eliminating vice. St. Paul emphasizes the necessary transformation of the individual Christian from his own selfish life into the very life of Christ. To become Christ-like is our common Christian goal.

The transformation of society Individuals make up society. As the individual changes, so does the society in which he lives. Dr. Barclay points to four noticeable directions in which Christianity transformed all life.

1. **The position of women**   In ancient civilizations, women were treated as inferiors, even in family life. The great philosopher, Aristotle, considered a woman to be a mistake of nature. The Jew, in his morning prayer, thanked God that he had not made him a Gentile, a slave, or a woman. Women were for childbearing and heavy manual labor. It was Christianity that elevated women to equal dignity as children of God. (Notice in the gospel accounts that many women attended to and accompanied Christ on his missions.) Christianity was the initial mover in the liberation of women.

2. **The treatment of the weak and the ill**   Says Barclay: "In heathen life, the weak and the ill were considered a nuisance. In Sparta a child, when he was born, was submitted to examiners; if he was fit, he was allowed to live; if he was weakly or deformed, he was exposed to death on the mountainside . . . The first blind asylum was founded by Thalasius, a Christian monk; the first free dispensary was founded by Apollonius, a Christian merchant; the first hospital of which there is any record was founded by Fabiola, a Christian lady. Christianity was the first faith to be interested in the broken things of life."

3. **The care of the aged**   Today, the problems and care of the aged are of major concern. We have specialists and homes for what we call "geriatrics." Not so in the past. Like the weak, the aged were a nuisance. Cato, the Roman writer, advises those taking over a farm. He tells them what to sell and to get rid of such as "an old slave, a sickly slave, and whatever else is superfluous." The old person whose day's work was done, was fit for nothing else than to be discarded on the rubbish heaps of life. Christianity was the first faith to regard men and women as persons and not instruments capable of doing so much work.

4. **Life for a child**   Today our society is almost child-centered. All agencies of social life, including government, concentrate on the needs of children. Again, it was not always so. Marriage was in a worse state then, with women taking a new husband every year. In such circumstances, children were a disaster and the custom of exposing children to death was tragically common. A Roman, writing to his wife from Alexandria, said, "If – good luck to you – you bear a child, if it is a boy, let it live; if it is a girl, throw it out."

How can anyone ask: "What has Christianity done for the world?" Modern civilization has been radically changed. Christians too have made mistakes in the course of the development of Western civilization. But the total effect has been a force for good in every area of human life. Of all the historical upheavals and changes in modern life, no force has been greater than the Christian transformation of the individual and of society.

THE HIDDEN TREASURE

Today almost everyone uses a bank to store valuables, including cash. Banks were not available to the ordinary citizen in ages past. People buried what they had in the ground. There was an old rabbinic saying that there was only one safe depositary for money—the earth. Notice in the parable of the talents the unworthy servant buried his portion in the ground instead of investing it for profit. When the Jewish people were in flight, they also buried their valuables in the ground hoping to retrieve them on their return. As for finding buried treasures, an old Jewish law stated, in its own way, "finders-keepers."

The main point of the example, however, is the high value of the servant's discovery. He gave up everything else to insure his continued possession of the treasure. Notice that the man finds it not by pure chance but as he was going about his daily work. The key to the kingdom of heaven is sacrifice, doing all that we can do to fulfill God's will on earth as it is in heaven. That means sacrificing our own will at times, our own inclination to selfishness.

THE PRECIOUS PEARL

Pearls attracted the attention of the Jews, not only because of their natural value, but also because of their natural beauty. Merchants, in their trading, always took a special interest in pearls.

Here the kingdom is compared to a pearl of great price, beautiful in itself, but also more valuable than other goods. Again, sacrifice is necessary for us to possess it.

THE CATCH AND THE SEPARATION

Net-fishing is indiscriminate. The large, weighted net is thrown into the sea and when it is drawn up, there is a mixture of things picked up—junk along with fish. Some of the items are good, some are bad, so they must be sorted out.

Jesus directs this parable to the good and the evil persons who are invited to the kingdom. Good persons will enter; evil ones will be rejected.

The Church, which represents the kingdom on earth, is not just for the good people. It is for all people and the final judgment is made by God as to who enters the kingdom and who does not. We cannot make such a judgment. Only God can. We may be tempted to judge the behavior of others, but we should avoid doing so. Only God knows enough about his creatures, his children, and judgment is for him alone to make.

THE SERVANT PARABLES

Many of the parables that Jesus tells involve servants, appropriate images of the children of God. In Israel, at that time, a servant was not a lowly slave. In fact, he was an honored member of a household. You may recall the story of a centurion who was so upset over the illness of his servant he sent friends to beg Jesus to heal the servant. The man was a Roman soldier but apparently a good person who had helped the Jews. And he recognized and respected authentic authority. He did not even ask Jesus to come to his home, saying, "I am not worthy to have you come under my roof . . . but say the word and let my servant be healed." Admiring the man's faith, Jesus cured the servant before the centurion's emissaries could return to the house (Luke 7:2-10).

The servant parables are six in number, two of them immediately pertinent; the others are eschata-logical in character. All are relevant to the kingdom, either in the present or at the end of the world (hence the word "eschatalogical," from the Greek *eschatos* meaning last or farthest). The servant parables are:

The Unmerciful Servant (Mt. 18:23-35)

The Unprofitable Servant (Lk. 17:7-10)

The Doorkeeper (Mk. 13:33-37)

The Watchful Servants (Lk. 12:35-38)

The Faithful and Unfaithful Servants (Mt. 24:45-51)

The Servants Entrusted with Talents (Mt. 25:14-30 and Lk. 19:12-27)

These servant parables obviously refer to our King and God's expectation of those who serve him. They are, then, lessons in conduct, how to serve so as to enter the kingdom of heaven. The first focuses on forgiveness.

The Unmerciful Servant (Matthew 18:23-35)

The parable of the unmerciful servant echoes the teaching of Christ in the prayer he taught us to say to Our Father in heaven: "Forgive us our trespasses as we forgive those who trespass against us." This statement is enforced by the passage that immediately follows the instruction on prayer: "For if you forgive men their trespasses, your heavenly Father also will forgive you; but if you do not forgive men their trespasses, neither will your Father forgive your trespasses" (Mt. 6:14).

This message transcends any particular time or place. It applies to us in our time. People are tempted to hold grudges against anyone who offends them. The Christian virtue of ready forgiveness is not easy to acquire because, like so many virtues of the super-

47

natural life, its practice goes against our natural grain. There are no limits to God's forgiveness, but we, at least, must be disposed to forgive if we expect God to forgive us.

Perhaps because of their lack of experience with human weakness, the young are especially inclined to resent and retaliate against any real or imaginary injury done to them. "Getting even" is almost an impulsive reaction. But virtue, on a supernatural level of life, harnesses and disciplines our natural impulses. Therefore, striving to live a life of grace, nourished by the sacraments, is so important. Otherwise we easily slip back onto a natural level which is already corrupted by sin. The Christian life is not easy and requires constant effort, as well as grace, if we are to survive on a supernatural level of life.

The Unprofitable Servant (Luke 17:7-10)

This story seems to paint a stark picture of the relation of servant to master, a different image from that given by the kind centurion; but Jesus uses it to criticize the attitude of the Jews who expected merit and reward. The servant should expect no reward; his service is taken for granted.

The Jews thought that God *owed* man salvation in view of the just man's fidelity to the law. But Jesus places man in *direct* relationship to God aside from the law itself. Today we have some of that demanding expectation in people who regularly go to church and do not violate the moral law in any grave or public way. But all that we have—creation, adoption, the kingdom itself—are God's gifts to us. He does not owe us anything. In that light, this parable emphasizes God's sheer goodness.

The Doorkeeper (Mark 13:33-37)

Watchfulness is obviously very relevant to the spiritual. We should always be prepared to face the judgment of God. Sometimes people will think and say, "I'll get straightened out some day." But, as St. Antoninus once wrote, "God promises us forgiveness but he doesn't promise us tomorrow."

As Scripture scholar, Wilfred Harrington, notes, the doorkeeper parable, as Mark found it, had already gone through a process of reshaping. It was recorded by Luke (12:35-38) in a more elaborated way with some unnecessary details. The core of the parable simply says a doorkeeper is commanded to keep watch, to open immediately as soon as the master knocks on his return from a banquet, and he is warned that it would be well for him if his master finds him watching at whatever the time of night he might return.

The point is that the doorkeeper should await the arrival of the master at no set time and always be in readiness to serve him. When will our own master come? He was among us, for Jesus said, "The time is fulfilled, and the kingdom of God is at hand" (Mk. 1:15). In this parable he calls on us to be ready for his final coming in judgment. But when that moment is to be cannot be forecast or reckoned. Watchfulness at all times is the only sensible attitude, indeed the necessary attitude. The warning is to live one's life at each moment in preparedness for our meeting with Christ.

The Watchful Servants (Luke 12:35-38)

This parable in Luke also appears in Mark (13:34-36). There are notable differences in the two accounts indicating a common source.

The outer garment worn by Jewish men was like a toga or smock. To move freely at work it would have to be tucked into the cincture, a rope-like gathering belt. The lamp must be ready and lighted, a longer process than simply turning on a light switch. The servants are expected to sit up waiting for their master who is returning from a wedding. Although similar to it, this story resembles the parable of the doorkeeper as told by Mark, except that the master has gone to a wedding, not just a banquet. This usually is a reference to the Messianic banquet when Christ brings his faithful into the heavenly kingdom.

Mark also is more detailed about this waiting of the servants, adding: "Watch therefore—for you do not know when the master of the house will come, in the evening or at midnight, or at cockcrow, or in the morning lest he come suddenly and find you asleep. And what I say to you, I say to all: watch" (13:35-37). He prefaces his account with an added element, "Watch and pray." So we should not be idle as we wait. We should pray, acknowledging always the hidden presence of our Lord.

Luke has an addition. Unlike an earthly master, this master will serve his faithful servants when he welcomes them to the Messianic feast. Two other related texts come to mind: "I am among you as one who serves" (Lk. 22:27) and "If I then, your Lord and Teacher, have washed your feet . . ." (Jn. 13:14).

There is still another version in Matthew, but known separately as:
The Faithful and Unfaithful Servants (Matthew 24:45-51 and Luke 12:42-48). The passages in Matthew and Luke are very similar. Consider Luke's account:

"Who then is the faithful and wise steward, whom his master will set over his household to give them their portion of food at the proper time? Blessed is the servant who when his master comes will find so doing. Truly I tell you, he will set him over all his possessions. But if that servant says to himself, `My master is delayed in coming' and begins to beat the menservants and the maidservants, and to eat and drink and get drunk, the master of that servant will come on a day when he does not expect him and at an hour he does not know, and will punish him, and put him with the unfaithful. And that servant who knew his master's will, but did not make ready or act according to his will shall receive a severe beating. But he who did not know, and did what deserved a beating, shall receive a light beating . . ." —Lk. 12:42-48

This parable deals with the alternative conduct of a servant whom his master would place in charge of his affairs while he himself was absent on a long journey. Especially significant in Luke's account is the change to the Greek word for *steward* in place of the word for *servant.* When Luke wrote his gospel, Greek Christians saw their leaders as stewards dispensing God's gifts, acting not in their own name, but in his. They are not, therefore, masters of the community, but men dedicated to its service. In Acts 20:17-35, Paul movingly outlines, in personal terms, the quality of community service. For Luke, service is the essence of office in the Church.

Luke's comment about proportionate guilt and punishment is obvious. The stewards are those who know the will of their Lord and have the duty to make it known. If they do not live according to this knowledge, they deserve a greater punishment than others. This is to summon those who hold office in the community to faithful and selfless service of their Lord and of the Christians entrusted to their care.

The Servants Entrusted with Talents (Luke 19:12-27 and Matthew 25:14-30)

The talent, sometimes translated as "pound" was not a coin but a weight. Precious metals were used in investments; their value depending on the type: copper, gold or silver. Silver was most commonly employed.

The emphasis is on the servant who buries his amount, a character depicting the scribes and Pharisees who claimed they tried to "build a fence around the law." There are obvious lessons to be learned here:

1. *That God gives people different gifts.* God does not demand from anyone what he does not have, but that a person uses to the full what has been given to him.

2. *That the reward of work well done is still more work to do.* The successful servants are given greater tasks and graver responsibilities.
3. *That the man who is punished is the one who will not try.*
4. *To him who has more will be given while he who has not will lose what he has.* As in all sports and crafts, skills must be exercised to develop and improve. Underdeveloped, they wither and die.

Despite differences in detail, Matthew and Luke agree in their accounts, especially those concerned with the cautious servant. In all the servant parables, the servant metaphor expresses man's relationship with God. This parable, as Fr. Harrington points out, "is not concerned with culpable indolence or inexcusable lack of enterprise; it is concerned with a man who has never really known his master."

In our relationship with God, we should not be "slothful" (Matthew's word) or be "afraid" (Luke's word). Too often, people are indifferent about religious duties (slothful) or see God as a severe tyrant; we are "afraid" we cannot please him. This leads people to respond to God legalistically.

C. H. Dodd, another commentator, sees the third servant as "the type of pious Jew who comes in for such criticism in the gospels. He seeks personal security in a meticulous observance of the law." They are like the elder son of the parable of the prodigal son: their service of God is loveless because they do not know him as Father.

The kingdom of God, we have read, is like a treasure, a very costly pearl, a seed that grows of itself. In this parable of the talents, the capital entrusted to the servants is not only a treasure but also is meant to increase. The master takes for granted that interest will accrue. The first two servants understood the nature of the gift—because they understood the nature of God and of the kingdom. The other understood neither God nor the nature of God's gift. The kingdom is not something one keeps for oneself.

In the preaching and life of Jesus, the kingdom is the manifestation of God's goodness, of his fatherly love and mercy.

Thinking it over • • •

1. Does Jesus refer to the present or the future when he speaks about "the kingdom"?

2. What is a parable?

3. When asked, how does he say that he teaches by parables?

4. Approximately how many parables did Jesus tell?

5. In your own words, tell the story of the sower and the seed and explain it.

6. What is the precise point of the parable about the leaven?

7. State some ways that Christianity has affected modern culture.

8. Why would anyone put a treasure in the ground?

9. How many servant parables are there?

10. What does the parable of the unmerciful servant teach us?

11. Why was the servant who buried his investment money so severely chastised?

12. What do the parables of the doorkeeper and the watchful servants teach us in a very personal way?

13. Just what is the difference between a steward and a servant?

14. Apply the parable of the talents to your own life.

Chapter 4

THE PASCHAL MYSTERY

The "Paschal Mystery" refers to the passion, death, and resurrection of Our Lord, Jesus Christ.

These events are mysterious, beyond our natural comprehension, because on our own we could never grasp the revealed fact that God incarnate, God become man, could undergo human suffering and his cruel death. Then, by raising himself from death he assured us that we too can rise to a new and far better life of glory with him.

The *Pasch* refers to the Jewish sacrifice of a lamb on their principal feast of the Passover. The rite of Passover, according to the book of Exodus, commemorates the passing over of the destroying angel sent to kill the firstborn of Egyptian families, a punishment for the enslavement of the Jews.

The Jewish rite over the centuries has been the celebration of a banquet in which a yearling lamb is eaten, as well as unleavened bread. And prayers recalling the original historical event are said. The lamb is a symbol of innocence and purity who meekly is led to his death. The Last Supper, observed by Christ and his apostles, signified that the symbol of the lamb is about to become the reality of the redeemer in the person of Jesus Christ, the innocent and pure victim who was led to his crucifixion. Appropriately, it was at this meal that Christ instituted the Eucharist by which we consume his body and blood sacramentally. As we re-enact his redemptive sacrifice, we are united with him. Just before that communion with him, we address him as "Lamb of God."

A THEOLOGICAL VIEW

Before examining the gospel accounts of the paschal mystery, a familiar story to us because of its retelling during Holy Week of Lent, it is interesting to see what implications are contained in the narrative. St. Thomas Aquinas, the Church's principal theologian, follows his usual method of raising and responding to questions. He first asks about the intensity and the universality of Christ's sufferings, then about their effects.

THE INTENSITY OF CHRIST'S SUFFERINGS

Did Christ suffer more than any other man? St. Thomas replies that both the sensible pain and the interior pain of the passion were the greatest in this life. He offers four reasons:

1. Because of the sources of his pain: the frightful pain of crucifixion, the sadness arising from the weight of the sins of the world, from the rejection of his own people, and from the cowardice of his disciples.

2. Because of his special susceptibility to suffering, both in soul and body: Christ's human nature was the miraculous result of the power of the Holy Spirit; it was more perfect than that of ordinary mortals. His sense of touch which experienced pain, and his interior faculties, which apprehended the causes of sadness, were more acute than ordinary.

3. Because he abandoned himself wholly to his passion, without any effort to mitigate his sufferings or to distract himself from his pain.

4. Because he embraced an amount of pain proportionate to the fruit of the Redemption, and that was universal.

Christ's sufferings, great as they were, did not interfere with his free will. Indeed, throughout the passion, the higher faculties of his soul continually enjoyed the Beatific Vision. But this supernatural peace and joy did not mitigate his sufferings, for it was not allowed to overflow either into the lower faculties of his soul or into his senses.

THE UNIVERSALITY OF CHRIST'S SUFFERINGS

The suffering of Christ was universal, inflicted by many persons, in many ways and in all senses:

1. On the part of the men who tormented him, he suffered from Jews and Gentiles; men and women; rulers, servants and the mob; friends and acquaintances.

2. On the part of the ways man can suffer, he suffered from his friends who abandoned him; in his reputation, from the blasphemies hurled at him; in his honor and glory, from the mockeries and insults heaped upon him; in his possessions, when he was stripped of his garments; in his soul, from sadness, weariness and fear; in his body, from wounds and scourging.

3. On the part of the members of his body, he suffered in his head, from the crown of thorns; in his hands and feet, from the nails; on his face, from blows and spittle; and throughout his body, from lashes. Every one of his senses was afflicted: touch, by the nails and scourges; taste, by vinegar and gall; smell, by being crucified in a malodorous place of execution; hearing, by the shouts of blasphemers; sight, by the tears of his mother and the disciple whom he loved.

There was, then, a kind of universal extent to the sufferings of Christ in a generic, rather than a specific, sense. Any one of his actions, even a wave of his hand, would have sufficed to redeem us. But Christ's action is our instruction, and he underwent the entire weight of his passion to teach us the horror of sin from which he saved us because of his love.

THE EFFECTS OF CHRIST'S SUFFERINGS

St. Thomas then asks what were the effects of Christ's passion. What was accomplished by intensely cruel suffering?

1. The passion delivered us from sin. Christ is the head; we are members of his Mystical Body. By laying down his life through love and obedience, he paid the price for our sins. Similarly, a man may repair by the work of his hands the damage he has caused by his feet.

2. The passion freed us from the devil's domination. Man became a slave of the devil through sin (Jn. 8:34; II Pet. 2:19). The passion paid the price for our sins, and hence freed us from the dominion of Satan.

3. The passion freed us from the debt of punishment. Christ's passion made superabundant satisfaction for all sin, and thus discharged the debt of punishment. However, this effect, like all the rest, must be applied to each individual soul by faith, charity, the sacraments, and good works.

4. The passion reconciled us to God. Sin made us enemies of God. But the passion destroyed sin and thus restored us to the divine friendship. This was not done by working a change in God, but by taking away the source of the divine hatred, and by making compensation through a more pleasing offering.

5. The passion opened the gates of heaven. Christ satisfied both for original and actual sin. These had kept the gates of heaven locked to mankind (Heb. 9:11-12).

6. The passion merited Christ's exaltation. ". . .he humbled himself, and became obedient unto death, even death on a cross. Therefore God has highly exalted him . . ." (Phil. 2:8-9). This exaltation was fourfold, including his resurrection, ascension, sitting at the Father's right hand, and his power of judgment over all men.

It is clear that Christ's redemption is universal. That means that the passion was sufficient to redeem all men, from all sins, and to restore all good things that were lost by sin.

What was accomplished by Jesus for our redemption is of no help to us unless we freely accept and practice the required way of living as a faithful Christian. It is not as simple as merely "accepting Jesus as our personal savior." This may be done at a critical time or in fervor of intense feeling. It is good but not good enough. There must be a follow-up of faithful practice.

Summing up the thought of St. Thomas on this point:

Although Christ satisfied sufficiently for all sins, this satisfaction must be effected in each individual by having the merits of Christ applied through faith, charity, the sacraments, and good works. No adult is ever saved without his cooperation. The means which Christ established must be used by each one.

Christ's passion restores to mankind all the goods lost through sin. This is a work begun in this life and completed in the next. Christ sufficiently merited for all not only habitual grace but also the actual graces that precede and follow justification, and eternal life itself. Likewise he merited whatever natural goods are conducive to salvation. The reason he did not will the restoration of the preternatural gifts of freedom from death, sickness, error, and concupiscence was to leave us with the opportunity to be united to the sufferings of Christ in this life. He did will that these defects should not conquer us, and that they shall be completely eliminated in heaven.

THE SCRIPTURAL ACCOUNT OF
THE PASCHAL MYSTERY

The principal source of theology is Sacred Scripture, and the accounts of Christ's passion and death as detailed by all the evangelists. There is no need to reprint the exact words describing these events. You can and should go directly to the New Testament. If you do not have a small paperback edition of the New Testament, you should have one; not only for the study of theology but as a basic reference work you can use throughout your education, now and always. If you could have only two required reference books in your personal library, they should be an English dictionary and a New Testament. As we go through this part of our textbook, you should have the gospels and the epistles handy for ready reference. Consider chronologically the events that are finally concluded in the glorious climax of the resurrection.

The council and betrayal   The chief priests and the scribes first plotted the arrest and death of Jesus. They did this with Judas Iscariot, one of Christ's own apostles, one of his especially chosen followers. A convenient opportunity was provided by our Lord's celebration of the Passover with his apostles.

The betrayal council is described by Luke 22:1-6. The preparation for the Passover meal is told by Luke 22:7-13.

The Passover meal   We have already mentioned the Passover celebration and its significance. Christ and his apostles celebrated the feast in anticipation, on Thursday, whereas the figure of its foreshadowing occured on Friday when the blood of the Lamb of God was shed for men that they might escape God's just wrath. The ceremony began with the blessing of the first cup of wine, herbs were brought in with a dish of sauce, and the Jews, using their fingers, dipped their herbs into the sauce and consumed them. Next, the paschal lamb was placed on the table and a prayer reminding them of God's mercy was said. The lamb was eaten with a second cup of wine and more herbs. The meal was concluded with a hymn, called the Hallel. Luke describes their observance in 22:14-18.

The institution of the Eucharist   To this ceremony, Christ added a very unusual element, the actual institution of the key Christian sacrament of the Eucharist, the changing of bread and wine into his own body and blood. This is a substantial change, not a change in appearance and taste just as it occurs daily in our celebration of the Mass. Read Luke 22:19-20. In verses 21-23, Jesus predicted his betrayal.

There are two important elements in Luke's short account of the institution of the Eucharist. He says "my body" and "my blood"not a symbol or figure of his body and blood as some separated Christians would interpret this passage. Further, he hands on to his apostles and their successors the power to repeat his words and consequent change. He tells men to "do this in remembrance of me." And so the paschal mystery is recalled and in this way re-enacted in every Mass.

Evidence of the practice of celebrating the Eucharist is found in the early apostolic Church. St. Paul bears witness to this fact and his word would confound any modern dissenter who claimed that our celebration of the Eucharist was a later addition in the history of the Church. It is very important to read this passage from St. Paul's first epistle to the Corinthians (11:23-29).

In this passage, St. Paul repeats the command of Jesus to do this (celebrate the Eucharist) "For as often as you eat this bread and drink the cup, you proclaim the Lord's death until he comes" (1 Cor. 11:26). He also emphasizes the *real presence* of Jesus in the Eucharist. "Whoever, therefore, eats the bread or drinks the cup of the Lord in an unworthy manner will be guilty of profaning the body and blood of the Lord" (1 Cor.

11:27). So no one should receive communion while aware of grave sin.

Clearly then, the apostolic Church and Christ's earliest disciples were certain Jesus had transmitted to his own followers the incomprehensible power to change bread and wine into his body and blood, using substantially the same words he had been the first to use. Therefore, when Jesus instituted the Eucharist he also appointed priests with the right and power to perpetuate it.

Following Luke, the evangelist goes on to record Peter's avowal of faith and the prediction of Christ that he would deny him three times before the cock crowed (Luke 22:31-34). There follows a brief instruction from Jesus to his apostles (Luke 22:35-38).

All of the evangelists give an account of some of the details of Christ's passion and death. St. John adds more. He faithfully records the final words of Jesus to his apostles. At the end of the meal they converse, but John alone repeats the last instructions of Jesus to those who will preach the kingdom after his death. Called "The Discourse," this series of intimate revelations to his chosen ones discloses the secrets of his heart. You will need to have the Gospel of John (chapters 14-17) to understand the entire account.

The promises   Jesus first assures his apostles that there will be a place for them in his Father's house. He tells them that he is "the way, and the truth, and the life" and that no one comes to the Father except through him. To Philip's question about seeing the Father the surprised Lord replies that "He who has seen me has seen the Father . . . I am in the Father and the Father in me." (Jn. 14:9-10) He goes on to say pointedly, "If you love me you will keep my commandments." (Jn. 14:15) (It is not enough to say that we love God; we have to prove it by our behavior.) He promises them "another advocate," the Holy Spirit who will remain with us forever.

Again he speaks of the union with the Father and of the test of love, the keeping of the commandments. He promises us the indwelling of the Trinity and the guidance of the Holy Spirit. He promises his peace which is not the peace of the world and advises them, and us, that we should not let our hearts "be troubled; believe in God, believe also in me." (Jn. 14:1)

Union with Christ   To show how closely we are united to Christ he illustrates that union with the figure of a vine and its branches. Again, he points out that our bond with him and the Father is founded on love. He tells us to extend that love to others especially by sacrificing our own selfishness. In his first letter to his followers, John expands on this theme of love for God by showing love in the kindness and generosity we express to others. We cannot see God directly, only our neighbors. Love, says St. John, is not expressed in mere words but in our actions (Jn. 15:1-17).

The world's hatred   First of all, read John 15:18-27 and 16:1-4. Our Lord here presents his listeners with a stern reality. They will suffer the hatred of the world, just as he had been hated by the Jewish leaders. Remember that ten of the original twelve apostles were severely persecuted and put to death in a cruel manner.

Today, as in the days of Jesus, "the world" stands for the great mass of humanity, the unbelievers who are often slaves to their own passions and are unwilling to submit their hearts and minds to God. They will not even be reasonable because they are selfish and seek only their own gratifications. Jesus will send his disciples into the world, for he wishes to convert it, and they will be hated for their efforts.

Their consolation will rest in this: they are illtreated for his sake. But he will send them a helper and defender, the Spirit of Truth, who proceeds from the Father and the Son. After Jesus has entered into his glory, the disciples will have to live by the spirit of faith. His bodily presence will be replaced by a spiritual presence, the action of the Holy Spirit in us. The Holy Spirit is promised for all time to the successors of the apostles, and to all who, under their guidance, will believe in Jesus.

He then speaks of the role of the advocate, the Holy Spirit, who "will guide you into all truth" (Jn. 16:13). He tells them of his resurrection: "A little while and you shall see me no more; again a little while and you will see me . . .", (Jn. 16:16) a statement misunderstood by the apostles. They will be saddened by his passion and crucifixion, but he likened their sadness to the pain of a woman in childbirth which is followed by great joy—the joy they will experience from his resurrection. Then, he says, he will speak to them plainly, not in parables. After their protestation of faith, he predicts that the time is coming when they will be scattered, each one to his own house, and leave him alone—which is what happened when he was put to death and they feared for their own lives (Jn. 16:16-33).

Finally, he offers what has been called his "priestly prayer" because it not only applied to the apostles, but to all priests, a passage often read by priests or read to them when they are on retreat. This passage, in John 17:1-26, should be read and considered by everyone.

Since his work was to be continued and spread by the apostles, he prayed for them and for all who would believe through them, all who would form what we now call the Church. And for the Church Jesus desired unity, a unity which is not to be realized by a simple imitation of a model; it is a union with the Father through Jesus that will make perfect oneness. Such a unity is one of the marks of the true Church founded by Jesus himself.

The agony in the garden Now we turn back to St. Luke's account. He tells us that after Jesus' prayer, the group made their way to the Mount of Olives, crossing the brook Kedron, to a place called Gethsemane where there was a garden. They were accustomed to spending the night in this way and so the apostles prepared to settle down. Jesus asked them to pray; then he took Peter, John, and James with him—as he had done on the day of his glorious Transfiguration—because as they had seen him in his glory they would also see in him his passion. Telling them to stay and watch, he went a bit farther, sank to the ground, and prayed to the Father. St. Luke describes Christ's agony which was caused by his apprehension of the impending great evil. It was so intense that ". . . his sweat became as drops of blood . . ." (Lk 22:44 NAB) Throughout this scene we are deeply conscious of the human nature of Jesus and the agonizing crisis he suffered as his two natures clashed—he abhorred suffering, yet he was determined to do his Father's will (Luke 22:39-46).

The arrest Judas knew where to find Jesus. He was acting as a guide for the police provided by the chief priests who had planned the arrest. To make sure there would be no chance of resistance, they requested and brought with them a section of the Roman cohort. After Judas had performed his traitorous job of distinguishing Jesus from the others in the dim light (by kissing him no less) Jesus identifies himself. St. John, in his account, tells us that at this moment those who had pushed forward fell back, overwhelmed by his majesty and somewhat ashamed to be seen by Jesus. After the incident of Peter and his futile attempt to use the sword to defend Jesus, the passion begins; the disciples desert their master and flee for safety. Jesus is left to his enemies (Luke 22:47-53).

THE TRIAL AND THE CROSS

Jesus before Annas and Caiphas Jesus was manacled and led to the house of Annas, the father-in-law of Caiphas; the latter was high priest that year. Why, then, was Jesus taken to Annas first? Probably because Annas' influence among the Jews had always been great, and Caiphas wished to show him deference. Jesus was then led to Caiphas. During this interrogation, Jesus was unlawfully struck by a guard. The law of the Jews provided penalties for judges who struck prisoners or who allowed others to do so.

> Then they seized him and led him away, bringing him into the high priest's house. Peter followed at a distance; and when they had kindled a fire in the middle of the courtyard and sat down together, Peter sat among them. Then a maid, seeing him as he sat in the light and gazing at him, said, "This man also was with him." But he denied it, saying, "Woman, I do not know him." And a little later someone else saw him and said, "You also are one of them." But Peter said, "Man, I am not." And after an interval of about an hour still another insisted, saying, "Certainly this man also was with you; for he is a Galilean." But Peter said, "Man, I do not know what you are saying." And immediately, while he was still speaking, the cock crowed." And the Lord turned and looked at Peter. And Peter remembered the word of the Lord, how he had said to him, "Before the cock crows today, you will deny me three times." And he went out and wept bitterly.
>
> —Lk. 22:54-62

In Jerusalem, during April, the first cock has been observed to crow as early as 2:30 a.m. Before the cock was to crow a second time at dawn, Peter had denied his association with Jesus three times. It should be noted that, although the circumstances which are reported differ, all the evangelists record three denials; they are in complete agreement as to the substance of the fact.

After Jesus' appearance before Caiphas, the Sanhedrin withdrew; then the outrageous scene took place when Jesus suffered the blows and insults at the hands of the servants.

Now the men who were holding Jesus mocked him and beat him;
they also blindfolded him and asked him, "Prophesy! Who is it that
struck you?" And they spoke many other words against him, revil-
ing him.

−Lk. 22:63-65

Before the Sanhedrin   Early in the morning the
whole Sanhedrin was called together. The high priest
presided; the elders represented the aristocracy and
landowners; and the party of the Pharisees was there
with its learned followers called the scribes. The
Roman governor alone had the power of inflicting
capital punishment. However, had a Jew been condemned to death by his own people for some crime,
Pilate doubtless would have made no fuss about sign-
ing the death warrant. But the Sanhedrin did not
wish to take the whole responsibility because they
were dealing with a question involving an "impostor
Messiah," and to the Romans this could mean a
political question.

The Jews considered the affair a religious trial,
but they were careful to give it the appearance of a
political case in order to win the understanding of the
Roman procurator, Pontius Pilate. First they had to
discover some charge, based on religious grounds,
which would involve a criminal action punishable by
death. The statements used against Jesus were words
that ought to have been explained rather than used
as an excuse for the accusation of blasphemy. Jesus
had spoken these words when he referred to the temple of his own body (predicting his resurrection) and
not to the destruction of the Temple of Jerusalem.
Caiphas questioned Jesus, hoping his answers would
decide his fate. Caiphas did succeed in eliciting from
Jesus a statement that he was the Messiah, but this
was still not enough for condemnation to death.
Anyone, if he liked, might lay claim to being the
Messiah, as long as he did not mind being looked upon
as a fool. Caiphas had to press further. More than once
Jesus had called himself the Son of God, and in a

67

sense which far surpassed what belonged to the idea of the Messiah. The question arose then: "Art thou, then, the Son of God?" Jesus' answer was blasphemous to their ears; it condemned him to death as far as the law was concerned.

When day came, the assembly of the elders of the people gathered together, both chief priests and scribes; and they led him away to their council, and they said, "If you are the Christ, tell us." But he said to them, "If I tell you, you will not believe; and if I ask you, you will not answer. But from now on the Son of man shall be seated at the right hand of the power of God." And they all said, "Are you the Son of God, then?" And he said to them, "You say that I am." And they said, "What further testimony do we need? We have heard it ourselves from his own lips."

–Lk. 22:66-71

Judas   Then Judas, who betrayed him, when he saw that he was condemned, repented and brought back the thirty pieces of silver to the chief priests and the elders, saying, "I have sinned in betraying innocent blood." But they said, "What is that to us? See to it yourself." (Mt. 27:4) And he flung the pieces of silver into the temple, and withdrew, and went away and hanged himself with a halter.

And the chief priests took the pieces of silver, and said, "It is not lawful to put them into the treasury, since they are blood money." (Mt. 27:6) And after they had consulted together, they bought with them the potter's field, as a burial place for strangers. For that reason that field has been called even to this day, Haceldama, that is, the Field of Blood. Then what was spoken through Jeremiah the prophet was fulfilled:

And they took the thirty pieces of silver,
    the price of him on whom a price had been set by some of the sons of Israel . . .

And they gave them for the potter's field,
as the Lord directed me.

–Mt. 27:9,10

The condemnation of Jesus to death must have shaken Judas considerably. Perhaps he did not realize the gravity of his crime until it was already committed. Still, he could not have been ignorant of the chief priests' intention to kill Jesus; hence he must have realized the consequences of his betrayal. Nevertheless, he did admit his crime: "I have sinned in betraying innocent blood" (Mt. 27:4). He returned the money, but his remorse went no further. Had he asked forgiveness it would have been granted, as it had been granted to Peter. But Judas doubted God's mercy and, in despair, hanged himself.

Jesus before Pilate and Herod   Pilate's attitude, it should be noted, showed that although he had no love for the Jews (his behavior toward them was that of a severe governor), he was probably not a vindictive man or a plunderer. Pilate despised the Jews and distrusted them. But he had to be cautious, because he realized that, while the official council, the Sanhedrin, was asking for Jesus' death, there might be other Jews who would use the occasion to denounce him to Rome for having caused innocent blood to be shed.

Ordinarily, the Jews would have taken Jesus to Pilate's residence, where he usually administered justice in the large courtyard. However, because the inhabitants of this place were pagans and the very place itself used for pagan administration, the Jews looked upon the place as ritually unclean. In order that they could remain ritually clean and be able to partake of the paschal supper in the evening, the Jews would not enter. Probably the Jews gathered outside the palace, at the arched entrances to the courtyard, and looked in through them. Here Pilate exchanged words with those who accompanied Jesus and his guards. At first, Pilate, when he was informed of the religious nature of the accusation, told the representatives of the Sanhedrin to take Jesus away and judge him according to their own law. The Jews were ready for this and told Pilate that Jesus was attempting to move into the sphere of his authority by forbidding men to pay tribute to Caesar and claiming himself to be the Messiah or king. Pilate ordered Jesus brought into his praetorium and questioned him there.

> Then the whole company of them arose, and brought him before Pilate. And they began to accuse him, saying, "We found this man perverting our nation, and forbidding us to give tribute to Caesar, and saying that he himself is Christ a king." And Pilate asked him, "Are you the King of the Jews?" And he answered him, "You have said so." And Pilate said to the chief priests and the multitudes, "I find no crime in this man." But they were urgent, saying, "He stirs up the people, teaching throughout all Judea, from Galilee even to this place."
>
> —Lk. 23:1-5

At the conclusion of their conversation, Pilate realized that he need not worry about Jesus being a political threat to the interests of Rome. He still considered it a religious matter. To be more certain, however, he decided to send Jesus to Herod Antipas to find out what he and the other Jewish princes thought of all this.

> When Pilate heard this, he asked whether the man was a Galilean. And when he learned that he belonged to Herod's jurisdiction, he sent him over to Herod, who was himself in Jerusalem at that time.
>
> —Lk. 23:6-7

Jesus before Herod   When Herod saw Jesus, he was exceedingly glad, for he had been a long time desirous to see him, because he had heard so much about him, and he was hoping to see some miracle done by him. He put many questions to him, but he made him no answer.

> The chief priests and the scribes stood by vehemently accusing him. And Herod with his soldiers treated him with contempt and mocked him; then, arraying him in gorgeous apparel, he sent him back to Pilate. And Herod and Pilate became friends with each other that very day, for before this they had been at enmity with each other.
>
> —Lk. 23:10-12

Jesus considered Herod a fox, cunning and vile, and did not answer his questions. Herod shared Pilate's opinion: Jesus was suffering from hallucinations. The guards made a joke of it and placed a bright garment on Jesus' shoulders and took him back to Pilate.

Jesus again before Pilate

Pilate then called together the chief priests and the rulers and the people, and said to them, "You brought me this man as one who was perverting the people; and after examining him before you, behold, I did not find this man guilty of any of your charges against him; neither did Herod, for he sent him back to us. Behold, nothing deserving death has been done by him; I will therefore chastise him and release him."

–Lk. 23:13-16

Barabbas   Pilate was reminded of a custom which had the force of law. On a feast day it was customary for the governor to release a prisoner, and the choice belonged to the people. Pilate thought this would be an opportunity to end the business. He imagined the people would be glad to free a man who had sacrificed himself for the cause of independence. He made the mistake of calling Jesus "King of the Jews," which infuriated the mob. The high priests and doctors of the law were present to call out their choice— Barabbas, in prison for murder. "What was to be done with Jesus?" Pilate asked. "Crucify him!"

So Pilate gave sentence that their demand should be granted. He released the man who had been thrown into prison for insurrection and murder, whom they asked for; but Jesus he delivered up to their will.

–Lk. 23:24-25

Who was guilty of condemning Jesus? Certainly some Jews incurred this guilt, but which Jews? They consisted of two groups: the members of the Sanhedrin, and the crowd who screamed for crucifixion. The guilt of the first group is surely more serious; leaders of the people, they saw the popularity of Jesus only as a threat to their own authority over the populace.

The crowd's guilt was less, because they did not become involved in the matter freely but only as their leaders incited them to do so. They honored their religious law and turned against Jesus when it seemed to them the law branded Jesus worthy of death. Pilate also shares the guilt. After all, he did have Jesus scourged, and he condemned him to death while convinced of his innocence. True, he acted under pressure from the Jewish leaders, but a judge should put justice before his personal safety or position.

Modern Jews are in no sense guilty of Jesus' death; Christians are guilty of bigotry when they form prejudices against the Jewish people.

Perhaps the question of guilt can be concluded by querying our own consciences. Without Christ's death there would be no salvation from sin. Why did Christ will to die? To redeem us we all share the guilt. Rather than look for a guilt in others, be they Roman or Jewish, we should humbly show our gratitude to him who had the power to prevent the crime from taking place and did nothing to interfere—for love of us sinners and our salvation.

The way of the Cross

And as they led him away, they seized one Simon of Cyrene, who was coming in from the country, and laid on him the cross, to carry it behind Jesus. And there followed him a great multitude of the people, and of women who bewailed and lamented him. But Jesus turning to them said, "Daughters of Jerusalem, do not weep for me, but weep for yourselves and for you children. For behold, the days are coming when they will say, 'Blessed are the barren, and the wombs that never bore, and the breasts that never gave suck!' Then they will begin to say to the mountains, 'Fall on us'; and to the hills, 'Cover us.' For if they do this when the wood is green, what will happen when it is dry?" Two others also, who were criminals, were led away to be put to death with him.

–Lk. 23:26-32

Fearing that Jesus would die before reaching the place of execution, the soldiers forced Simon of Cyrene to carry the Cross. A group of women indicated their compassion for Jesus, motivated perhaps by a sense

72

of the enormity of the crime. Two criminals were also dragged to execution by the soldiers. As soon as the procession passed the city gate, they arrived at the place of execution, Golgotha or "The Skull."

THE DEATH OF CHRIST

The crucifixion   The Romans executed their victims close to the city gates, so that all could see and learn a lesson. The place of execution was barbaric and repulsive. Early Christians had a horror of seeing the image of Christ on the Cross, for they had seen the sight of poor, naked bodies fastened to a plank and hoisted to the top of a large post, forming the shape of a "T." The body would sink from its own weight, the head swinging back and forth while the victims in their extreme torment and burning thirst uttered pitiful cries. The body would become rigid with pain; the chest would swell; and the lungs, heart, and head would become congested. The agony was frightful.

Mary was present at the foot of the Cross, suffering with her Son, thus adding to his torture but consoling him in his desertion. The chief priests who had come to witness the death of Jesus shouted insults at him, thus fulfilling verses of one of the messianic psalms: "But I am a worm, not a man; / the scorn of men, despised by the people. / All who see me scoff at me . . .: / 'He relied on the LORD; let him deliver him, / let him rescue him, if he loves him'" (Ps. 22:7-9 NAB). And Jesus' crucifixion between two thieves fulfilled Isaiah's prophecy that the Messiah would be numbered among the wicked (Is. 53:12). Even the soldiers who gambled for Jesus' clothing unknowingly fulfilled another prophecy: ". . . they divide my garments among them, and for my vesture they cast lots" (Ps. 22:19 NAB).

Shortly before his death, Jesus, in his native Aramaic tongue, intoned messianic Psalm 21, which contained many details concerning the death of the Messiah. Of those present, only the doctors of the Law realized Jesus was quoting a psalm; the others, the simpleminded, thought Jesus was calling Elijah. When Jesus sighed: "I thirst" (Jn. 19:28), the soldiers offered him a mixture of vinegar and water. Thus they fulfilled Psalm 69:22 NAB, concerning the suffering of the Messiah: ". . . in my thirst they gave me vinegar to drink."

And when they came to the place which is called The Skull, there they crucified him, and the criminals, one on the right and one on the left. And Jesus said, "Father, forgive them; for they know not what they do." And they cast lots to divide his garments. And the people stood by, watching; but the rulers scoffed at him, saying, "He saved others; let him save himself, if he is the Christ of God, his Chosen One!" The soldiers also mocked him, coming up and offering him vinegar, and saying, "If you are the King of the Jews, save yourself!" There was also an inscription over him, "This is the King of the Jews."

One of the criminals who was crucified railed at him, saying, "Are you not the Christ? Save yourself and us!" But the other rebuked him, saying, "Do you not fear God, since you are under the same sentence of condemnation? And we indeed justly; for we are receiving the due reward of our deeds; but this man has done nothing wrong." And he said, "Jesus, remember me when you come in your kingly power." And he said to him, "Truly, I say to you, today you will be with me in Paradise."

It was now about the sixth hour, and there was darkness over the whole land until the ninth hour, while the sun's light failed.

–Lk. 23:33-45a

The death of Jesus   It was three o'clock, and as the Passover ceremony was beginning in the temple, Jesus bowed his head and died; his work was consummated, completed. He had paid the price for our redemption. He had accomplished his Father's will. Israel at this very moment was engaged in the rites whose meanings were being changed completely. All the centuries of God's preparing Israel for his Son were climaxed; all the prophecies intended to prepare the people were now fulfilled and became history. Thus was accomplished the most important event in the history of the human race.

At the moment of his death the veil of the sanctuary in the temple was torn down the middle, as if to signify that what was holy and sacred before was now open to all men. An earthquake struck, and many tombs were opened. A soldier drove a lance into Jesus' side to make sure of his death. St. John, who witnessed it, says that blood and water flowed from the wound. Perhaps the lance point pierced the part of the heart containing the colorless pericardial fluid collected there during the agony.

> . . . and the curtain of the temple was torn in two. Then Jesus, crying with a loud voice, said, "Father, into thy hands I commit my spirit!" And having said this he breathed his last. Now when the centurion saw what had taken place, he praised God, and said, "Certainly this man was innocent!" And all the multitudes who assembled to see the sight, when they saw what had taken place, returned home beating their breasts. And all his acquaintances and the women who had followed him from Galilee stood at a distance and saw these things.
>
> —Lk. 23:45b-49

Now at this tremendous moment in the history of Salvation let us pause for reflection, as the Church does when the passion is read during Holy Week. A man, branded and convicted by his own nation as a religious and political criminal, has been unjustly put to death: the Jews have legally murdered their king. The Messiah of the Promise, expectation of the ages, has been definitively rejected by the Covenant People of God. Lifted up between heaven and earth that the Son of Man might draw all things to himself, God has died . . . for you.

The burial

> Now there was a man named Joseph from the Jewish town of Arimathea. He was a member of the council, a good and righteous man, who had not consented to their purpose and deed, and he was looking for the kingdom of God. This man went to Pilate and asked for the body of Jesus. Then he took it down and wrapped it in a linen shroud, and laid him in a rock-hewn tomb, where no one had ever yet been laid. It was the day of Preparation, and the sabbath was

beginning. The women who had come with him from Galilee followed and saw the tomb, and how his body was laid; then they returned, and prepared spices and ointments.

—Lk. 23:50-56a

Joseph of Arimathea was successful in obtaining Pilate's permission to arrange for the burial of Jesus' body. Joseph and Nicodemus washed the body and wrapped it in linen bands sprinkled with mixed spices. The body was then laid in a nearby tomb which Joseph had prepared for himself. His act of generosity also relieved Jesus' friends of the task of transporting the body at night, and forestalled possible Jewish interference. They rolled a stone over the entrance and left. Meanwhile, the holy women who had remained with Mary at the Cross had been preparing more spices and perfumed oil with the hope of making their contribution to the burial of Jesus. There was no time, however, before darkness arrived, and they left with the intention of returning. They remained at home the next day, Saturday, for fear of breaking the Law concerning the Sabbath.

And on the Sabbath they rested according to the commandment.

—Lk. 23:56b

Next day, that is, after the day of Preparation, the chief priests and the Pharisees gathered before Pilate and said, "Sir, we remember how that impostor said, while he was still alive, 'After three days I will rise again.' Therefore order the sepulchre to be made secure until the third day, lest his disciples go and steal him away, and tell the people, 'He has risen from the dead,' and the last fraud will be worse than the first." Pilate said to them, "You have a guard of soldiers; go, make it as secure as you can." So they went and made the sepulchre secure by sealing the stone and setting a guard.

—Mt. 27:62-66

THE RESURRECTION OF CHRIST

The day of resurrection   The Sabbath ended on Saturday evening. Early the following morning the devoted women made their way to the tomb to anoint Jesus' body. There were two groups of women, the second arriving later than the first. The difficulty of harmonizing the four diverse accounts of what took place that day disappears if we do not dwell on unimportant details and realize that each writer was giving his own account of what took place as he observed the happenings or learned about them. The important thing is that Jesus had risen, and each account explains in its own way how the fact was made known to his disciples. When we read St. Paul we see what an exalted position the resurrection had in its time, indeed throughout the entire history of the Church. The disciples had not understood that Jesus was to rise again, even though he had foretold it to them. But now it dawned on them that this was the fulfillment of what he had told them.

The women at the grave

But on the first day of the week, at early dawn, they went to the tomb, taking the spices which they had prepared. And they found the stone rolled away from the tomb, but when they went in they did not find the body. While they were perplexed about this, behold, two men stood by them in dazzling apparel; and as they were frightened and bowed their faces to the ground, the men said to them, "Why do you seek the living among the dead? He is not here, but has risen." Remember how he told you, while he was still in Galilee, that the Son of man must be delivered into the hands of sinful men, and be crucified, and on the third day rise." And they remembered his words, and returning from the tomb they told all this to the eleven and to all the rest. Now it was Mary Magdalene and Joanna and Mary the mother of James and the other women with them who told this to the apostles; but these words seemed to them an idle tale, and they did not believe them. (Lk. 24:1-12) When Peter and John arrived at the tomb they observed the linen cloths set apart. Puzzled, they then returned home in awe.

Mary Magdalene

Now when he rose early on the first day of the week, he appeared first to Mary Magdalene, from whom he had cast out seven demons. She went and told those who had been with him, as they mourned and wept. But when they heard that he was alive and had been seen by her, they would not believe it.

–Mk. 16:9-11

When Mary Magdalene recognized Jesus in the garden she fell at his feet, weeping for joy. This was no time for emotion, and furthermore, Jesus' body was in a glorified state; he was soon to ascend to his Father, and the disciples needed to be warned of the fact. This apparently explains Jesus' remark:

"Do not hold me, for I have not yet ascended to the Father; but go to my brethren and say to them, I am ascending to my Father . . ."

–Jn. 20:17

Jesus appears at Emmaus   Probably most of Jesus' followers looked upon the report that Jesus was alive again as an old wives' tale. Two of them decided to return to their native village, Emmaus. Jesus appeared on the road as a fellow traveler. They did not recognize him; indeed, his questioning about what had taken place indicated he was a complete stranger. Jesus explained to them (as he had previously done to his disciples) that, as Isaiah had prophesied, the Messiah would suffer before entering his glory. Jesus also explained the Scriptures which spoke of him, both in the Law of Moses and in the prophets.

Recognizing Jesus, the disciples were carried away with joy and left immediately to inform the eleven apostles in Jerusalem.

That very day two of them were going to a village named Emmaus, about seven miles from Jerusalem, and talking with each other about all these things that had happened. While they were talking and discussing together, Jesus himself drew near and went with them. But their eyes were kept from recognizing him. And he said to them, "What is this conversation which you are holding with each other as you walk?" And they stood still, looking sad.

Then one of them, named Cleopas, answered him, "Are you the only visitor to Jerusalem who does not know the things that have happened there in these days?" And he said to them, "What things?"

And they said to him, "Concerning Jesus of Nazareth, who was a prophet mighty in deed and word before God and all the people, and how our chief priests and rulers delivered him up to be condemned to death, and crucified him. But we had hoped that he was the one to redeem Israel. Yes, and besides all this, it is now the third day since this happened. Moreover, some women of our company amazed us. They were at the tomb early in the morning and did not find his body; and they came back saying that they had even seen a vision of angels, who said that he was alive. Some of those who were with us went to the tomb, and found it just as the women had said; but him they did not see."

And he said to them "O foolish men, and slow of heart to believe all that the prophets have spoken! Was it not necessary that the Christ should suffer these things and enter into his glory?" And beginning with Moses and all the prophets, he interpreted to them in all the scriptures the things concerning himself.

So they drew near to the village to which they were going. He appeared to be going further, but they constrained him, saying, "Stay with us, for it is toward evening and the day is now far spent." When he was at table with them, he took the bread and blessed, and broke it, and gave it to them. And their eyes were opened and they recognized him; and he vanished out of their sight. They said to each other, "Did not our hearts burn within us while he talked to us on the road, while he opened to us the scriptures?" And they rose that same hour and returned to Jerusalem; and they found the eleven gathered together and those who were with them, who said, "The Lord has risen indeed, and has appeared to Simon!" Then they told what had happened on the road, and how he was known to them in the breaking of the bread.

–Lk. 24:13-35

Jesus appears to the eleven

As they were saying this, Jesus himself stood among them, and said to them, "Peace to you." But they were startled and frightened, and supposed that they saw a spirit.

And he said to them, "Why are you troubled, and why do questionings rise in your hearts? See my hands and my feet, that it is I myself; handle me, and see; for a spirit has not flesh and bones as you see that I have." And when he had said this he showed them his hands and his feet. And while they still disbelieved for joy, and wondered, he said to them, "Have you anything here to eat?" They gave him a piece of broiled fish, and he took it and ate before them.

–Lk. 24:36-43

Apparitions in Galilee   After the days of sorrow and joy, the apostles had to resume their ordinary occupations. They knew they were to see him again in Galilee, and their work with the souls of men could not begin until then. Therefore, they returned to their nets, and Jesus appeared to them. Jesus asked Peter three times for a proclamation of his love, perhaps alluding to Peter's threefold denial. Peter was consecrated universal shepherd; the whole flock, lambs and sheep, were to be subject to Peter's pastoral care. The plan for the future was contained in a few lines: Go and baptize all nations and teach them to live the moral life Jesus had taught them; he would be with them at all times.

After this Jesus revealed himself again to the disciples by the Sea of Tiberias; and he revealed himself in this way. Simon Peter, Thomas called the Twin, Nathanael of Cana in Galilee, the sons of Zebedee, and two others of his disciples were together. Simon Peter said to them, "I am going fishing." They said to him, "We will go with you." They went out and got into the boat; but that night they caught nothing.

Just as day was breaking, Jesus stood on the beach; yet the disciples did not know that it was Jesus. Jesus said to them, "Children, have you any fish?" They answered him, "No." He said to them, "Cast the net on the right side of the boat, and you will find some." So they cast it, and now they were not able to haul it in, for the quantity of fish. That disciple whom Jesus loved said to Peter, "It is the Lord!" When Simon Peter heard that it was the Lord, he put on his clothes, for he was stripped for work, and sprang into the sea. But the other disciples came in the boat, dragging the net full of fish, for they were not far from the land, but about a hundred yards off.

When they got out on land, they saw a charcoal fire there, with fish lying on it, and bread. Jesus said to them, "Bring some of the fish that you have just caught." So Simon Peter went aboard and hauled the net ashore, full of large fish, a hundred and fifty-three of them; and although there were so many, the net was not torn. Jesus said to them, "Come and have breakfast." Now none of the disciples dared ask him, "Who are you?" They knew it was the Lord. Jesus came and took the bread and gave it to them, and so with the fish. This was now the third time that Jesus was revealed to the disciples after he was raised from the dead.

—Jn. 21:1-14

The primacy of Peter

When they had finished breakfast, Jesus said to Simon Peter, "Simon, son of John, do you love me more than these?" He said to him, "Yes, Lord; you know that I love you." He said to him, "Feed my lambs." A second time he said to him, "Simon, son of John, do you love me?" He said to him, "Yes, Lord; you know that I love you." He said to him, "Tend my sheep." He said to him the third time, "Simon, son of John, do you love me?" Peter was grieved because he said to him the third time, "Do you love me?" And he said to him, "Lord, you know everything; you know that I love you." Jesus said to him, "Feed my sheep. Truly, truly, I say to you, when you were young, you girded yourself and walked where you would; but when you are old, you will stretch out your hands, and another will gird you and carry you where you do not wish to go." (This he said to show by what death he was to glorify God.) And after this he said to him, "Follow me."

–Jn. 21:15-19

Peter turned and saw following them the disciple whom Jesus loved, who had lain close to his breast at the supper and had said, "Lord, who is it that is going to betray you?" When Peter saw him, he said to Jesus, "Lord, what about this man?" Jesus said to him, 'If it is my will that he remain until I come, what is that to you? Follow me!" The saying spread abroad among the brethren that this disciple was not to die; yet Jesus did not say to him that he was not to die, but, "If it is my will that he remain until I come, what is that to you?"

–Jn. 21:20-23

Now the eleven disciples went to Galilee, to the mountain to which Jesus had directed them. And when they saw him they worshiped him; but some doubted. And Jesus came and said to them. "All authority in heaven and on earth has been given to me. Go therefore and make disciples of all nations, baptizing them in the name of the Father and of the Son and of the Holy Spirit, teaching them to observe all that I have commanded you; and lo, I am with you always, to the close of the age."

–Mt. 28:16-20

Final instructions

Then he said to them, "These are my words which I spoke to you, while I was still with you, that everything written about me in the law of Moses and the prophets and the psalms must be fulfilled." Then he opened their minds to understand the scriptures, and said to them, "Thus it is written, that the Christ should suffer and on the third day rise from the dead, and that repentance and forgiveness of sins should be preached in his name to all nations, beginning from Jerusalem. You are witnesses of these things. And behold, I send the promise of my Father upon you; but stay in the city, until you are clothed with power from on high."

–Lk. 24:44-49

The ascension   The apostles returned to Jerusalem to await the beginning of their apostolic labors. Jesus must have appeared to them several times there to instruct them. On the day of his ascension we learn that he gave them their final lesson, dealing with the meaning of the Scriptures, which would prove so helpful in their teaching and preaching. The time for their work had not yet come, and Jesus told them to remain in Jerusalem until the Holy Spirit would visit them. The group then traveled toward Bethany. At some location on the route, Jesus lifted his hands and blessed his followers, and ascended to heaven. A great joy filled the hearts of the witnesses, the joy Jesus had promised them at the Last Supper, and they returned to Jerusalem to await the Holy Spirit.

> Then he led them out as far as Bethany, and lifting up his hands he blessed them. While he blessed them, he parted from them and was carried up into heaven. And they worshipped him, and returned to Jerusalem with great joy, and were continually in the temple blessing God.
>
> —Lk. 24:50-53

Where is Jesus Christ? St. Mark says he is at the right hand of the Father. This is a mystery for our minds, one of the unfathomable features of the mystery of the ascension. Our faith, in this matter, is not concerned with the geographical question of Christ's location. Our faith is in the mystery of Christ's exaltation, his establishment in the power of the Holy Spirit. Christ reigns now with his Father and sends his Spirit upon those who are to form his Mystical Body on earth. This is what we believe; this is the object of our faith. Jesus has become a life-giving spirit, victory over death and sin, the "firstborn among many brethren."

CONCLUSION

No consideration of the exaltation of Christ would be complete were mention not made of St. Paul's classic statement on the subject. In fact, quoting the entire passage from his first letter to the Corinthians may well supply the conclusion to the present chapter.

It will serve a twofold purpose: first, it will provide a remarkable statement of the doctrine that sustained the hope of the early Christians—and of all Christians; secondly, it will provide a solid doctrinal basis for the matters to be discussed in the following chapter.

Christ's resurrection

Now I would remind you, brethren, in what terms I preached to you the gospel, which you received, in which you stand, by which you are saved, if you hold it fast—unless you believed in vain.

For I delivered to you as of first importance what I also received, that Christ died for our sins in accordance with the scriptures, that he was buried, that he was raised on the third day in accordance with the scriptures, and that he appeared to Cephas, then to the twelve. Then he appeared to more than five hundred brethren at one time, most of whom are still alive, though some have fallen asleep. Then he appeared to James, then to all the apostles. Last of all, as to one untimely born, he appeared also to me. For I am the least of the apostles, unfit to be called an apostle, because I persecuted the Church of God. But by the grace of God I am what I am, and his grace toward me was not in vain. On the contrary, I worked harder than any of them, though it was not I, but the grace of God which is with me. Whether then it was I or they, so we preach and so you believed.

—1 Cor. 15:1-11

The false doctrine

Now if Christ is preached as raised from the dead, how can some of you say that there is no resurrection of the dead? But if there is no resurrection of the dead, then Christ has not been raised; if Christ has not been raised, then our preaching is in vain and your faith is in vain. We are even found to be misrepresenting God, because we testified of God that he raised Christ, whom he did not raise if it is true that the dead are not raised. For if the dead are not raised, then Christ has not been raised. If Christ has not been raised, your faith is futile and you are still in your sins. Then those also who have fallen asleep in Christ have perished. If for this life only we have hoped in Christ, we are of all men most to be pitied.

—1 Cor. 15:12-19

Christ the first fruits

But in fact Christ has been raised from the dead, the first fruits of those who have fallen asleep. For as by a man came death, by a man has come also the resurrection of the dead. For as in Adam all die, so also in Christ shall all be made alive. But each in his own order: Christ the first fruits, then at his coming those who belong to Christ. Then comes the end, when he delivers the kingdom to God the Father after destroying every rule and every authority and power. For he must reign until he has put all his enemies under his feet. The last enemy to be destroyed is death. "For God has put all things in subjection under his feet." But when it says, "All things are put in subjection under him," it is plain that he is excepted who put all things under him. When all things are subjected to him, then the Son himself will also be subjected to him who put all things under him, that God may be everything to every one.

−1 Cor. 15:20-28

For not all flesh is alike, but there is one kind for men, another for animals, another for birds, and another for fish. There are celestial bodies and there are terrestrial bodies; but the glory of the celestial is one, and the glory of the terrestrial is another. There is one glory of the sun, and another glory of the moon, and another glory of the stars; for star differs from star in glory.

So is it with the resurrection of the dead. What is sown is perishable, what is raised is imperishable. It is sown in dishonor, it is raised in glory. It is sown in weakness, it is raised in power. It is sown a physical body, it is raised a spiritual body.

−1 Cor. 15:39-44

The natural and the spiritual body

If there is a physical body, there is also a spiritual body. Thus it is written, "The first man Adam became a living being"; the last Adam became a life-giving spirit. But it is not the spiritual which is first but the physical, and then the spiritual. The first man was from the earth, a man of dust; the second man is from heaven. As was the man of dust, so are those who are of the dust; and as is the man of heaven, so are those who are of heaven. Just as we have borne the image of the man of dust, we shall also bear the image of the man of heaven.

−1 Cor. 15:44B-49

Final glory of the body

I tell you this, brethren: flesh and blood cannot inherit the kingdom of God, nor does the perishable inherit the imperishable. Lo! I tell you a mystery. We shall not all sleep, but we shall all be changed, in a moment, in the twinkling of an eye, at the last trumpet. For the trumpet will sound, and the dead will be raised imperishable, and we shall be changed. For this perishable nature must put on the imperishable, and this mortal nature must put on immortality. When the perishable puts on the imperishable, and the mortal puts on immortality, then shall come to pass the saying that is written:

"Death is swallowed up in victory.
O death, where is thy victory?
O death, where is thy sting?"

The sting of death is sin, and the power of sin is the Law. But thanks be to God who gives us the victory through our Lord Jesus Christ.

Therefore, my beloved brethren, be steadfast and immovable, always abounding in the work of the Lord, knowing that your labor is not in vain in the Lord.

—1 Cor. 15:50-58

Thinking it over • • •

1. What is the "paschal mystery"?
2. How does it relate to the Jewish rite of Passover?
3. Describe some of the ways by which Jesus suffered.
4. Name four of the effects of Christ's passion.
5. How can we realize these effects in us?
6. Besides an English dictionary, what book is essential which we should have?
7. Which two evangelists do we follow more closely in their accounts of the events leading to the crucifixion of Our Lord?
8. For those who would speak only of the symbolism of the Eucharist, what phrases or words of Christ would we point out?
9. Where would we find the earliest record of the practice of celebrating the Eucharist in apostolic times?
10. What was "The Discourse" of Jesus? Which of the evangelists records it?
11. What did Peter do when Jesus was arrested?
12. Who shares responsibility for the death of Jesus?
13. There are four evangelical accounts of the resurrection of Our Lord differing in details. What is the most important message that all of them are telling us?

Chapter 5

THE ROLE OF MARY
IN OUR REDEMPTION

A Popular Daily Prayer to Mary Asking
Her Intercession For Us

MEMORARE

Remember, O most holy Virgin Mary, that never
was it known, that anyone who fled to your protec-
tion, implored your help, or sought your intercession, was left unaided. Inspired with this confidence,
I hasten to you, O Virgin of Virgins, my mother. To
you I come; before you I stand, sinful and sorrowful.
O Mother of the Word Incarnate, despise not my
petitions, but in your mercy, hear and grant my
prayer. Amen.

MARY, OUR MOTHER

When you want something from your dad, what do you usually do? You go to your mother and ask her to intercede for you, to put in a good word to your dad in favor of your request. This is what we do in relation to Jesus. He is our Lord but he is also our brother. Knowing that Mary is closer to Jesus than any other creature, we go to her in prayer to ask for her intercession with him in all our needs because nothing is granted to us from heaven except through the Lord Jesus Christ. We always pray through him, for he has merited for us the gifts of our redemption.

In speaking of, or writing about, the Virgin Mary, we should follow closely the official teaching of the Church about her role in our redemption. That role was clearly defined by the Pope and the bishops of the world in their last ecumenical (world-wide) council which was held in Rome between 1963 and 1965. The council was convened by the very popular Pope John XXIII when he was 80 years old and after only 90 days of his reign. It was continued and concluded by Pope Paul VI. The gathering of all the bishops was pastoral in intent—to better clarify and communicate the Church's doctrine—but involved many teachings of the Church in its sixteen constitutions, or sections. It was called Vatican Council II because the previous council, which also was held in Rome (1869-70), was referred to as Vatican Council I. Let us consider the most recent teaching of Mary's role which is found in chapter eight of the constitution on the Church.

Mary's position   The Church first reminds us that God planned our redemption "when the fullness of time came" and then he "sent his Son, born of a woman . . . that we might receive the adoption of sons" (Gal. 4:4-5). His incarnation was accomplished by the Holy Spirit from the Virgin Mary. This divine mystery is revealed to us and continued in the

Church, which the Lord established as his own body. Adhering to Christ, the head, and having communion with all his saints, the faithful must also venerate the memory "above all of the glorious and perpetual Virgin Mary, Mother of our God and Lord, Jesus Christ."

Therefore, our veneration of Mary is founded on her being truly the Mother of God and Mother of the Redeemer. Thus "she is united to him by a close and indissoluble tie . . . a favorite daughter of the Father and the temple of the Holy Spirit." She surpasses all other creatures both in heaven and on earth. Because she belongs to the offspring of Adam, she is one with all human beings in their need for salvation. She is, as St. Augustine wrote, "The mother of the members of Christ . . . who are members of Christ their head." She is a pre-eminent and altogether singular member of the Church, and is the Church's model and exemplar in faith and charity. Taught by the Holy Spirit, the Catholic Church honors her with filial affection and piety as a most beloved mother.

Mary's role in the plan of salvation   Her figure is foreshadowed in the Old Testament and now comes into a gradually sharper focus. She is prophetically foreshadowed in that victory over the serpent promised to our first parents after their fall into sin. She is seen as the virgin who was to conceive and bear a son whose name will be called Emmanuel (Is. 7:14). The Father of mercies willed that the consent of the pre-destined mother should precede the Incarnation, so that just as a woman contributed to death, so also a woman should contribute to life. She gave to the world that very life which renews all things, and she was enriched by God with gifts befitting such a role.

From the earliest apostolic times, the Fathers viewed Mary as entirely holy and freed from all stain of sin. This freedom begins at her conception. Unlike us, and in anticipation of the merits won by our redemption through her son, she is addressed by the angel at the Annunciation as "full of grace." Her willingness to serve as God's handmaiden is simply expressed by her words, "Let it be done to me according to your word." (Lk. 1:38) "In subordination to him and along with him," say the Council Fathers, "by the grace of Almighty God she served the mystery of the redemption." And so the early Fathers of the Church saw her as used by God, not merely in a passive way, but as cooperating in the work of human salvation through free faith and obedience. Together they would say, "death through Eve, life through Mary." The contrast between the roles of Mary and Eve has been a constant theme in Christian writing.

The Virginity of Mary   Mary's uniqueness in God's plan of salvation is further demonstrated by her perpetual virginity. St. Augustine sums up Mary's perpetual virginity by teaching us that she "remained a virgin in conceiving her Son, a virgin in giving birth to him, a virgin in carrying him, a virgin in nursing him at her breast, always a virgin." In St. Augustine's words we learn that Mary's maternal relationship with her Son was very human in that she nurtured him as any other human mother cares for her child. Yet, we also note that hers was more than just a human relationship with Jesus; it was also divine as attested to by her perpetual virginity.

No other mother on earth remained a virgin before, during and after the birth of her child. This unique privilege was a gift given the Blessed Mother by God's grace as a testimony to the divinity of his Son. Mary's virginity on the one hand demonstrates her unequaled cooperation with God's will and grace. On the other hand, Mary's virginity also confirms the divinity of her Son, born as no other human being before or after him.

Furthermore, Mary's virginity is the sign of her total fidelity to God. By giving herself entirely to God's will for her in his plan of salvation, Mary shows herself to be the perfect disciple. She reserves her whole being, physically, spiritually and mentally, for God. She is for us the model disciple whom we seek to emulate in our own relationship with Christ. Mary is for us the ideal follower of Christ, an example of total and free obedience to God's Will. It is shown:

1. In her visit to Elizabeth who greeted her as blessed while John in joy leaped in Elizabeth's womb;

2. At the birth of our Lord, who did not diminish his mother's integrity but sanctified it, when the mother of God joyfully showed her first-born Son to the shepherds and Magi;

3. When she presented him to the Lord in the temple and heard Simeon foretell that her Son would be a sign of contradiction and that a sword would pierce her soul;

4. When the child Jesus was lost, and they sought him sorrowing, they found him with the teachers in the temple. When his parents told him of their natural anxiety, he enigmatically replied, "Did you not know that I must be in my Father's house?" (Lk. 2:49) They did not understand fully what he meant, but, says St. Luke, "His mother kept all these things in her heart" (Lk. 2:41-51);

5. When Mary's compassion for friends at the marriage feast in Cana impelled her to ask her son to work his first miracle as Messiah;

6. When he declared publicly that those who heard and kept the Word of God, as she was faithfully doing, were blessed (Mk. 3:35, Lk. 11:27-28, and Lk. 2:19, 51);

7. When she followed him to his cross, suffering with him in the company of the one courageous apostle, John;

8. When she united herself with a maternal heart to the sacrifice of her Son, consenting to his immolation, and when Jesus gave her to his disciple, John, as his mother and the mother of us all: ". . . he said to his mother, 'woman, behold your son', and to John and us, 'Behold your mother' " (Jn. 19:26-27);

9. When God manifested solemnly the mystery of the salvation of the human race at Pentecost, we read that in the preceding days the apostles continued "with one accord devoted themselves to prayer, together with the women and Mary the mother of Jesus, and with his brothers. (Acts 1:14);

10. When finally, preserved from all guilt of sin, the Immaculate Virgin was taken up body and soul into heavenly glory upon the completion of her earthly sojourn. She was exalted by the Lord as Queen of All, in order that she might be the more thoroughly conformed to her son, the Lord of Lords. Her Assumption anticipates the promise of our own bodily resurrection and gives us hope in the fulfillment of that promise.

The Blessed Virgin and the Church   We have, of course, only one Mediator between God and men: "For there is one God, and there is one mediator between God and men, the man Christ Jesus, who gave himself as a ransom for all . . ." (1 Tim. 2:5-6). Mary's position in no way obscures or diminishes this unique mediation of Christ, but rather shows its power. For her intercessory powers come not from her own nature, but from the divine pleasure. They flow forth from the superabundance of the merits of Christ, rest on his mediation, depend entirely on it and draw all their power from it. In no way do they impede the immediate union of the faithful with Christ. Rather, they foster this union. In an utterly singular way, she cooperated by her obedience, faith, hope, and burning charity in the Savior's work of restoring supernatural life to souls. For this reason, she is a mother to us in the order of grace.

Mary was eternally predestined, in conjunction with the incarnation of the divine Word, to be the mother of God. This maternity of Mary in the order of grace began with the consent which she gave in faith at the Annunciation and continued all the way to the Cross. Her role continues on until the end of time by her many acts of intercession to win for us the gifts of eternal salvation. By her maternal charity she cares for the brethren of her Son who still journey on earth surrounded by dangers and difficulties, until they are led to their happy home in heaven. Thus Mary is invoked by the Church under the titles of Advocate, Auxiliatrix, Adjutrix, and Mediatrix.

These titles are understood neither to take away nor to add anything to the dignity and efficacy of Christ the one Mediator. The unique mediation of the Redeemer does not exclude but rather gives rise among creatures to a manifold cooperation which is but a sharing in this unique source; the Church does not hesitate to profess this subordinate role of Mary. She commends it to the hearts of the faithful, so that encouraged by her maternal help they may more closely adhere to the Mediator and Redeemer.

St. Ambrose taught that the Mother of God is a model of the Church in the matters of faith, charity, and perfect union with Christ. She is also, in a singular fashion, an exemplar of both virginity and motherhood, and is hailed as the unique virgin mother. The Church herself becomes a mother by accepting God's word in faith. By her preaching and by baptism she brings forth to a new and immortal life children who are conceived of the Holy Spirit and born of God. The Church herself is a virgin, who keeps whole and pure the fidelity she has pledged to her spouse. Imitating the Mother of her Lord and by the power of the Holy Spirit, she preserves with virginal purity an integral faith, a firm hope, and a sincere charity.

The followers of Christ strive to increase in holiness by conquering sin. And so they raise their eyes to Mary who shines forth to the whole community of the elect as a model of the virtues. For Mary in a certain way unites and mirrors within herself the central truths of the faith. Hence, when she is being preached and venerated, she summons the faithful to her Son and his sacrifice and to love for the Father.

Devotion to the Blessed Virgin   Because she was so involved in the mysteries of Christ and so exalted by divine grace above all angels and human beings, Mary has always been venerated by the Church. She attracts the devotion of the faithful as the person closest to her divine Son. Thus we frequently "go to Jesus through Mary." To her we direct many of our prayers of intercession. All of us are attracted to many different saints as we make our prayers of petition, but Our Lady holds our highest priority as the Intercessor for all Christians. She predicted that continuing devotion when she said at the time of her visit to her cousin, Elizabeth: "For behold, henceforth, all generations will call me blessed; for he who is mighty has done great things for me" (Lk. 1:48-49a).

The Church has endorsed many forms of piety toward the mother of God, provided they are within the limits of sound and orthodox doctrine and do not substitute for or distract us from our one Mediator, Our Lord Jesus Christ. These sound forms of devotion have varied according to the circumstances of time and place and have reflected the diversity of native characteristics and temperament among the faithful. While honoring Christ's mother, these devotions cause her Son to be rightly known, loved, and glorified, and all his commands observed.

At Vatican Council II, the bishops of the world warned against promoting misunderstandings of Mary's role in the Redemption among both the Catholic faithful and our separated brethren:

> This Synod earnestly exhorts theologians and preachers of the divine word that in treating of the unique dignity of the Mother of God, they carefully and equally avoid the falsity of exaggeration on the one hand, and the excess of narrow-mindedness on the other. Pursuing the study of Sacred Scripture, the holy Fathers, the doctors, and liturgies of the Church, and under the guidance of the Church's teaching authority, let them rightly explain the offices and privileges of the Blessed Virgin which are always related to Christ, the Source of all truth, sanctity, and piety.

> Let them painstakingly guard against any word or deed which could lead separated brethren or anyone else into error regarding the true doctrine of the Church. Let the faithful remember moreover that true devotion consists neither in fruitless and passing

emotion, nor in a certain vain credulity. Rather, it proceeds from true faith, by which we are led to know the excellence of the Mother of God, and are moved to a filial love toward our mother and to the imitation of her virtues ("The Church," n. 67).

OUR LADY IN THE ROSARY

Above all prayer is the Eucharist, the Paschal Mystery represented to us sacramentally. Within this redemptive offering all four kinds of prayer are included: adoration, reparation, thanksgiving and petition. The Mass also includes the most perfect prayer, given to us by Jesus himself, the Our Father. The most popular devotional prayer is the Rosary, for it provokes our meditation on the fundamental mysteries of our Christian faith.

As a prayer form it was begun in the Middle Ages by men and women working in the fields on the hillsides of little towns. Atop each of these hillside towns was a monastery, and as they worked the fields, the peasants could hear the monks chanting their Divine Office during different parts of the day. The Office is composed of lessons, mostly from the Scriptures, and the Psalms of the Old Testament. In all, there are 150 psalms. The people could not read these while they worked, but they were very familiar with the Hail Mary, so they divided their Hail Marys into tens, or decades. The decades were divided into three groups of 50, a total of 150, the number of psalms. The three groups of decades were for the joyful, sorrowful, and glorious mysteries of Christ. The Rosary has all the necessary ingredients of sound prayer. It is scriptural in origin because the events recalled are from the gospels. The Lord's Prayer was revealed by Jesus himself and the first half of the Hail Mary is the Angel Gabriel's salutation to Mary.

Devotion to Mary through the Rosary has been urged by Mary herself through those chosen ones to whom she appeared. Popes and bishops have urged the faithful to go to Jesus through Mary's Rosary. A faithful follower of Jesus always has and usually carries a rosary.

The beads help us to number our decades, keeping track of our prayerful progress. But our repetition of the Our Fathers and Hail Marys is not senseless mumbling, as some might suspect. For this prayer is mental as well as oral. As we finger our beads we reflect on the whole Paschal Mystery. Meditation is a necessary part of the recitation. We are aided in our understanding of the various mysterious events if we are familiar with their scriptural origins. To know Jesus one must know the gospels that inspire the topics of our meditation.

All five joyful mysteries involve Mary and her role in our redemption. The last two glorious mysteries are focused on Mary and her place with Jesus. To continue our study of Mary's role in our redemption and to deepen our knowledge of the subjects of our meditations, let us examine closely the five joyful mysteries of the Rosary.

THE ANNUNCIATION

"In the sixth month the angel Gabriel was sent from God to a town of Galilee called Nazareth, to a virgin betrothed to a man named Joseph, of the house of David, and the virgin's name was Mary" (Lk. 1:26 NAB). It was the cherished hope of every Jewish woman that she would be chosen by God to be the mother of the Messiah. Finally God chooses, and he sends his angel to announce his choice. The one chosen is a humble virgin from Nazareth, and her name is Mary. Until this moment history knows nothing of Mary; tradition states that her parents were Joachim and Anne, but that is all.

" 'Behold, you will conceive in your womb and bear a son.' . . . 'The Holy Spirit shall come upon you

and the power of the Most High will overshadow you
. . .' " (Lk. 1:31, 35). The angelic message is brief but
clear. Mary is asked by God to assent to his invitation that she become the mother of the Messiah. The
whole of creation waited in anxious expectation. The
sinful human race was now, in the person of Mary,
asked to consent freely to its redemption. One of the
great moments of history was at hand. "And Mary
said, 'Behold I am the handmaid of the Lord; let it be
done to me according to your word.' And the angel
departed from her" (Lk. 1:38). At that moment, in a
quiet little village in northern Palestine, witnessed
only by the virgin and the choirs of heaven, "your all-
powerful word from heaven's royal throne bounded
. . ." (Wis. 18:15 NAB). This was one of the supreme
moments of the history of Salvation; now the perfect
revelation of God to man was accomplished. The Son
of God—"God of God, Light of Light, true God of true
God"—assumed human nature in the womb of the
Virgin Mary.

Truly a mother   "While they were there, the time
came for her to be delivered. And she gave birth to
her firstborn son and wrapped him in swaddling
clothes, and laid him in a manger, because there was
no place for them in the inn" (Lk. 2:6-7). It is obvious
from these words that Mary is truly the mother of
Jesus. He was conceived in her womb; she bore him
for several months; and when the time came for her
to be delivered, she gave birth to him. Jesus had no
human father, but by the miraculous intervention of
the Holy Spirit all the factors of human conception
usually provided by the father were supplied. Mary
provided all that any human mother provides for her
child. *Mary is in the true and literal sense the mother
of Jesus, the mother of God.*

The conception of Jesus is at the same time
miraculous and natural. It is entirely natural as far
as the mother's part is concerned; it is supernatural,

since the Holy Spirit miraculously supplies the factors usually provided by the human father. Although the conception is usually attributed to the Holy Spirit, like all of the divine actions outside of the Godhead, this miraculous conception was the work of all three persons of the Blessed Trinity. Nor is the Holy Spirit ever called the "father" of Jesus; although the miraculous action is attributed to him, Christ did not become man from matter received from the Holy Spirit.

The Mother of God   ". . . the child to be born shall be called holy, the Son of God" (Lk. 1:35). Mary is the mother of Jesus Christ. Jesus Christ is true God. Mary is the mother of God. Sacred Scripture does not explicitly state that Mary is the mother of God; it is, nevertheless, explicitly stated that Jesus Christ is true God, and that the Blessed Virgin is the mother of Jesus Christ. This doctrine was formally defined at the Council of Ephesus: "If anyone does not confess that Emmanuel is truly God, and therefore, the holy virgin is the mother of God (for she gave birth according to the flesh to the word of God made flesh), let him be anathema."

Mary truly conceived and gave birth to Jesus Christ, who is a divine person. Mary is not, of course, the mother of the divinity; she did not give birth to the divine nature. She gave birth to a divine person, not in his divinity, not in his eternal being nor in his divine character, but according to the substance of his flesh, his humanity, his temporal being, his temporal birth. But Mary is mother of God in a very proper sense of the word. She is not merely the mother of one who was afterwards to receive divinity. The mother of a man who late in life is elected president is "mother of the president," but not in the proper sense that she gave birth to a president. Mary did not give birth to a human person who was later made divine; she gave birth to Jesus Christ who was true God. Mary is truly the mother of God.

The fullness of grace   "Rejoice, O highly favored daughter, the Lord is with you. Blessed are you among women" (Lk. 1:28 NAB). In the execution of his solemn mission the angel Gabriel chose to address Mary by the title "full of grace." In a very special way, then, this must be Mary's prerogative, her most personal title. You have seen that the absolute plenitude of grace belongs only to Jesus; he possessed grace in the fullest measure that anyone could possibly possess it. Mary had a fullness of grace that corresponded to her vocation to be the mother of God. This grace places her at the very apex of creation. She is God's masterwork, the greatest thing (besides the human nature of her son) in all his creation. The fullness of her grace places her above all other creatures.

Mary did not receive the fullness of her grace at one moment. She grew in grace continually throughout her life. No doubt her grace grew most especially at certain moments in her life; for example, it may be presumed that she received a veritable flood of grace at the moment of the Incarnation.

THE VISITATION

Fra Angelico, the great artist saint, painted many murals on the walls of his Dominican priory in Florence, Italy, the art center of his country. In depicting the Annunciation to Mary that she would be the mother of the Messiah, Fra Angelico shows her kneeling in an attitude of prayer—as if to remind us that God speaks to us in quiet times of reflection and prayer. Then Mary is shown hastening to the hill country to visit a close relative, Elizabeth, who is bearing a child even though she is advanced in age and had been considered barren, or sterile. When the angel Gabriel told Zechariah that his wife Elizabeth was to bear a child the elderly temple priest expressed his doubt that this could happen. He was punished for his doubt by losing the use of his voice until the birth of his son. The son was John the Baptist, the precursor, or forerunner, of Jesus. (Read Luke 1:5-24 for the full account of these events.)

When the angel announced to Mary that she would be the mother of Jesus and Mary unhesitatingly accepted the word and will of God as expressed by Gabriel, he also said to her: "And behold, your kins-woman Elizabeth in her old age has also conceived a son; and this is the sixth month with her who was called barren. For with God nothing will be impossible." It was then that Mary accepted the angel's announcement, saying, "Behold, I am the handmaid of the Lord, let it be done to me according to your word" (Lk. 1:36-38).

Luke continues:

> In those days Mary arose and went with haste into the hill country, to a city of Judah, and she entered the house of Zechariah and greeted Elizabeth. And when Elizabeth heard the greeting of Mary, the babe leaped in her womb; and Elizabeth was filled with the Holy Spirit and she exclaimed with a loud cry, "Blessed are you among women, and blessed is the fruit of your womb! And why is this granted me, that the mother of my Lord should come to me? For behold, when the voice of your greeting came to my ears, the babe in my womb leaped for joy. And blessed is she who believed that there would be a fulfillment of what was spoken to her from the Lord."
>
> –Luke 1:39-46

Mary then expressed her own thanksgiving and humility. This is probably the most beautiful and profound prayer ever said by any mere mortal. With flawless words, under the influence of the Holy Spirit, she describes God's relation to his people. The prayer is popularly called The Magnificat (Latin for "magnifies"). It deserves your closest concentration and consideration.

My soul magnifies the Lord,
  and my spirit rejoices in God my savior,
For he has regarded
  the low estate of his handmaiden,
For behold, henceforth all generations
  will call me blessed;
For he who is mighty has done
  great things for me, and holy is his name.
And his mercy is on those who fear him
  from generation to generation.
He has shown strength with his arm,
  he has scattered the proud in the imagination of their hearts,
He has put down the mighty from their thrones,
  and exalted those of low degree;
He has filled the hungry with good things,
  and the rich he has sent empty away.
He has helped his servant Israel,
  in remembrance of his mercy, as he spoke
to our Fathers, to Abraham and to his posterity forever.
                                        –Luke 1:47-56

Then Luke tells us that Mary remained with Elizabeth about three months and then returned to her home.

There is so much that Our Blessed Mother teaches us when she shows us how to follow Jesus, her Son, who is the way to salvation and eternal happiness. She indicates the importance of prayer in our lives, accepting and doing God's will as we know it to be, the necessity of humility as a foundation of our faith and of perseverance in hope, even to the foot of the cross. We can learn a great deal about Christ by saying and meditating on the Rosary which she proposed and promoted among us. If we are to follow Jesus, we can do so only by her side and through her intercession.

THE NATIVITY, OR BIRTH OF OUR SAVIOR

For almost everyone, the happiest time of the year is Christmas. There is a festive spirit, a good feeling, lots of good will around. We wish it would last all year long. Why is there so much joy at this time, and why all the gift-giving?

Many people seem to forget what Christmas is all about. The season has become secularized and commercialized. The featured person of the season is Santa Claus, a figure of fantasy, purely mythical and unreal. Sometimes he is confused with St. Nick. There really was a St. Nicholas, a bishop of the early Church, a holy man who brought gifts to the needy, leaving his gifts at the homes of the recipients without taking credit for them as a benefactor.

The true meaning of Christmas is in the name itself. Christmas refers to the Mass of Christ which celebrates his birth. In our churches, of course, we do have displays of Jesus lying in the manger (a little cave shelter) with his mother Mary and his foster father Joseph hovering over him. Perhaps there are animals around them, and angels with trumpets above them. This is a scene taken from the scriptural account of the birth of Christ. St. Luke, in his gospel, gives us the familiar account of this event. He must have obtained this detailed information from Our Blessed Mother, for the writer says that Mary "kept all these things, pondering them in her heart." (Read the nativity story in Luke 2:1-20.) St. Matthew introduces the Wise Men from the East (Mt. 2:1-12), and tells about other circumstances preceding Christ's birth (Mt. 1:18-25).

Theologians study the Word of God as revealed and recorded in the Bible. On the basis of the writings of the early Fathers of the Church and doctrinal decisions of Church councils, they speculate on the many possible implications contained in the Sacred Scriptures. The authors of a previous theology textbook for college students *(A Primer of Theology)*, which was published by The Priory Press in 1957, summarized these theological speculations very succinctly. We follow these traditional opinions and quote them as they were given:

THE CIRCUMSTANCES OF CHRIST'S BIRTH

Of all cities, Bethlehem enjoyed a special suitability as the birthplace of the Savior. Bethlehem was the birthplace of King David, from whose lineage Christ came and to whom a special promise of the Messiah was made (2 Kings 23:1). His birth in the City of David indicated that the promise was fulfilled. Then, as St. Gregory points out, "Bethlehem means 'The House of Bread.' It is Christ himself who said, 'I am the living bread which came down from heaven' " *(Eighth Homily on the Gospels).*

The simple fact that Christ chose the time of his own birth is sufficient proof that it occurred at the moment best suited to the divine plan. St. Thomas offers some reasons which point up the suitability of the time of the Nativity. Christ became man to lead us from bondage to spiritual liberty, and by being born at the time when he would be enrolled in Caesar's census, he thus submits himself to bondage for the sake of our freedom. He was born at a time when the world was at peace, a fitting time for the birth of him who ". . . himself is our peace. . ." (Eph. 2:14). Again, at the time of Christ's birth Augustus was the sole ruler of the civilized world, and this was a suitable time for him who came ". . . that he might gather into one the children of God who were scattered abroad. . ." (Jn. 11:52), that there might be ". . . one fold and one shepherd. . ." (Jn. 10:16). Finally, he chose to be born in winter to begin at once his sufferings for us.

THE MANIFESTATION OF CHRIST'S BIRTH

The Gospel account of Christ's birth indicates that this most important event was made known to few people. It seems strange that the Savior of Mankind should enter upon his work so quietly. Yet the fact that his coming was not heralded immediately to everyone fits in well with the plan of Redemption. Universal knowledge of Christ would have interfered with the crucifixion, ". . . for if they had known it, they would never have crucified the Lord of glory" (I Cor. 2:8). Secondly, widespread manifestation of Christ's birth would have deprived mankind of the merit of divine faith, which is ". . . the evidence of things that are not seen . . ." (Heb. 11:1).

Christ's birth was manifested to a few, and through these to many, for ". . . faith depends on hearing . . ." (Rom. 10:17). The universality of the salvation which Christ brought was reflected in those to whom his birth was first made known. The shepherds were Israelites; the Magi were Gentiles. The shepherds were simple and humble; the Magi wise and powerful. Simeon and Anna were saintly; the Magi were sinners. Thus the first messengers of the Incarnation represented all classes and conditions of men. It would not have been suitable for Christ himself to manifest his birth, for that would have shaken confidence in the reality of his human nature, because no human infant manifests his own birth.

The very means used to signalize the birth of the Savior were carefully chosen. To Simeon and Anna who were leading an interior life, his coming was made known by the inspiration of the Holy Spirit. To the shepherds who, as Jews, were accustomed to divine signs in religious matters, he was made known by the message of angels. To the Magi, who were astrologers, he was manifested by a star. The order in which the Incarnation was revealed is most suitable. The shepherds represent the Apostles and the first Jewish converts, among whom ". . . there were not many wise according to the flesh, not many mighty, not many noble" (I Cor. 1:26). The faith of Christ came next to the fullness of the Gentiles represented by the Magi. Finally faith came to the fullness of the Jews represented by the righteous Simeon and Anna who learned of Christ in the Temple at Jerusalem (Lk. 2:22-38).

It is the opinion of St. Thomas that the star which led the Magi to adore Christ, as a sign of the faith and devotion of the nations who were to come to Christ from afar, was a heavenly body created specially for this purpose. [God also could use a natural phenomenon for this purpose, such as Halley's Comet. Remember that these are *speculations*. Ed. note]

–A Primer of Theology,
pp. 135-137

THE PRESENTATION OF JESUS IN THE TEMPLE

The Jews had many time-honored rituals and customs, most of them originating in divine instructions set down in the first five books of the Old Testament. Some of these were concerned with the birth of a child, considered a great gift of God. According to one law (Exodus 13:2), every firstborn male, both of human beings and of cattle, was sacred to God. That law may have been a recognition of the gracious power of God in giving his gift of procreation. There was, therefore, a ceremony called "the Redemption of the Firstborn" (Numbers 18:16). Symbolically, this was a buying back of their son from God who gave him life. It could not be done sooner than thirty-one days after the birth of the child, and it should not be long delayed after that.

The detailed narrative of this event in the life of Jesus is given to us by Luke in the second chapter of his gospel:

And when the time came for their purification according to the law of Moses, they brought him up to Jerusalem to present him to the Lord (as it is written in the law of the Lord, "Every male that opens the womb shall be called holy to the Lord") and to offer a sacrifice according to what is said in the law of the Lord, "a pair of turtledoves or two young pigeons." Now, there was a man in Jerusalem, whose name was Simeon, and this man was righteous and devout, looking for the consolation of Israel, and the Holy Spirit was upon him. And it had been revealed to him by the Holy Spirit that he should not see death before he had seen the Lord's Christ. Inspired by the Spirit, he came into the temple; and when the parents brought in the child Jesus, to do for him according to the custom of the law, he took him up in his arms and blessed God and said, "Lord, now let your servant depart in peace, / according to your word; / for my eyes have seen the salvation / which you have prepared in the presence of all peoples, / a light for revelation to the Gentiles, / and for glory to your people Israel." / And his father and his mother marveled at what was said about him; and Simeon blessed them and said to Mary his mother, "Behold, this child is set for the fall and rising of many in Israel, / and for a sign that is spoken against / (and a sword will pierce through your own soul also), that thoughts out of many hearts may be revealed." (Luke 2:22-35)

Verses 34 and 35 of this passage predict the future of Jesus and Mary. Our Lord will cause many to rise and many to fall, depending on their reaction to Christ and his kingdom. As a commentator on this passage says: "It is not so much God who judges a man; a man judges himself; and his judgment is his reaction to Jesus Christ. If, when he is confronted . . . his heart runs out in answering love, he is within the kingdom. If, when so confronted, he remains coldly unmoved or actively hostile, he is condemned." Many will rise because the children of God who are faithful will rise out of an old life into the new, out of sin into goodness, out of shame into glory. He will be "a sign that is spoken against" (in other translations: "a sign which will meet with much opposition"—"a sign of contradiction"). Towards Jesus there can be no neutrality. We either surrender to him or are at war with him. And it is the tragedy of life that our pride often keeps us from making that surrender which leads to victory. The "pierced soul of Mary" is a traditional image, sometimes graphically portrayed in old processions by a statue of the Blessed Mother with real swords plunged into the heart of the figure. Mary did indeed share in the passion and sufferings of her divine son, up to the lonely vigil at the foot of the cross.

After the hymn of Simeon (sometimes called by the Latin words *Nunc Dimittis*—"now you dismiss"), another person approaches the Holy Family. She is a woman named Anna, a widow of eighty-four; Luke tells us that "she did not depart from the temple, worshiping with fasting and prayer night and day. And coming up at that very hour, she gave thanks to God, and spoke of him to all who were looking for the redemption of Jerusalem" (Luke 2:37-38).

To all of this Mary was not only a witness but an essential part of the story of Christ's redemption of us all. No one was closer to Jesus then. No one is closer to him now.

Luke concludes this infancy account by noting their observance of the law and returning to the town of Nazareth in Galilee. As for the growing up of the divine child, he simply tells us: "And the child grew and became strong, filled with wisdom; and the favor of God was upon him" (Luke 2:40).

THE FINDING OF JESUS IN THE TEMPLE

The wisdom of Jesus was from three sources. He had a keen spiritual insight, a kind of angelic intuition, and, like any other human, he learned and developed an acquired knowledge. Beyond these natural sources, he possessed divine knowledge. As a man, he had human knowledge. As God, he had divine knowledge. These forms of knowledge did not come in spurts, nor were they suddenly turned on at will. Rather, they blended in the perceptions experienced on various occasions. We first encounter this in the boyhood event narrated by St. Luke in his gospel. Informed by Mary's remembrances, he records an unusual occasion in the life of Jesus as a child.

Every year, according to Jewish law, men living within fifteen miles of the temple in Jerusalem were obliged to celebrate the Passover in the holy city. Manhood was reached at the age of twelve. And so after the twelfth birthday of Jesus, the Holy Family made this pilgrimage. They were joined by other families among their relatives and friends, and formed a caravan of wagons and carts carrying their tents and food and clothing. As in the days of the Old West in America, they formed a long line along the dusty road from Nazareth to Jerusalem. The men naturally tended to cluster together in the front with the women behind them and the animals following. The children mixed together to run back and forth along the winding trail. This scene must be recalled as we read of the lost child who caused so much anguish to his parents. Losing a child, who might be harmed when drifting off from a group, is one of the great worries of all parents.

St. Luke tells the story:

> Now his parents went to Jerusalem every year at the feast of the Passover. And when he was twelve years old, they went up according to custom; and when the feast was ended, as they were returning, the boy Jesus stayed behind in Jerusalem. His parents did not know it, but supposing him to be in the company they went a day's journey, and they sought him among their kinsfolk and acquaintances; and when they did not find him, they returned to Jerusalem, seeking him. And after three days they found him in the temple, sitting among the teachers, listening to them and asking them questions; and all who heard him were amazed at his

understanding and his answers. And when they saw him they were astonished; and his mother said to him, "Son, why have you treated us so? Behold, your father and I have been looking for you anxiously." And he said to them, "How is it that you sought me? Did you not know that I must be in my Father's house?" And they did not understand the saying which he spoke to them. And he went down with them and came to Nazareth, and was obedient to them; and his mother kept all these things in her heart. And Jesus increased in wisdom and in stature and in favor with God and man.

–Luke 2:41-52

This incident describes one of those great sorrows that Simeon had predicted for the Blessed Mother, the temporary loss of her divine Son. This is an experience of many mothers—a child lost. But this is a very special child and he is absent for three days! We can barely imagine the anguish of this mother. We can see her going forward to discover whether Jesus is with Joseph or not, then the two parents going back along the long line of the moving caravan. They thought he would be with relatives or friends, but he was nowhere to be found. Now feeling desperate, they began the journey back to Jerusalem and there at last they search the city.

After three days of separation they find him in the midst of some of the scholarly teachers in the temple. He is not teaching them; he is listening and learning and responding. He is acquiring knowledge, as any student does — a natural process of acquiring wisdom. The doctors are amazed at his understanding, his supernatural insight into the questions raised and the responses given. Typical of a mother's reaction to finding him, she asks why he has done this to his parents, causing them so much grief. "Behold," she says, "your father and I have been looking for you anxiously." He replies by expressing his divine knowledge in distinguishing his foster father from his divine Father in heaven. (Note the small "f" for Joseph, the capital "F" designating God the Father.)

He must be in his Father's house, which is the temple, the house of God at that time.

They, his mother and father, did not understand his response, although they knew from the time of his conception that he was not an ordinary child, that he was from the beginning united with God in a way which they could not comprehend.

Notice that when he went home, he "was obedient to them" — a divine Person subjecting himself to human authority. Again, we are told that his mother "kept all these things in her heart." She later disclosed these early events to Luke who recorded them in his gospel. We are also told again that he increased not just physically—growing up—but also in wisdom; for he had much to learn naturally. He also grew in favor—with both God and man.

In 1946, Father John Lynch wrote a book-length poem about Mary called *A Woman Wrapped in Silence*. Describing Mary's loss during that sad pilgrimage, he imagines the frantic search and the pain of that experience:

> This was the ache that had no feel or sight of him
>   to make it seem much less than pain.
> This was a road that could not be. A place that was not. This was
>   darkness come when she was walked and pushed beyond the edge
>   of possibilities, and clutched with scratching fingers at the stones
>   of dreams.
> This was a screech shrieked down in fever from the
>   topmost swirls of night.
> He was not here! *He was not here!* Alone! Not
>   here! She'd lost him.
> She had lost . . .

–p. 130

On that treacherous road back to Jerusalem Mary and Joseph searched in vain for Jesus as they encountered other travelers. Fr. Lynch vividly describes the scene:

They'd come upon a few old wanderers like thicker
dark that loomed up suddenly more near to them.
And they had paused a moment while the horses neighed, and
voices spoke to them strangely for the question they had asked.
No, they'd not seen a child, nor found a child
who'd looked to them.
And when they'd gone beyond, and speech and murmured echo
then had passed into the night, her lifted search was ended.
And the hopes that only were half hopes, and scanned their faces
wearily, died down again, and were no more than further pain
that stirred a little to become more keen.

–p. 131

There were more sorrows to come, climaxed by the shared pain and passion of her divine Son. But all of this suffering brought her closer to the suffering Savior of all mankind. And now Mary reigns as Queen of Heaven, ever ready to respond to our pleas of intercession.

Jesus brings us to him through his chosen mother, and Mary looks upon us and protects us as her other children.

Thinking it over • • •

1. A good project for you: commit the *Memorare* to your own memory so that you can easily say this prayer daily. Such devotional prayers may be said anywhere, at any time.

2. Why is Mary a more influential intercessor with Jesus than any of the other saints?

3. How many years did Vatican Council II last, and who was the pope who called for this council?

4. Sometimes non-Catholics misunderstand our devotion to Mary, saying it is exaggerated and that we worship her instead of Our Lord. How would you reply to this objection?

5. What does the Rosary have to do with God's revelation in the Bible?

6. How did Mary reply to Gabriel's annunciation that she was to become the mother of the Messiah?

7. Why did Mary visit her cousin Elizabeth?

8. What is the Magnificat hymn?

9. Where does the word "Christmas" come from?

10. Why did Joseph and Mary present the infant Jesus in the temple?

11. What did Simeon predict would happen to Jesus and to Mary?

12. What was the occasion for taking Jesus to Jerusalem when he was twelve years old?

13. What kinds of knowledge does Jesus manifest in this incident of his separation from Mary and Joseph?

THE MYSTERY OF THE CHURCH

"Peter, standing with the eleven, lifted up his voice and addressed them, 'Men of Judea and all who dwell in Jerusalem, let this be known to you, and give ear to my words . . . know assuredly that God has made him both Lord and Christ, this Jesus whom you crucified.' Now when they heard this they were cut to the heart, and said to Peter and the rest of the apostles, 'Brethren, what shall we do?' And Peter said to them, 'Repent and be baptized, every one of you in the name of Jesus Christ for the forgiveness of your sins; and you shall receive the gift of the Holy Spirit. For the promise is to you and to your children and to all that are far off, every one whom the Lord God calls to him.' . . . So those who received his word were baptized, and there were added that day about three thousand souls. And they devoted themselves to the apostles' teaching and fellowship, to the breaking of bread and the prayers . . . And day to day, attending the temple together and breaking bread in their homes, they partook of food with glad and generous hearts, praising God and having favor with all the people. And the Lord added to their number day by day those who were being saved."

—Acts 2:14-47

Chapter 1

THE NATURE OF THE CHURCH

Why a study of the Church   The importance of
the study of the Church cannot be overestimated. So
many changes have taken place in the "bark of Peter"
over the centuries that we need principles for guiding
both theologians who confront the problems of the
Church and lay people who desire to know more about
this mystery of their spiritual lives. This is especially true in our own day when Church policy and
discipline often seem to depend more on the whim or
feeling of this or that teacher than on what God has
revealed concerning this mystery, and indeed on what
the Church, through faith, has affirmed of itself.

Certainly, the Spirit breathes where he will as St.
Paul tells us (1 Cor. 12:11). But it must be remembered that the Spirit comes to us only because Christ,
fulfilling his promise, sends him. And the purpose of
Christ sending such an advocate is precisely to guide
his Church, to keep it safe from error, and to bring
its members to holiness in truth. Indeed, Christ promised at the Last Supper that the Spirit "will guide
you into all the truth" (Jn. 16:13). This means that
the life of the Church, and its guiding Spirit, and its
members who are faithful, are joined to Christ and

are inseparable from him. Hence, if we desire to receive the fullness of Christ's redeeming and grace-filled gifts to us, then we cannot neglect the study of the mystery of the Church. To do so would be to fail to recognize the movement of the Holy Spirit in the whole Church. St. Irenaeus, an early Father of the Church, highlights this truth most beautifully when he writes: "Where the Church is, there is the Spirit of God, and where the Spirit of God is, there is the Church and all grace, and the Spirit is truth" (*Adversus Haereses* 3. 24. 1).

The meaning of the word "church"   The English word "church" had its origin in the Greek word *kiriakon,* which can be translated as "a place pertaining to the Lord." The Latin word for church, *ecclesia,* is an exact transliteration of another Greek word meaning "an assembly of the people." These root words certainly do not provide any profound definitions of the nature of the Church. However, they do give indications of the direction to be taken in order to achieve some understanding of the mystery of the Church. That is, "an assembly of the people in a place pertaining to the Lord" at least provides a familiar image to the student who is seeking principles by which the Church can be known more fully. The science that pursues such knowledge of the Catholic Church is called ecclesiology (from *ecclesia,* church, and *logos,* study; therefore, the study of the Church).

Theology and mystery   The work of theology is to give a rational interpretation of revelation, under the light of faith. When the science of theology is applied to the mystery of the Church, then that mystery is seen as fundamentally the revelation of God's eternal plan for the salvation of the entire universe, and particularly for the salvation of mankind. The Christian understanding of the word "mystery" is also important. In the Christian sense, a mystery is not something hidden or secret, but something revealed

116

though beyond full human understanding. Thus, the science of theology permits the student, the person with faith, to appreciate the Church as a multi-dimensional phenomenon. That is, the Church as mystery is both human and divine, visible and invisible, legal and mystical, earthbound and destined for heaven.

The important thing to remember, however, is that through the wisdom of theology, the mystery, the revelation, can be reasonably interpreted. In this present chapter, we shall concentrate on three interwoven ideas whose clarification will give us sure and solid knowledge concerning the nature of the Church. These ideas are:

1. the Church as sacrament;
2. the Church as the People of God;
3. the Church as the Mystical Body of Christ.

The Baltimore Catechism defined the Church as "the congregation of all baptized persons united in the same true faith, the same sacrifice, and the same sacraments, under the authority of the Sovereign Pontiff and the bishops in communion with him."

This definition is precise and informative, listing the components that go into making up the visible Church. However, because it seems to speak of the Church only in terms of structure and organization — the institutional Church — it fails to express the entire reality needed for an understanding of the Church founded by Christ. The Second Vatican Council, realizing the need for men and women of today to better understand the nature of the Church, produced two documents on the Church: one simply called "The Church"; another called "The Church in the Modern World."

The Preface to the second-named document sets a more pastoral tone and provides a more complete description of the Church's desires for mankind:

The joys and hopes, the griefs and the anxieties of the men of this age, especially those who are poor or in any way afflicted, these too are the joys and hopes, the griefs and anxieties of the followers of Christ. Indeed, nothing genuinely human fails to raise an echo in their hearts. For theirs is a community composed of men united in Christ, they are led by the Holy Spirit in their journey to the kingdom of their Father, and they have welcomed the news of salvation which is meant for every man. This is why this community, the Church, realizes that it is truly and intimately linked with mankind and its history . . . Hence, the Second Vatican Council, having probed more profoundly into the mystery of the Church . . . yearns to explain to everyone how it conceives of the presence and activity of the Church in the world today ("The Church in the Modern World," nn. 1-2).

However, it is the first of the documents, "The Church," that proposes a broader view of the nature of the Church. This document gives two fundamental concepts that provide not only a more complete definition of the Church, but also a greater emphasis on its spiritual life and interior structure. The first of these concepts is that the Church is actually a *sacrament* of Christ:

By her relationship with Christ, the Church is a kind of sacrament of intimate union with God, and of the unity of all mankind, that is, she is a sign and an instrument of such union and unity. For this reason, following in the path laid out by its predecessors, this Council wishes to set forth more precisely to the faithful and to the entire world the nature and encompassing mission of the Church. The conditions of this age lend special urgency to the Church's task of bringing all men to full union with Christ, since mankind today is joined together more closely than ever before by social, technical, and cultural bonds ("The Church," n. 1).

What the Council meant is this: since Christ established an inseparable union between himself and the Church, the Church is something more than a society of men and women; rather, it has a sacred dimension.

The Church as sacrament A sacrament is a sacred sign. In Catholic use and practice, the word "sacrament" is usually reserved for the seven sacraments. These are the sacred signs Christ gave to his Church as the channels of his saving graces.

By Christ's will, sacraments such as baptism, penance and the Eucharist, use visible realities (water, bread, wine, etc.) which are made effective signs of his saving gifts. Part Three of this book details the meaning of the seven sacraments and their institution. The point to be made here concerning the Church is that the Church is a more universal and comprehensive sacrament. It is something visible that Christ has founded in this world as a sacred sign of his presence. But it is also a sign of his authority and of his mission. That is, as a sacrament, the Church is the means Christ uses to *give* the unity and the holiness he actually confers through it.

The Church is a family that has been called to share the life of the Trinity for all eternity. Until the final *parousia,* the Second Coming of Christ, takes place, this family is in its time of pilgrimage on earth. It is in the context of the pilgrim Church that the truth of the Church as sacrament emerges. For a sacrament is a "sign," and the very purpose of a sign is to lead beyond itself—that is, to signify something. In the case of the Church as sacrament, it must lead the believer to what it signifies, namely, to Christ, to God.

The Church in heaven, in eternity, will no longer exist as a sacrament. Why? Because then, the faithful, having been led *finally* to God with Christ, will no longer need the "sign." In eternity, every instrument, whether sacrament or minister of the sacraments, will cease to be needed. Then, they will be drawn up into the heavenly realities they served on earth. In heaven, the Church will be the union of the saints with the Father and the Son and the Holy Spirit. This eternal reality is known now by faith and by God's love given to us through his graces. The reality of such glorification, however, is left to the life hereafter and to the final resurrection.

This is what the Second Vatican Council means when it describes the mission of the Church as being

filled both with joy and with sorrow as it leads the
faithful toward eternal happiness:

> The Church, "like a pilgrim in a foreign land presses forward amid
> the persecutions of the world and the consolations of God" (St.
> Augustine, *The City of God*), announcing the cross and death of the
> Lord until he comes (1 Cor. 11:26). By the power of the risen Lord,
> she is given strength to overcome patiently and lovingly the afflic-
> tions and hardships which assail her from within and without, and
> to show forth in the world the mystery of the Lord in a faithful though
> shadowed way, until at last it will be revealed in full light.
>
> —"The Church," n. 8

Thus, the Church as sacrament, the sign leading
to God, will continue, as Christ promised, until the
end of time when its work is finished and glory in
Christ is achieved. After all, this sign is Christ's own
visible gift to the world, making it both precious and
indispensable for salvation.

The People of God   The second fundamental concept that gets to the heart of the meaning of the
Church is the expression, "The People of God"; or, to
be more precise, "The new People of God." This title
has solid foundations in the Scriptures, as will be
shown. But, the point to be made here is that, in its
desire to explain more fully the nature of the Church,
the Council wanted to speak on the human and communal aspect of the Church. It did so in the document
on "The Church," pointing out that the Church is not
merely an intangible idea, nor is it just an isolated
association of men in authoritarian positions. Rather,
the Council wanted to exhibit the Church's warm and
expansive qualities. Therefore, the members of the
Church are seen as one people united within the family of faith. Taken together, this family is the Church,
with each member the recipient of the Holy Spirit's
gifts of grace. And, as one united family, the *people*
are called to continue the saving work of Christ in
the world.

The Council proposed this basic idea of the Church
clearly and succinctly in the following words:

Christ instituted this new covenant, that is to say, the new testament in his blood (1 Cor. 11:25), by calling together a people made up of Jew and Gentile, making them one, not according to the flesh but in the Spirit.

This was to be the *new People of God.* For those who believe in Christ, who are reborn not from a perishable but from an imperishable seed through the Word of the living God (1 Pt. 1:23), not from the flesh but from water and the Holy Spirit (Jn. 3:5-6), are finally established as "a chosen race, a royal priesthood, a holy nation, a purchased people . . . You who in times past were not a people, but are now the *People of God* (1 Pt. 2:9-10).

—"The Church," n. 9

These words punctuate the notion that *we* are Christ's people, the *People of God.* Gathered together in Christ, the Word who both reveals this new relationship between God and his people, and *is* the revelation, the link binding the members together with God—all together make up a unique, united people. Men, women, religious, priests, bishops, pope— members from every vocation and with various dignities—all bound together in Christ, are the Church. It is true, of course, that each person has his or her own special vocation or mission. It is also true that each person, because of that special call, has certain works to perform and definite responsibilities to be shouldered. Nevertheless, considered together in Christ, all are united as one People. Why? Because it is one and the same Holy Spirit received by all, no matter how great are the diversity of vocations and responsibilities. All share the one Bread of Life in the Eucharist and receive the same nourishment in the eating and drinking of Christ's body and blood. All yearn for the same goal, striving forward toward eternal life. Where there is one Faith, there is one Hope urging all toward a closer relationship with Christ. Hence, no matter what the status of the individual may be, the idea "People of God" provides a new dignity and equality among the children of God.

The Church as communion   Joined to and flowing from these ideas is the impetus in the document on "The Church" toward a study of the Church based on "communion."

The mystery of the Church is presented as rooted in the Trinity, with the universal Church seen as "a people made one from the unity of the Father and of the Son and of the Holy Spirit" ("The Church," n. 4); a *people* "established by Christ as a *communion* of life, love, and truth"; one holy community, both priestly and prophetic, in which "all the faithful scattered throughout the world lead a common life with the rest in the Holy Spirit," and in which all so united "both labor and pray that the fullness of the world be transformed into the People of God, the Body of the Lord, and the temple of the Holy Spirit" ("The Church," n. 17).

Old Testament origins   The title, "People of God," was given first to Israel; therefore, the title has to be seen in the light of the New Testament's dependence on the Old Testament. In the beginning, according to the Book of Genesis (chapters 1-4), mankind was called by God to form and live in society. God's direction of this society included multiplying itself, subduing and having dominion over the earth and its creatures, and living closely together—in a familiar way—with God.

Sin, however, destroyed his special relationship to God. Yet, even before God banished us from the garden of Eden, he mercifully promised, in a primitive but clear way, deliverance. Nevertheless, the consequences of our sin included the manifestation of hatred toward one another within society, inordinate pride, and the loss of friendship with God.

The formation of the People of God in the Old Testament commenced with the selection of Abraham by God and was sealed by a covenant:

When Abram was ninety-nine years old, the LORD appeared to Abram and said to him, "I am God Almighty; walk before me, and be blameless. And I will make my covenant between me and you, and will multiply you exceedingly." Then Abram fell on his face; and God said to him, "Behold, my covenant is with you, and you shall be the father of many nations. No longer shall your name be Abram, but your name shall be Abraham; for I have made you the father of a multitude of nations. I will make you exceedingly fruitful; and I will make nations of you, and kings shall come forth from you. And I will establish my covenant between me and you and your descendants after you throughout your generations for an everlasting covenant, to be God to you and to your descendants after you."

–Gn. 17:1-8

This covenant or agreement made between Abraham and God was renewed and clarified during the Exodus from Egypt of some of Abraham's descendants led by Moses (Ex. 19-24). In spite of God's care for his people, however, the Israelites were not always faithful to him. Their fidelity as the Chosen People of God was particularly offensive during the Exodus (Ex. 35:1-6). Often, Israel violated God's laws and betrayed the covenant made with him.

Because of the faithlessness of the Chosen People, the prophets often foretold, down through the centuries, that only a portion of the people would be the inheritors of the promises of salvation made by God to them. This portion came to be known as the "remnant," the holy and faithful ones who would realize the need for salvation and seek it (Is. 4:3; Amos 3:12 and 9:8-10). At some time in the future God would make a new covenant with his people (Jer. 31:31-34), a promise reaffirmed during the centuries following the Babylonian exile. Hence, these two ideas, the holy and faithful remnant and the promise of a new covenant fed the hopes of Israel for a Messiah, a savior (Is. 54:9-10).

The new and final covenant was sealed by the death and resurrection of Jesus. The Church began at that time. But only in a gradual way was the nature of this new community, this new People of God, seen as separate from Judaism and as possessing its own identity and structure. Nevertheless, the title "People of God" certainly refers to the Church as the fulfillment of the Old Testament prophecies. Jesus truly fulfills all of the prophecies and promises concerning the Messiah and given to the world through the Jewish people. Therefore, because the Church possesses Christ and the new gifts—the sacraments as channels of grace—that he brings and because the Church is the inheritor of the Old Testament prophecies and can be seen as the communion of the faithful remnant, we can say of ourselves as members in union with one another in the Church that *we are the People of God.*

A People called together   Thus the words "People of God," founded on the Old Testament and brought to perfect fruition in the New Testament, remind us that we are like one another in being members of this "assembly" of God's people. The people *are* the Church. Each and every member shares in its dignity; and each and every member is called to continue the heavenly mission of Christ, the Founder—Priest, Prophet, and King.

The teaching of the Old Testament concerning the calling of God's people made it clear that they were a "congregation called together" only because God had made them such. The same thing is true of the Church; it was and had to be "called together" by Jesus. Hence, "the people" can be a Church only because they are joined together by the grace of Christ. This means that the Church is not so much men and women joining together as it is men and women joined together. Jesus is the Builder and the Joiner. Clearly then, he also determines how his people are to be united and gathered together.

The Body of Christ   In the next chapter, well-known images or metaphors of the Church will be examined to enhance knowledge about the mystery of the Church. In this chapter, however, the image of the Church as the Body of Christ is so necessary to an understanding of the intrinsic nature of the Church that it will be discussed here.

Up to this point, the nature of the Church has centered on two ideas: the Church as Sacrament, leading man to eternal life in God; and the Church as the new People of God, united together in and by Christ. A complementary reality, communion, has also been introduced to fill out the picture of this mystery.

Pope Pius XII, in his encyclical *Mystici Corporis* says that the Church is "a society whose head and ruler is Christ" (n. 64) and is the Mystical Body of Christ. In the Old Covenant, God dwelt among his Chosen People: first in the Ark of the Covenant, later in the Temple of Jerusalem. In the New Covenant, God wished to dwell in the community of believers who love him — in the Body of Christ, his Church. St. Paul introduced the idea of the Body of Christ as essential for understanding the nature of the Church. The notions he wished to enhance by this image were twofold. First, he wanted to show that the People of God were given a status beyond that of the Old Covenant. This new status had as its foundation the giving of the Holy Spirit personally to the members united in faith in the glorified Lord. Secondly, St. Paul wanted to emphasize that this same Spirit was given to all, to the whole Church, not simply because it was constituted as the People of God, but because it had been constituted, newly and marvelously, in Christ as his Body. Now this "people" is not simply the People of God, but *the People of God who form the Mystical Body of Christ.*

The metaphor in the epistles   In the epistles of St. Paul we discover the body metaphor used in two ways. Sometimes St. Paul compares the Church to the trunk of the body, to contrast it with the head, Christ. Hence, the Church and Christ—trunk and head—form two parts of one and the same unit. This sense is found in all of the passages from the Pauline epistles, in which the person of Christ is compared to the head; thus: ". . . and he has put all things under his feet and has made him the head over all things for the Church, which is his body, the fullness of him who fills all in all" (Eph. 1:22-23). And again: "He is the head of the body, the church" (Col. 1:18).

At other times, the term "Body of Christ" is not used to distinguish it from Christ as the Head, but includes it. The best example of this joining of the head and the body as one whole is found in St. Paul's first letter to the Corinthians:

> For just as the body is one and has many members, and all the members of the body, though many, are one body, so it is with Christ. For by one Spirit we were all baptized into one body—Jews or Greeks, slaves or free—and all were made to drink of one Spirit.
>
> For the body does not consist of one member but of many. If the foot should say, "Because I am not a hand, I do not belong to the body," that would not make it any less a part of the body. And if the ear should say, "Because I am not an eye, I do not belong to the body," that would not make it any less a part of the body. If the whole body were an eye, where would be the hearing? If the whole body were an ear, where would be the sense of smell? But as it is, God arranged the organs in the body, each one of them, as he chose. If all were a single organ, where would the body be? As it is, there are many parts, yet one body. The eye cannot say to the hand, "I have no need of you," nor again the head to the feet, "I have no need of you." On the contrary, the parts of the body which seem to be weaker are indispensable, and those parts of the body which we think less honorable we invest with the greater honor, and our unpresentable parts are treated with greater modesty, which our more presentable parts do not require. But God has so adjusted the body, giving the greater honor to the inferior parts, that there may be no discord in the body, but that the members may have the same care for one another. If one member suffers, all suffer together; if one member is honored, all rejoice together. Now you are the Body of Christ and individually members of it.
>
> —1 Cor. 12:12-27

Gospel indications   The Gospels do not explicitly use the words Body of Christ; further, the title "Mystical Body" is of medieval origin. Nevertheless, Christ did express the same doctrine under the figure of the vine and the branches: "I am the vine, you are the branches. He who abides in me, and I in him, he it is that bears much fruit, for apart from me you can do nothing . . . You did not choose me, but I chose you" (Jn. 15:5, 16).

The picture of the total Christ, head and members, emerges from this imagery. What also emerges is the truth that this unity is based on Christ's choosing, not ours. This reinforces the doctrine that there is no Church, no Body, without Christ's willing it and bringing it into being.

Another passage, from the Gospel of St. Matthew, uses our Lord's account of the Last Judgment to prove his identification with the members he has chosen:

When the Son of man comes in his glory, and all the angels with him, then he will sit on his glorious throne. Before him will be gathered all the nations, and he will separate them one from another as a shepherd separates the sheep from the goats, and he will place the sheep at his right hand, but the goats at his left. Then the King will say to those at his right hand, "Come, O blessed of my Father, inherit the kingdom prepared for you from the foundation of the World; for I was hungry and you gave me food, I was thirsty and you gave me drink, I was a stranger and you welcomed me, I was naked and you clothed me, I was sick and you visited me, I was in prison and you came to me." Then the righteous will answer him, "Lord when did we see you hungry and feed you, or thirsty and give you drink? And when did we see you a stranger and welcome you, or naked and clothe you? And when did we see you sick or in prison and visit you?" And the King will answer them, "Truly, I say to you, as you did it to one of the least of these my brethren, you did it to me." Then he will say to those at his left hand, "Depart from me, you cursed, into the eternal fire prepared for the devil and his angels; for I was hungry and you gave me no food, I was thirsty and you gave me no drink, I was a stranger and you did not welcome me, naked and you did not clothe me, sick and in prison and you did not visit me." Then they also will answer, "Lord, when did we see you hungry or thirsty or a stranger or naked or sick or in prison, and did not minister to you?" Then he will answer them, "Truly, I say to you, as you did it not to one of the least of these, you did it not to me." And they will go away into eternal punishment, but the righteous into eternal life.

—Mt. 25:31-46

It is easy to see from this passage that St. Paul derived his doctrine on the Body of Christ from the teaching of Christ himself.

Therefore, the unity of the faithful with one another and with Christ is unbroken. Further, this same unity is visible to all who will examine the Church. This means that, even though the Church as the Body of Christ is one organism, nevertheless it can support a great diversity of members. Each member has his or her own God-given talents and intelligence and abilities and personality. And all are bound together, being of benefit to each other and indeed being of benefit to the entire community of believers. "For as in one body we have many members, and all the members do not have the same function, so we, though many, are one Body of Christ, and individually members one of another" (Rom. 12:4-5).

Thomas Aquinas' explanation   The metaphor of Head and Body has been beautifully and simply interpreted by St. Thomas Aquinas, O.P., in his summa of theology:

> As the whole Church is called one Mystical Body from its likeness to the natural body of man, which has different acts according to its different members, as the Apostle teaches, so Christ is called the Head of the Church from a likeness with the human head. In this head we may consider three things: order, perfection, and power:
>
> *Order,* because the head is the first part of man, beginning with the higher. And thus every principle is customarily called the head.
>
> *Perfection,* because it is in the head that all the senses, interior and exterior, are found, whereas in the other members there is only the sense of touch.
>
> *Power,* because it is the head which, by its sensitive and motive power, gives strength and movement to the members and governs them in their actions. It is in this sense that the ruler of the people is called their head.

These three functions of the head belong in a spiritual manner to Christ:

First, by reason of his closeness to God, his grace is more exalted and prior to all other graces (even though not in time). For all have received grace on account of his grace, as St. Paul points out: "For those whom he foreknew he also predestined to be conformed to the image of his son, in order that he might be the first-born among many brethren" (Rom. 8:29).

Second, he possesses the perfection of grace, the fullness of all graces, according to St. John: "And the word became flesh and dwelt among us, *full of grace and truth; we have beheld his glory,* glory as of the only son from the Father" (Jn. 1:14).

Third, he possesses the power of communicationg grace to all the members of the Church, according to John 1:16: "And from his fullness have we all received, grace upon grace."

So it is clear that Christ is fittingly called the "Head" of the Church.

—Summa, III, q. 8, a. 1

The diversity of roles   In another place, St. Paul shows how intimately connected are the members of the one Body of Christ: "If one member suffers, all suffer together; if one member is honored, all rejoice together. Now you are the Body of Christ and individually members of it" (1 Cor. 12:26-27).

Truly, then, there is a wide diversity of roles to play in the Church: "God has appointed in the Church first apostles, second prophets, third teachers, then workers of miracles, then healers, helpers, administrators, speakers in various kinds of tongues. Are all apostles? Are all prophets? Are all teachers? Do all work miracles? Do all possess gifts of healing? Do all speak with tongues? Do all interpret?" (1 Cor. 12:28-31). Some, then, have more important roles to play, such as the apostles and teachers; others, lesser roles, such as the helpers and those who speak in tongues. Still, the diversity of roles adds to the unity of the Body rather than detracting from it. Again we are reminded by St. Paul that, "As it is, there are many parts, yet one body" (1 Cor. 12:20).

Thus, the Church, in order to continue Christ's work as teacher, prophet, apostle, etc., will need both hierarchical and communal elements if it is to show forth the beauty and holiness of the one Body of Christ. To live as a Christian, understanding one's own responsibilities in the midst of the whole Christian community, means that each member must contribute to the whole by becoming more and more identified with Christ. The richness and holiness of Christ's life must permeate each one, in order to maintain the health of the Body of which Christ is the Head. "Rather, speaking the truth in love, we are to grow up in every way into him who is the head, into Christ, from whom the whole body, joined and knit together by every joint with which it is supplied, when each part is working properly, makes bodily growth and upbuilds itself in love" (Eph. 4:15-16).

This formula, "to grow up in every way into . . . Christ," signifies that whatever life the members have is received from him. Further, each member is under Christ's influence and receives movement from him. Consequently, all of the actions of each member are really Christ's actions. They act on his account; they belong to that sphere of being and action which he animates and inspires. This amounts to saying that the members are in his Body.

A corresponding formula, "Christ in you," is also original with St. Paul: "My little children, with whom I am again in travail until Christ be formed in you" (Gal. 4:19). It means that Christ is as intimate to the member as that member's very life. He is the interior source of all holy actions. This idea strengthens one of St. Paul's major themes, namely, the Christian life demands that Christ be imitated, both by possessing the sentiments of Christ and by having Christ formed in the believer.

The two ideas, "in Christ" and "Christ in us," express the same basic truth: whatever the Christian does is an act of Christ, because the Christian is a member of Christ. Hence, taken together, all Christians, animated by the same Spirit and acting in the name of and under the impulse of the same Lord, form the one Body of Christ. To make a comparison: just as the human organism is animated by the soul, so also the Church is animated by Christ. The Church is simply Christ in tangible form, the visible Body of his Spirit.

As each member of that Body learns to appreciate and to imitate Christ, the Head, each member can learn also to love the Church more deeply and earnestly. Pope Pius XII makes this point most clearly:

> That such a love, solidly grounded and undivided, may abide and increase in our souls, we must accustom ourselves to see Christ in the Church. It is Christ who lives in the Church, who teaches, governs, and sanctifies through her. It is Christ too who manifests himself differently in different members of his society. Once the faithful try to live in this spirit of conscious faith, they will not only pay due honor and reverence to the higher members of this Mystical Body, especially those who by Christ's mandate will have to render an account of our souls, but they will take to their hearts those members who are the object of our Savior's special love: the weak, the troubled, the wounded and the sick, who are in need of natural or supernatural assistance; children whose innocence is so easily exposed to danger these days and whose little hearts are wax to be moulded; and finally the poor, in helping whom we touch, as it were, through his supreme mercy the very person of Jesus Christ (*Mystici Corporis,* nn. 104-105).

Interpreting "Mystical" Body   Of course, the Church as the Body of Christ cannot be identified with the glorious Christ who even now is sitting at the right hand of the Father in heaven, and who is contained sacramentally in the Eucharist. Nor is the Church simply a social or moral Body, like General Motors or the government of the United States. Rather, the Church is the *Mystical* Body of Christ.

All the various parts of a physical body unite to form one independent existing thing. Each part has meaning and purpose when united in the whole. In the Mystical Body of Christ, however, even though the individual members are united by intrinsic and supernatural bonds, each still retains his or her own personality. Another difference is this: the different parts of a physical body exist solely to contribute to the good of the whole organism. In the Mystical Body, each member individually is of inestimable value in the eyes of God.

On the other hand, the elements of a social or moral body are also present in the Church. For example, the Church exists both for the good of the individual member and for the good of the society as a whole. However, it would be wrong to assert that the union of Christ and the faithful is *merely* moral or social.

The Church, embracing all of its members, is like any moral body in the sense that the Church's unity is based on a common goal — the sanctification of its members — and the mutual cooperation of all its members (pope, bishops, laity) striving to achieve that goal. If this were the only difference, however, the Church would still be simply a moral body. What raises the society of Christians above all other societies is the presence within this Body of the Spirit of Christ. His Spirit penetrates every part of the Church. This Spirit is active within the Church until the end of time as the source of every grace and every gift and every supernatural power. Thus, even though the social structure of the Church reflects the infinite wisdom of its Divine Founder, the social organization itself is still inferior in comparison to the spiritual gifts which give it life and the Divine Source from whence they flow.

The Spirit of Jesus   The Church is unique among all societies because of the presence within it of the Holy Spirit, the third Person of the Trinity. Just as every faculty and member of the human body is perfected and animated by the human soul, so also all of the members of the Mystical Body are united, insofar as the Holy Spirit—the ultimate and principal perfection of the entire Mystical Body—is in them. In essence, then, the Holy Spirit is the soul of this Body of Christ. The union that results is real and intimate and vivifying.

Obviously the unity between Christ and the Christian is more binding than that existing between the head and the members of an ordinary moral body such as a corporation or a state. Each member of the faithful keeps his own individuality and does not become a part of Christ's physical body. Nevertheless, the members depend upon Christ for a real communication of supernatural life and being. For on his life and being the actual existence and growth of Christ's Church depends.

The unique and mysterious qualities of this union, as well as its sometimes inexpressible and hidden nature, justify the use of the word "Mystical" to describe it. Therefore, it is proper to speak of that union between Christ and his members as a "mystical union," or simply as the Mystical Body of Christ.

People of God and Mystical Body   It is easy to see that Christian revelation has infinitely enriched the Old Testament concept of the People of God. Christ was not an earthly king, nor was his kingdom born of a political movement. Rather, his kingdom, his community, depends on faith in him. This adds a new element to the history of salvation. Divine faith causes Christ's own life to pass into Christians and the Spirit of Christ lives in them. Therefore, *faith* and the *life of Christ* through grace and the *Spirit of God* are the essential elements of a *new People of God.*

The idea of a People of God—externally identifiable as such—remains. But the idea becomes more interior and spiritualized. Now, instead of the Christian community being just God's People, it is also the Mystical Body of Christ. Its unity flows from Christ's life and from his Spirit who dwells within each member. Living by the life of Christ in the Spirit, the new People possesses the ideal toward which Israel could only strive.

Membership in the Church   The aims of the Church, both as a structured institution and on the social level, are in perfect harmony with the interior workings of the mission of Christ's Spirit within the Body of the Church. Nevertheless, one can live within the visible unity of the Church and at the same time have lost the life of sanctifying grace. It is also true that a soul can be justified interiorly and possess the grace of a living faith without visible union with the Church. The distinction just given affects individual souls, never the Church as a whole.

Pope Pius XII pointed out that visible communication with Christ is made up of three elements: 1) outward profession of faith; 2) the sacrament of baptism; 3) external submission to legitimate Church authority:

> Since its founder willed this social Body of Christ to be visible, the cooperation of all its members must also be externally manifest through their profession of the same faith and their sharing the same sacred rites, through participation in the same sacrifice, and the practical observance of the same laws. Above all, it is absolutely necessary that the Supreme Head, that is, the Vicar of Jesus Christ on earth, be visible to the eyes of all, since it is he who gives effective direction to the work which all do in common in a mutually helpful way towards the attainment of the supposed end. As . . . the Spirit of Truth . . . should govern the Church in an invisible way, so, in the same manner, Christ commissioned Peter and his successors to be his personal representatives on earth and to assume the visible government of the Christian community (*Mystici Corporis,* n 4).

The Second Vatican Council found that there was no need to amend the teaching of Pope Pius XII on this matter when it declared:

> They are fully incorporated in the society of the Church who, possessing the Spirit of Christ, accept her entire system and all the means of salvation given to her, and are united with her as part of her visible bodily structure and through her with Christ, who rules her through the Supreme Pontiff and the bishops. The bonds which bind men to the Church in a visible way are profession of faith, the sacraments, and ecclesiastical government and communion ("The Church," n. 14).

Invisible union with Christ   By the invisible bonds of faith, hope, and charity, the individual soul enters into a spiritual union of shared life with God. This "shared life" is animated by the theological virtues (faith, hope, and charity, which have God as the direct object of their acts). And it becomes even more integrated with God through the healing balm of the infused moral virtues (prudence, justice, fortitude, temperance). Just as the exterior organization of the Church stands on a foundation laid by Christ, so also the interior life of the soul is directed and vivified by God himself. The Holy Spirit, the Spirit of Christ, is the source and the driving power of this interior supernatural life of the soul. He guides it toward its goal. The Holy Spirit is the uncreated soul of the Church. He is present in the whole Church and dwells in every member who is in the state of sanctifying grace.

Consideration of the twofold bond that holds the full member of the Mystical Body to the Head, Christ, is a reminder of the phrases of St. Paul, "We in Christ," and "Christ in us." Visible and invisible bonds ensure a life-giving union between the Head and the member. This union is both unique and wondrous. It was attested to by Christ himself at the Last Supper when, in his Priestly prayer, he likened the union to that mysterious unity by which the Son is in the Father and the Father in the Son: "I do not pray for these only (the disciples), but also for those who believe in me through their word, that they may all be one; even as you, Father, are in me, and I in you, that they also may be in us . . ." (Jn. 17:20-21).

Requirements for real membership   Who may be members in this Body which is the true Church of Christ? Before it can express its governmental authority, the Church needs subjects. The Body, in order to exercise its vital function, requires members. The question, then, concerns the manner in which men and women are constituted subjects and members of the Church of Jesus Christ.

Pope Pius XII pointed out an important truth: "Actually, only those are to be included as members of the Church who have been baptized and profess the true faith, and who have not been so unfortunate as to separate themselves from the unity of the Body, or been excluded by legitimate authority for grave faults committed" (*Mystici Corporis,* n. 16). Baptism is surely the beginning of membership, "For by one Spirit we were all baptized into one Body—Jews or Greeks, slaves or free—and all were made to drink of one Spirit" (1 Cor. 12:13). Where there is no baptism, where divisions on points of faith exist, where people refuse to accept the authority of the Church, there is no life in union with the Body of Christ.

The membership of which Pope Pius XII spoke, however, is membership defined in terms of an external and legal bond. It excludes any mention of the invisible bonds linking the soul to God, such as sanctifying grace and the theological virtues. Mortal sin does not necessarily sever a person from this external, legal connection with the Body of the Church. Only the sins of schism, heresy, and apostasy separate a member from visible unity with the Church. Visible or legal membership consists, therefore, in the three external, sensible realities mentioned above: the reception of the sacrament of baptism; the external profession of the true faith; and the evident submission to lawful ecclesiastical authority. And, as has been mentioned before, the Second Vatican Council did nothing to change these basic requirements.

Degrees of membership   The degree of membership in the Mystical Body of Christ, as described thus far, is very limited and imperfect. We have spiritual souls, and the only kind of living, vital union which the soul can enjoy with God is primarily a spiritual one. Important as a person's visible connections or bonds with the Church may be (and their importance must not be underestimated), these bonds are always limited and partial. It has always been the common teaching of the Church that those who, through no fault of their own, fail to satisfy the requirements for full visible – or external – union with the Catholic Church are not, by that very fact alone, excluded from that far more important interior or spiritual union with God and Christ through sanctifying grace. Men and women are made partakers of the divine nature essentially by means of sanctifying grace. The instruments by which this participation in the life and nature of God is effected are the visible, organizational aspects of Christ's Body, the Church, as well as the sacraments of the Church.

Sanctifying grace, "the created soul of the Church," establishes the soul's vital bond or link with Christ and with the Spirit of Christ—the uncreated soul of the Mystical Body of Christ. Despite the fact that an individual may manifest the three external signs of communion with the Body of the Church, no one will be saved who does not fulfill the following requirements that are interior:

> He is not saved, however, who, though he is a part of the Body of the Church, does not persevere in charity. He remains indeed in the bosom of the Church, but, as it were, only in a "bodily" manner and not "in his heart." All the sons of the Church should remember that their exalted status is to be attributed not to their own merits but to the special grace of Christ. If they fail moreover to respond to that grace in thought, word, and deed, not only will they not be saved but they will be more severely judged ("The Church," n. 14).

The point made by the Council is that an individual may indeed remain in the bosom of the Church, as it were, but only in a bodily manner and not interiorly.

Full and perfect union with Christ implies both visible and invisible bonds with Christ. Perfect membership in the Church, or Mystcial Body of Christ, is defined in terms, first, of sanctifying grace and charity (an invisible bond) and second, in terms of the three external conditions laid down by Pope Pius XII and the Second Vatican Council. Those individuals who, fulfilling only the three conditions for visible membership, are at the same time guilty of grave sin, and are imperfect visible members of the Mystical Body. Those who are lacking either one or all of the three visible bonds, while yet in the state of sanctifying grace and joined interiorly to God by charity, are members, though invisibly and in an imperfect manner. They can be said to be members only potentially.

Membership in the People of God   Who then comprise that People of God which forms the Body of Christ? The document on "The Church" states that the Catholic faithful who possess the Holy Spirit are fully incorporated into the society of the Church. These are certainly full members of the Body of Christ. But, since the document on "The Church" mentions that by baptism others are united to Christ, even though they may be lacking in one or more of the visible connections with the Church, it is clear that there must be various ways or degrees of belonging to her. Consequently, the People of God who constitute the Body of Christ is a wider though less precise concept than that of "Catholic Church."

The People of God includes those baptized in other Christian denominations. The Second Vatican Council seems to imply this when it declares:

The Church recognizes that in many ways she is linked with those who, being baptized, are honored with the name of Christian, though they do not profess the faith in its entirety or do not preserve unity of communion with the successor of Peter. For there are many who honor Sacred Scripture, taking it as a norm of belief and of action, and who show a true religious zeal. They lovingly believe in God the Father Almighty and in Christ, Son of God and Savior. They are consecrated by baptism, through which they are united with Christ. They also recognize and receive other sacraments within their own churches or ecclesial communities. Many of them rejoice in the episcopate, celebrate the Holy Eucharist, and cultivate devotion toward the Virgin Mother of God. They also share with us in prayers and other spiritual benefits ("The Church," n. 15).

Thus, the Second Vatican Council did not change substantially the requirements for membership in the Mystical Body of Christ. It did modify the definition of membership in the Mystical Body formulated by Pope Pius XII. The definition adopted by the Council is a more fluid one, speaking rather of membership in the People of God. In *Mystici Corporis,* Pope Pius XII provided guidelines that pinpointed membership or non-membership. However, the Second Vatican Council, by interpreting membership based on the concept "People of God," has shown that a person's relationship to Christ and to his Church admits of degrees.

An outline for remembering   In light of the discussion and qualifications presented above, the following diagram may be helpful in remembering the various degrees of membership in the Mystical Body of Christ:

Membership in the Mystical Body of Christ

Perfect: three external bonds, grace, and charity

Imperfect:
- *Visible:* three external conditions
- *Invisible:* grace and charity without any, or with only one or two, of the external conditions

139

The necessity of visible membership   Certainly, invisible membership in the Mystical Body is sufficient for salvation. This is not the same as saying that such a Christian belongs to an invisible Church. Christ's Church is necessarily a visible organization. The question then arises: Why is visible membership in the Catholic Church necessary?

Membership in the Mystical Body according to the three conditions laid down in the encyclical *Mystici Corporis* is the normal and only secure visible relationship to the Church that is favorable for the interior sanctification of the soul—for interior union with God. Christ said to his apostles: "Go therefore and make disciples of all nations, baptizing them in the name of the Father and of the Son and of the Holy Spirit, teaching them to observe all that I have commanded you; and lo, I am with you always, to the close of the age" (Mt. 28:19-20).

The command to incorporate members by baptism into the Mystical Body of Christ was given by Christ himself to the apostles. In other words, Christ decreed by personal command that men and women should enter his Church. Membership was not left up to mere personal preference. In a letter issued from the Vatican in 1949, the declaration was made that "no one will be saved who, knowing the Church to have been divinely established by Christ, nevertheless refuses to submit to the Church or withholds obedience from the Roman Pontiff, the Vicar of Christ on earth." The Second Vatican Council reaffirmed this position when it declared:

> This sacred Synod turns its attention first to the Catholic faithful. Basing itself on Sacred Scripture and tradition, it teaches that the Church, now sojourning on earth as an exile, is necessary for salvation. For Christ, made present to us in his Body, which is the Church, is the one Mediator and the unique Way of salvation. In explicit terms he himself affirmed the necessity of faith and baptism (Mk. 16:16; Jn. 3:5) and thereby affirmed also the necessity of the Church, for through baptism as through a door men enter the church. Whosoever, therefore, knowing that the Catholic Church was made necessary to God through Jesus Christ, would refuse to enter her or to remain in her could not be saved.   —"The Church," n. 14

And, in another document, the Council gives further affirmation to this position:

> Nevertheless, our separated brethren, whether considered as individuals or as Communities and Churches, are not blessed with that unity which Jesus Christ wished to bestow on all those whom he has regenerated and vivified into one Body and newness of life – that unity which the holy Scriptures and the revered tradition of the Church proclaim. For it is through Christ's Catholic Church alone, which is the all-embracing means of salvation, that the fullness of the means of salvation can be obtained. It was to the apostolic college alone, of which Peter is the head, that we believe our Lord entrusted all the blessings of the New Covenant, in order to establish on earth the one Body of Christ into which all those should be fully incorporated who already belong in any way to God's People. During its pilgrimage on earth, this People, though still in its members liable to sin, is growing in Christ and is being gently guided by God, according to his hidden designs, until it happily arrives at the fullness of eternal glory in the heavenly Jerusalem ("Ecumenism," n. 3).

These documents show that visible adherence to the Church is something necessary, not only because of Christ's command, but also because Christ has "decreed the Church to be a means of salvation, without which no one can enter into the kingdom of eternal glory." In other words, the Lord has decreed two things: 1) he has commanded all men to enter his Church, becoming full members of his Mystical Body; and 2) he has established this visible society as the supernatural resource apart from which no man can be united to him interiorly.

Hence, the important dogmatic truth: "Outside of the Church there is no salvation."

The extension of the Body of Christ   It is important to take note of the fact that the Second Vatican Council did not make a simple identification between the Body of Christ and the Catholic Church. The document on "The Church" says that "the Church constituted and organized in the world as a society, subsists in the Catholic Church." In other words, the People of God forming the Body of Christ extends beyond the Catholic Church. The previous discussion of the degrees of membership in Christ's Body makes it clear that membership is by no means limited to Catholics. Thus, in the light of the Second Vatican Council, the statement that "Outside the Church there is no salvation," may be amended and interpreted to read: "Outside of the People of God who form the Body of Christ there is no salvation."

The important thing to realize is that "all men are called to be part of this catholic unity of the People of God, a unity which is the harbinger of the universal peace it promotes. And there belongs to it or are related to it in various ways, the Catholic faithful as well as all who believe in Christ, and indeed the whole of mankind. For all men are called to salvation by the grace of God" ("The Church," n. 13).

Those who do not wish to be saved will not be saved. No one fails unless he freely and deliberately rejects the offer of God's gift of life. Other Christians besides Catholics are certainly incorporated into the People of God which forms Christ's Body on earth. Even though their membership may be deficient in the sense of belonging to an institution, nevertheless, if they possess supernatural charity, salvation is theirs. Such groups exist in the world as partial realizations of Christ's Church. Such separated Christians are joined to Catholics as brothers and sisters in Christ. Certainly they share the gift of the same Holy Spirit.

Conclusion   The Christian life is a life lived as a member of a Body, the Church. Union with Christ in charity, which is the interior life (and, simultaneously, the goal of the individual soul), is to be lived and acquired socially as a member of the Body which is the Church. This "life in Christ" is especially expressed, embodied, and nourished by the visible rites of initiation and sacramental worship instituted by Christ himself. *Life* in the Body-Church is admirably sustained from birth to death by baptism, the Eucharist, and the other sacraments. *Faith* is expressed in and nourished by the dogmas of the Church. *Religion* finds its outlet in liturgical prayer. *Love,* which brings about mutual help and service, is strengthened and sustained by submission to law.

The chief elements of the Church-community are both served and directed by a hierarchy invested, as will be seen in the final chapter of this section, with the threefold power of *teaching magisterium, the priesthood,* and *pastoral governance.* These elements constitute a single Church (Body) that is both spiritually and externally one. That is, the one Church is both the center of the personal union of souls with God and the social embodiment of life in the Body of Christ.

The Church Christ established was to be like a city set on a mountain, a visible reality for all to see. It was to be a society with flesh and blood members, exercising an authority derived from Christ. It was to have a visible rite for worship and sacrifice. Furthermore, it was to embrace elements experienced with the satisfying assurance of the senses: things that could be seen, heard, touched, smelled, and tasted. But it was to be much more for the eyes of faith. The complete reality of the Church was to be invisible to the senses; this reality could be seized only by the mind through the gift of divine faith.

The total picture of the Church is more completely filled in by a variety of metaphors. In this chapter we have treated the metaphor "Body of Christ." The notion of the vine and the branches has also been touched on. In the next chapter, this latter metaphor, plus several others, will be explained more fully. However, as a kind of summary, all of the images or metaphors of the Church cause the believer to realize that the community of life between himself and Christ is one of total dependence on Christ. He is the beginning and the foundation of all supernatural life and growth. And his activity does not stop here; it is interior and continuing. Indeed, union with Christ is the absolutely necessary condition for fruitful works and for salvation. This dependence is especially manifested in Christ's influence on the soul through grace, but it includes as well his role as the exemplar and goal of each person's life.

The total view of the Church, therefore, must include this invisible and supernatural union with Christ. It is a union of life and love, manifested and caused by the Eucharist. It is both individual and communal, for it depends both upon Christ and upon the hierarchy that he has established.

Christ's universal call to holiness

The Lord Jesus, the divine Teacher and Model of all perfection, preached holiness of life to each and every one of his disciples of every condition. He himself stands as the author and consummator of this holiness of life: "Be you therefore perfect, even as your heavenly Father is perfect" (Mt. 5:48). Indeed he sent the Holy Spirit upon all men that he might move them inwardly to love God with their whole heart and their whole soul, with all their mind and all their strength (Mk. 12:30) and that they might love each other as Christ loves them (Jn. 13:34; 15:12). The followers of Christ are called by God, not because of their works, but according to his own purpose and grace. They are justified in the Lord Jesus, because in the baptism of faith they truly become sons of God and sharers in the divine nature. In this way they are really made holy. Then too, by God's gift, they must hold onto and complete in their lives this holiness they have received. They are warned by the Apostle to live "as becomes saints" (Eph. 5:3), and to put on "as God's chosen ones, holy and beloved, a heart of mercy, kindness, humility, meekness, patience" (Col.3:12), and to possess the fruit of the Spirit in holiness (Gal. 5:22; Rom. 6:22). Since truly we all offend in many things (Jas. 3:2), we all need God's mercies continually and we all must daily pray: "Forgive us our debts" (Mt. 6:12).

–"The Church," n. 40

The Catholic Church, then, is not an organization which is optional, which one may choose or reject.

Christ's main concern as lived out in the Church's mission in the world, is that men and women believe his entire word, obey his saving commands, and be unified with one another in his family. Anyone who recognizes the truth of the Catholic faith and the reality of Christ's will that he live in and according to that faith, and yet deliberately ignores so important a call, would cut himself off from Jesus as Savior and from salvation. This is not a question simply of loyalty to human beings, but of fidelity to Christ. He invites all to eternal life in him, "And there is salvation in no one else, for there is no other name under heaven given among men by which we must be saved" (Acts 4:12).

Thinking it over • • •

1. What is "mystery" in the Christian sense? Apply this sense to the "mystery of the Church," explaining the dependence of the Church on revelation.

2. Give the two etymological definitions of the Church and explain how each one and both together provide an important insight into understanding the nature of the Church.

3. The three closely-linked ideas of the Church as sacrament, as People of God, and as Mystical Body of Christ are the basis of a theology of the Church. Give reasons why.

4. Name the two documents on the Church that, in a particular way, interpret the meaning of the Church for people of today.

5. Where does the document called "The Church" first speak of the Church as a sacrament? What is the meaning of the word "sacrament"? Apply the word "sacrament" to the Church and explain how this application is the same as, and how it differs from, applications to the seven sacraments.

6. Who were the first People of God? Explain the distinction between "People of God" and the "new People of God." Read again Genesis 17:1-8 and give the basic ideas contained in the contract made between Abraham and God.

7. There is emphasis in the document "The Church" on the notion of "communion." What does this notion mean in relationship to the study of the Church as People of God?

8. What does the word "metaphor" mean? Explain the title "Body of Christ" by applying the definition of metaphor.

9. Pope Pius XII wrote an encyclical called *Mystici Corporis.* Give a definition of the word "encyclical" and give reasons why this particular encyclical is so very important to the study of the nature of the Church.

10. Who wrote the epistles upon which *Mystici Corporis* depends so heavily? What was this inspired writer's explanation of the words "Head" and "Body" insofar as these words pertained to the Body of Christ, the Church.

11. St. Thomas Aquinas also gave an explanation of the metaphors of the Head and Body. What were the points he wanted to explain?

12. Apply the teaching of St. Thomas Aquinas to the workings of the human body; apply the same teaching to the Church's doctrine of the Body of Christ.

13. What are basic requirements for membership in the Catholic Church? What is the difference between an actual member and a potential member? Is it possible for an individual to be a member of the People of God and yet not a member of the Mystical Body of Christ? Explain "Mystical."

14. Outside the Church there is no salvation. Is this still a valid teaching of the Church? Is it just? Why? Explain the Church's reasons for speaking in this manner.

15. "So it is that this messianic people, although it does not actually include all men, and may more than once look like a small flock, is nonetheless a lasting and sure seed of unity, hope, and salvation for the whole human race" ("The Church," n. 9). Relate this quotation to the yearning of all peoples for salvation through being somehow part of the People of God.

Chapter 2

THE CHURCH IN IMAGES

In the previous chapter, Christ's Church was presented as a sacrament, the new People of God, and the Mystical Body of Christ. Recreated from the Israel of the Old Testament, the Church is merely one phase in the overall history of salvation. Neither a beginning nor an end, but lying between the Old Covenant which it fulfills and the heavenly Church which it anticipates, the Church on earth is the harbinger of the New Covenant established by Christ.

There are things about this society that are so extraordinary—so lofty and elevated—that often it is impossible to explain adequately the idea of the Church simply by definitions. Sometimes, the best that human words and speech can do to express these realities is to speak in comparisons, to resort to the use of metaphors and images. Indeed, the supernatural quality of the Church is so sublime that the metaphorical method of expression is necessary. Christ's identification of himself with the Church suggests that there is more to the Church than can be told by ordinary, direct speech. It is insufficient to represent the Church simply as a society endowed with legislative power, or as the custodian of a sacred teaching and sanctifying rite, like a marvelous bureaucracy in charge of an institution founded by Christ himself. This represents only the external architecture, an outer framework—the Church perhaps as viewed from outside. In its hidden, invisible, inner nature this Church *is* Jesus Christ; it *is* Christ himself, always active, ever living, continually unfolding within her and by her all the riches of divine life. In an effort to gain further insights into this important truth, the Second Vatican Council urged the study of the metaphors of the Church which are found in the New Testament:

> The mystery of the holy Church is manifest in her very foundation, for the Lord Jesus inaugurated her by preaching the good news, that is, the coming of God's kingdom, which, for centuries, had been promised in the Scriptures: "The time is fulfilled, and the kingdom of God is at hand" (Mk. 1:15; Mt. 4:17). In Christ's word, in his works, and in his presence this kingdom reveals itself to us. The word of the Lord is like a seed sown in a field (Mk. 4:14). Those who hear the word with faith and become part of the little flock of Christ (Lk. 12:32) have received the kingdom itself. Then, by its own power the seed sprouts and ripens until harvest time (Mk. 4:26-29).

> The miracles of Jesus also confirm that the kingdom has already arrived on earth: "If I cast out devils by the finger of God, then the kingdom of God has come upon you" (Lk. 11:20; Mt. 12:28).

> Before all things, however, the kingdom is clearly visible in the very person of Christ, Son of God and Son of Man, who came "to serve, and to give his life as a ransom for many" (Mk. 10:45).

> When Jesus rose up again after suffering death on the cross for mankind, he manifested that he had been appointed Lord, Messiah, and Priest forever (Acts 2:36; Heb. 5:6; 7:17-21), and he poured out on his disciples the Spirit promised by the Father (Acts 2:33). The Church, consequently, equipped with the gifts of her Founder, and faithfully guarding his precepts of charity, humility, and self-sacrifice, receives the mission to proclaim and to establish among all peoples the kingdom of Christ and of God. She becomes on earth the initial budding forth of that kingdom. While she slowly grows, the Church strains toward the consummation of the kingdom and, with all her strength, hopes and desires to be united in glory with her King.

In the Old Testament the revelation of the kingdom had often been conveyed by figures of speech. In the same way the inner nature of the Church was now to be made known to us through various images. Drawn from pastoral life, agriculture, building construction, and even from family and married life, these images serve a preparatory role in the writings of the prophets.

—"The Church," nn. 5-6

The metaphor of the Mystical Body of Christ was treated in the last chapter. This was necessary because of the close relationship of that image with the concept of the new People of God. In this chapter, drawing heavily on the Scriptures and the use of the Scriptures by the Second Vatican Council, we shall examine the images of the Church as the Kingdom of God, the Spouse of Christ, his Flock, the Vineyard of God, and the Temple of the Holy Spirit.

Metaphor and similar terms   To avoid confusion in the consideration of these various images of the Church, the following glossary of terms may be helpful:

1. Parable: a short, simple story from which a moral lesson may be drawn; it is usually an allegory, or an extended allegory.

2. Allegory: a story in which people, things, and happenings have another meaning, as in a parable or fable. Allegories are used for teaching or explaining.

3. Fable: a fictitious narrative intended to teach some moral truth or precept, in which animals and sometimes inanimate objects are represented as speakers or actors.

4. Metaphor: a figure of speech in which one thing is likened to another, by speaking of it as if it were that other.

5. Image: a symbol or type of a picture in the mind.

6. Symbol: something that stands for or represents another thing.

THE KINGDOM OF GOD

Old Testament promises and prophecies

> And Moses went up to God, and the Lord called to him out of the mountain, saying, "Thus you shall say to the house of Jacob, and tell the people of Israel: You have seen what I did to the Egyptians, and how I bore you on eagles' wings and brought you to myself. Now therefore, if you will obey my voice and keep my covenant, you shall be my own possession among all peoples; for all the earth is mine, and you shall be to me a kingdom of priests and a holy nation. These are the words which you shall speak to the children of Israel."
> —Ex. 19:3-7

Having promised Abraham that he would make of him a great nation, God intervened in the history of Abraham's descendants in a special manner when they were in bondage in Egypt. With a great display of power he overwhelmed their Egyptian captors and led the Israelites across the Red Sea from slavery to freedom. Then at Mt. Sinai, through Moses, he began to mold a nation out of these children of Abraham. He gave them a law which would bind them to one another and bind the whole community of Israel to God.

The ruler of the new nation would not be a patriarch as formerly, nor a king as was the case in other nations. Yahweh would be the ruler of this nation, governing it through his chosen representatives, such as Moses, Joshua, and Samuel. Ultimately, because of the weakness of his people, he would permit them to be ruled by a king; but even then God would not cease to direct his people through his prophets.

Therefore, God ruled Israel; Yahweh was the only king; the kingdom was a kingdom of priests, a holy nation subject to the reign of the Lord God himself. Theirs was a true *theocracy (Greek: government by God). No longer were they a people enslaved by Pharaoh nor were they servants of an earthly master. They were truly the People of God,* "a people holy to the Lord . . . chosen . . . out of all the peoples that are on the face of the earth" (Dt. 7:6).

The idea "people" is closely allied to that of "kingdom." In Sacred Scripture the words are interchangeable. A kingdom denotes a domain subject to the rule of a monarch. The entire created universe constitutes a domain over which God alone is the sovereign. The entire universe is God's kingdom. With much more right, therefore, could Israel, the beloved People of God, Yahweh's holy nation, be called the kingdom of God, a supernatural kingdom of God. Israel was a kingdom made up of men and women who had subjected themselves to the supernatural law which God had communicated to them in a supernatural way—through the process of divine revelation.

The development of the kingdom   During the Old Testament period, the organization of the kingdom of God as a religious and social reality was gradually perfected. At the same time, the interpretation of the content of the revealed message constantly increased. In the beginning, the men and women who believed in the divine promises concerning the Messiah were not completely organized into one universal religious community. The divine worship commanded by the revealed message was conducted along patriarchal lines. Gradually, however, the nature of the kingdom was more fully revealed. God promised that the coming Redeemer would be of the seed of Abraham, a descendant of Isaac, of Jacob, and of Judah. Eventually the offspring of Jacob were organized into a racial, political, and religious body with which God entered into a special covenant. Clearly, God loved this society and cared for it in a special way, for out of it the Savior was to come. As a nation, Israel governed its activities according to the law given by God. The organized worship of Yahweh according to laws revealed to Moses was a special prerogative of this community. Israel could properly be designated as God's kingdom on earth, the special domain of which he was the only monarch.

The New Covenant in prophecy   After the Jews settled in Canaan, God sent them a continuing line of leaders. These men unified the newly-formed nation of God, fashioning it into a fully-developed human society—the final preparation for the coming of the Messiah. With the coming of the Promised One, God and his Messiah would form a new people, bringing to fulfillment and to perfection the individual, the family, the nation. The Messiah would establish his Church, the perfect religious and sacred society for which he had prepared men during so many ages. Then the words of Jeremiah would be fulfilled:

> Behold, the days are coming, says the Lord, when I will make a new covenant with the house of Israel and the house of Judah, not like the covenant which I made with their fathers when I took them by the hand to bring them out of the land of Egypt, my covenant which they broke, though I was their husband, says the Lord. But this is the covenant which I will make with the house of Israel after those days, says the Lord; I will put my law within them, and I will write it upon their hearts; and I will be their God, and they shall be my people. And no longer shall each man teach his neighbor and teach his brother, saying, "Know the Lord," for they shall all know me, from the least of them to the greatest, says the Lord; for I will forgive their iniquity, and I will remember their sin no more.
>
> —Jer. 31:31-34

The vocation of Israel, the People of God of the Old Testament, was received and willingly accepted at the time of the Exodus. Israel was called to be a people unique among the nations and this for a single purpose: to bear witness to the Promise. Israel was to keep alive the idea of the coming of the Lord's anointed, the Messiah, the one who would reign forever. It was the glory of the Jewish people that, despite the frequent defections from God's law, they were faithful to this calling. Gradually, through the teaching of the prophets, it could be seen that this old alliance would be superseded at a future time. The words of Jeremiah are but one example of this. There was to be a new order of things in the messianic era to come. This new order would be characterized, according to the prophets, by the extension of Yahweh's reign through Israel to the whole world and by a new kingdom of wisdom, gentleness, and peace.

False interpretations of the prophecies   This view of the future kingdom was not accepted by the majority of the Jews. They did not abandon their role of divine witness to the promise of Yahweh. However, the time and manner of Israel's redemption was not clear. Some envisaged a rising against foreign rule after the fashion of the Machabees, but in a decisive and final battle. Others thought that the triumph would not take place until an angry Lord came with his heavenly host to smite the world.

Israel was ever conscious of its supernatural calling, taking great pride in Yahweh's particular concern for his people. Inevitably, then, Israel's notion of the Messiah was that he would be a glorious and victorious king, a great warrior chief leading the nation to victory. Visions of the former grandeur of Israel under David and Solomon fueled such ideas. But, to the ears of this people, exalted by their messianic expectations and stultified by routine pietistic observances, came John the Baptist, "the voice of one crying in the wilderness: Prepare the way of the Lord, make his paths straight" (Mk. 1:3).

Preaching the new kingdom   The voice of John the Baptist, preaching "a baptism of repentance for the forgiveness of sins" (Mk. 1:4), brought to a close the centuries of preparation for God's kingdom. A new era was dawning, a new phase in the kingdom of God was to be inaugurated. "The law and the prophets were until John; since then the good news of the kingdom of God is preached, and every one enters it violently" (Lk. 16:16). Jeremiah had prophesied: "Behold, the days are coming, says the Lord, when I will make a new covenant with the house of Israel and the house of Judah, not like the covenant which

I made with their fathers . . ." (Jer. 31:31-32). The day of the New Covenant had arrived; the Baptist was its forerunner. Concerning John, the Messiah would say: "This is he of whom it is written, 'Behold, I send my messenger before your face, who shall prepare your way before you' " (Mt. 11:10).

The Jews of John's day knew the Scriptures well. They knew of the promises made to their fathers through the prophets. But no prophet had addressed this People of God for many centuries. An air of impatience imbued the expectations of God's people. Now came the words awaited by centuries of Jews: "Prepare the way of the Lord, make his paths straight" (Mt. 3:3), "for the kingdom of God is at hand" (Mt. 3:2).

The people flocked to hear the preaching of the Baptist, "and all men questioned in their hearts concerning John, whether perhaps he were the Christ" (Lk. 3:15). His disavowals were immediate and clear, for he declared: "But he who is mightier than I is coming, the thong of whose sandals I am not worthy to untie" (Lk. 3:16). To the priests and Levites dispatched officially from the Sanhedrin, John replied: "I am not the Christ . . . I am the voice of one crying in the wilderness, 'Make straight the way of the Lord' " (Jn. 1:20, 23).

Nevertheless, the people heard what they wanted to hear, and they saw in the preaching of John the Baptist the beginnings of an intervention by Yahweh himself. This, they believed, would bring about the political deliverance of Israel and the defeat of her enemies. When John cried out, "Repent, for the kingdom of heaven is at hand" (Mt. 3:2), he was delivering a message that was understood immediately. Finally, the despised Romans would be stripped of their power and driven out of the holy places. A great national leader would arise to crush the Gentiles under the feet of Yahweh's Chosen People. Famine, pestilence, and war would cease; the kingdom of God would be theirs.

Certainly, the prophets had spoken of such a Messiah—a victorious king. But the prophets also foretold a poor and lowly Messiah, a suffering servant, a lamb led to the slaughter. John's listeners were looking for a kingdom molded to their personal hope, and they were wrong.

The Messiah comes   Onto this scene prepared by John the Baptist came the person toward whom the history of salvation had pointed from the very beginning—the Redeemer, Jesus the Christ. His earthly beginnings were not marked by great notoriety, but the power of his words and of his works set him apart. While John preached repentance for the forgiveness of sin, Jesus began to gather disciples around him and to spread the good news of the kingdom of God: "Truly, truly, I say to you, unless one is born anew, he cannot see the kingdom of God" (Jn. 3:3).

After John's imprisonment by Herod, Jesus withdrew into Galilee, to Capernaum on the northwestern shore of the Sea of Galilee. "From that time Jesus began to preach, saying, 'Repent, for the kingdom of heaven is at hand' " (Mt. 4:17). Christ inaugurated his public ministry in Galilee. Until that time he had spoken only to a few close followers, to one Jewish leader in a private interview, and to a woman encountered by chance at Jacob's well in Samaria. Now he spoke to crowds of men and women, displaying the powers which his Father had given to him. To his chosen disciples he promised: "Follow me, and I will make you fishers of men" (Mt. 4:19). Thus, at the very beginning of his public ministry, Jesus indicated the future; that is, in the kingdom that he had come to establish, we will be saved by others who share in his saving power.

The kingdom preached by Jesus   From the beginning of his ministry Jesus preached that he was the legate sent by God. Later he would assert that he was the Messiah and Savior. The people were looking for a political Messiah, one who would restore the kingdom of Israel and lead the nation to temporal dominance over all the nations of the world. Jesus had to correct these erroneous notions; he had to prove that, indeed, he was the Messiah announced by the prophets, but that he was not a temporal leader. In the face of this general misunderstanding, Jesus delivered his Sermon on the Mount. This sermon, as recorded in the Gospel according to St. Matthew, contains ten references to the kingdom of heaven (Matthew's equivalent for "kingdom of God"; since he wrote for Jewish readers, he used this term out of deference to their reverence for the holy name of God, which prevented them from using it).

A reading of this sermon reveals that the term "kingdom of heaven" does not have the same signification each time it is used. The difficulty arises because the English word "kingdom" is used to denote the place or country in which a ruler exercises his authority. Formerly, the word "kingdom" meant the reign or rule itself, and denoted the power or authority of the king. In the Sermon on the Mount both meanings are implied: "Not everyone who says to me, 'Lord, Lord,' shall enter the kingdom of heaven, but he who does the will of my Father who is in heaven" (Mt. 7:21). This would seem to imply a place or country. "Your kingdom come . . ." (Mt. 6:10), on the contrary, implies the establishment of the dominion or authority of God.

Meanings of "kingdom of God (heaven)"   Jesus continually alternated between the two meanings of "kingdom." Sometimes it is the messianic kingdom of God on earth to which he refers; at other times he means the culmination of, or highest development of, that kingdom in heaven. In these instances the reference is to a place—either on this earth or in heaven. Frequently, Jesus speaks of "kingdom" in the sense of the recognition of God's dominion.

Thoughtful consideration of Christ's preaching, however, particulary his Sermon on the Mount, leads to the conclusion that he wanted to emphasize the spiritual character of the kingdom. Internal holiness is its chief characteristic. Jesus describes the true subjects of the kingdom and their spirit. He outlines what is required of those who would become his followers, and what is expected of those who wish to enter his kingdom. To enter the kingdom of God (the *place*) requires that the follower acknowledge God's dominion over his mind, heart, and will. This holiness, outlined in Christ's discourse on the Beatitudes, is summed up in his preaching by two all-inclusive commandments: "You shall love the Lord your God with all your heart, and with all your soul, and with all your mind . . . And a second is like it, You shall love your neighbor as yourself" (Mt. 22:37, 39).

Whether man dwells on this earth or in heaven, his acknowledgment of God's reign over him is the key to perfection. God's kingdom is *within* a person, in the internal holiness of each individual soul. This is the unmistakable message of the Sermon on the Mount. This is the theme of the keynote address in which Christ laid down the charter for his future Church. Christ emphasized the spiritual character of the kingdom in order to offset Israel's ambition for an earthly kingdom. That the kingdom Christ was to establish would be visible as well as invisible was yet to be revealed.

The parables of the kingdom   Because of the possibility of misunderstandings arising from the use of the expression "kingdom of heaven," Christ had to speak guardedly about the topic. Instead of looking for an invincible political leader who would lead the nation to temporal victory, the Israelites had to grasp a spiritual teaching that would affect all mankind. A critical moment would come when those who listened to him must abandon their own expectations and accept his view of the kingdom of God. To prepare his people for this moment, Christ spoke in parables (refer to the glossary for the definition of this term). This literary device compelled his hearers to ponder his message; it also furnished occasions for asking Christ questions concerning the kingdom.

Jesus prefaces his parables concerning the kingdom with that of the *sower,* found in the gospel of St. Mark (4:1-20). The details of this parable must have been easily understood by those who lived near the fertile fields of Galilee. The farmer goes out to plant his field. As he sows the seed it falls onto four different kinds of ground. The ground determines the way the seed will grow and how much it will produce. Some falls by the wayside and is rapidly eaten by birds. The seed that falls on rocky ground shoots up quickly, but because its roots are not deep it is soon withered by the sun. The farmer is not concerned that some seed falls among thorns, for when the crop grows he can cut down the weeds. But the thorns overcome the wheat and choke it. Finally, the fertile soil produces a perfect place in which the seed can grow and produce an abundant yield.

Since a parable is a comparison, the situation in the story must be compared with another situation. This next step is the *interpretation* of the parable. Jesus himself explains the Parable of the Sower in this way: the effect of the seed falling on different kinds of ground is similar to what happens when people with different dispositions receive the word of God. In this instance, the word of God is the revelation of the kingdom by Christ. Some hear Christ's preaching, but do not try to understand it; they are distracted, paying little attention to him. The devil snatches away the word from their hearts and minds. Others immediately accept the preaching with great joy; but their delight is superficial and their acceptance of the word is shallow; in time of temptation and trial they fall away. Others listen attentively enough, but before the word can mature in them, the attractions of pleasure and of riches stifle it. But finally, many souls receive the word wholeheartedly and it takes root deep within them. They cultivate the word, and the result is a yield of abundant goodness.

The master preacher contrasts the universal spread of the good news of the kingdom and the need of human cooperation to establish it in souls. He then speaks of the kingdom itself. The kingdom of heaven is like a man who sowed good seed in his field and his enemy came and sowed weeds among the good seed . . . It is like a grain of mustard seed . . . like leaven buried in three measures of flour . . . like a treasure hidden in a field . . . like a merchant in search of fine pearls . . . like a net cast into the sea . . . like a householder . . . etc.

The parables of the weeds and of the net

Another parable he put before them, saying, "The kingdom of heaven may be compared to a man who sowed good seed in his field; but while men were sleeping, his enemy came and sowed weeds among the wheat, and went away. So when the plants came up and bore grain, then the weeds appeared also. And the servants of the householder came and said to him, 'Sir, did you not sow good seed in your field? How then has it weeds?' He said to them, 'An enemy has done this.' The servants said to him, 'Then do you want us to go and gather them?' But he said, 'No; lest in gathering the weeds you root up the wheat along with them. Let both grow together until the harvest; and at harvest time I will tell the reapers, 'Gather the weeds first and bind them into bundles to be burned, but gather the wheat into my barn'" (Mt. 13:24-30).

Then he left the crowds and went into the house. And his disciples came to him, saying, "Explain to us the parable of the weeds of the field." He answered, "He who sows the good seed is the Son of man; the field is the world, and the good seed means the sons of the kingdom; the weeds are the sons of the evil one, and the enemy who sowed them is the devil; the harvest is the close of the age, and the reapers are angels. Just as the weeds are gathered and burned with fire, so will it be at the close of the age. The Son of man will send his angels, and they will gather out of his kingdom all causes of sin and all evildoers, and throw them into the furnace of fire; there men will weep and gnash their teeth. The righteous will shine like the sun in the kingdom of their Father. He who has ears, let him hear" (Mt. 13:36-43).

"Again, the kingdom of heaven is like a net which was thrown into the sea and gathered fish of every kind; when it was full, men drew it ashore and sat down and sorted the good into vessels but threw away the bad. So it will be at the close of the age. The angels will come out and separate the evil from the righteous, and throw them into the furnace of fire; there men will weep and gnash their teeth" (Mt. 13:47-50).

The parable of the weeds sown among the wheat and the parable of the net cast into the sea show two phases of God's kingdom—earthly and heavenly—as well as the coexistence of good and evil in the first phase. In the earthly kingdom, good and evil will live side by side; in the eternal kingdom, they will be separated. It should be noted that these two parables, together with that of the sower, present the kingdom of God under two aspects. In the parables of the weeds and of the net, the kingdom is a *social* one; in the parable of the sower, the kingdom is in the *individual.* In the first two parables, members of the kingdom of God (an organized group) tend toward a common goal. In its temporal phase, this kingdom is made up of both good and bad members; in its final phase, the kingdom will be marked by the complete triumph of good.

In the parable of the sower, the kingdom is the reign of God within souls; it is the individual's personal, private affair. Although the two points of view can be considered separately, they are not independent of each other. God reigns in the individuals only to the extent that they are members of his kingdom which he came to establish on earth.

The mustard seed and the leaven

Another parable he put before them, saying, "The kingdom of heaven is like a grain of mustard seed which a man took and sowed in his field; it is the smallest of all seeds, but when it has grown it is the greatest of shrubs and becomes a tree, so that the birds of the air come and make nests in its branches."

He told them another parable. "The kingdom of heaven is like leaven which a woman took and hid in three measures of meal, till it was all leavened" (Mt. 13:31-35).

According to Hebrew tradition, the kingdom of God would arrive suddenly and sensationally, with the visible triumph of God's Chosen People. The parable of the mustard seed denies this tradition by pointing out that the kingdom will have small, almost insignificant, beginnings, and will spread gradually—but inexorably—throughout the world. The parable of the leaven adds to this idea that the kingdom will bring itself about in silence and secretly, before the world even becomes aware of its existence and action.

The treasure and the pearl

"The kingdom of heaven is like treasure hidden in a field, which a man found and covered up; then in his joy he goes and sells all that he has and buys that field.

"Again, the kingdom of heaven is like a merchant in search of fine pearls, who, on finding one pearl of great value, went and sold all that he had and bought it" (Mt. 13:44-46).

These two parables are brief, but they show the inestimable value of the kingdom. In both parables the teaching is the same: the kingdom of heaven has great value, measurable only by the sacrifice one should be willing to undergo in order to obtain it. To the merchant's eyes, the pearl itself is worth more than all of the rest of his property; and the small field with the treasure in it is worth more than the land surrounding the field. Here, Jesus wishes to teach that the kingdom of heaven can never be purchased at too high a cost; no sacrifice or surrender is too great to gain entrance to it.

Characteristics of the kingdom Jesus Christ had a purpose. Gradually but unmistakably, he made it clear that he came to establish the kingdom of God prophesied in the Old Testament. This was the mission given him by the Father: "I must preach the good news of the kingdom of God . . ." (Lk. 4:43). A summary of the principal elements of Christ's teaching on the kingdom of God will show the relationship of the kingdom to the idea of the People of God:

1. The kingdom of God began simultaneously with the preaching of Christ. "The kingdom of God has come near to you" (Lk. 10:9).

2. The dominant note of the kingdom is interior holiness, as summarized in the command to love God and love neighbor. The ideal expression of this holiness is found in the Beatitudes.

3. The means by which the kingdom will grow is the preaching of the good news of Christ.

4. In relationship to its members, the kingdom produces external growth, gradual interior transformation, coexistence of good and evil until the final judgment, and, at the final judgment, a separation of the good and bad, followed immediately by the glorious consummation of the kingdom in heaven.

Meanings of the kingdom in summary   The kingdom of God, is:

An external kingdom: a collection of men and women brought to the knowledge of, and at least some outward acceptance of, the kingdom of God through the apostolic teaching. This is primarily the social aspect of the kingdom.

An internal kingdom: a kingdom whose purpose is to produce interior holiness. This aspect primarily concerns the individual.

An eschatological kingdom: the final state of this kingdom is glory with God after death for all those who, aided by Christ, have achieved the purpose of the kingdom.

This view of the kingdom of God embraces all that Christ said of it. It is a view which reveals the many facets of the kingdom and yet embraces and unifies them all. By defining the kingdom-Church in this way, one escapes a charge frequently leveled against the Catholic position, namely, that of reducing the Church solely to its exterior, juridical, and transitory elements. The Church, in a true and legitimate sense, is not merely the instrument of salvation nor the collection of means ordered to salvation. In its widest signification, the church is redeemed humanity. To this notion corresponds theology's classic definition of the Church as the assembly of those who have received the gift of faith and, through it, have been made sharers of the divine life. The Church is substantially one, unbroken in its movement through time.

Schematically, therefore, the kingdom-Church preached by Christ includes the *Church of the Old Testament,* the *Church of the New Testament,* and the *heavenly Church.* To understand the New Testament Church demands that it be seen neither as a beginning nor an end; rather it lies between the Old Testament which it fulfills, and the heavenly Church for which it prepares. "Think not that I have come to abolish the law and the prophets; I have come not to abolish them but to fulfill them" (Mt. 5:17).

Further images of the Church   As mentioned in the opening paragraphs of this chapter the other images of the Church to be treated here are the Church as the *Flock of Christ,* the *Vineyard of God,* the *Temple of the Holy Spirit,* and the *Spouse of the Immaculate Lamb.* Commentaries on these images will include and follow the order of the Second Vatican Council found in the document on "The Church."

THE CHURCH: FLOCK OF CHRIST

"Thus, the Church is a sheepfold whose one and necessary door is Christ" ("The Church," n. 6):

> "Truly, truly, I say to you, he who does not enter the sheepfold by the door but climbs in by another way, that man is a thief and a robber; but he who enters by the door is the shepherd of the sheep. To him the gatekeeper opens; the sheep hear his voice, and he calls his own sheep by name and leads them out. When he has brought out all his own, he goes before them, and the sheep follow him, for they know his voice. A stranger they will not follow, but they will flee from him, for they do not know the voice of strangers." This figure Jesus used with them, but they did not understand what he was saying to them. So Jesus again said to them, "Truly, truly, I say to you, I am the door of the sheep. All who came before me are thieves and robbers; but the sheep did not need them. I am the door; if any

one enters by me, he will be saved, and will go in and out and find pasture. The thief comes only to steal and kill and destroy; I came that they may have life, and have it abundantly" (Jn. 10:1-10).

The Church is a flock of which God himself foretold that he would be the shepherd: "He will feed his flock like a shepherd, he will gather the lambs in his arms, he will carry them in his bosom, and gently lead those that are with young" (Is. 40:11). Although guided by human shepherds, his sheep are nevertheless ceaselessly led and nourished by Christ himself, the Good Shepherd and the Prince of Shepherds (Jn. 10:11; 1 Pt. 5:4), who gave his life for the sheep: "I am the good shepherd. The good shepherd lays down his life for the sheep. He who is a hireling and not a shepherd, whose own the sheep are not, sees the wolf coming and leaves the sheep and flees; and the wolf snatches them and scatters them. He flees because he is a hireling and cares nothing for the sheep. I am the good shepherd; I know my own and my own know me, as the Father knows me and I know the Father; and I lay down my life for the sheep" (Jn. 10:11-15; "The Church," n. 6).

THE CHURCH: VINEYARD OF GOD

The Church is a tract of land to be cultivated, the field of God: "For we are fellow workers for God; you are God's field, God's building" (1 Cor. 3:9). On that land grows the ancient olive tree whose holy roots were the patriarchs and in which the reconciliation of Jew and Gentile has been brought about and will be brought about:

> Now I am speaking to you Gentiles. Inasmuch then as I am an apostle to the Gentiles, I magnify my ministry in order to make my fellow Jews jealous, and thus save some of them. For if their rejection means the reconciliation of the world, what will their acceptance mean but life from the dead? If the dough offered as first fruits is holy, so is the whole lump; and if the root is holy, so are the branches (Rom. 11:13-16).

The Church has been cultivated by the heavenly Vinedresser as his choice vineyard (Mt. 21:33-41). The true vine is Christ who gives life and fruitfulness to the branches, that is, to us. Through the Church, we abide in Christ, without whom we can do nothing:

> I am the true vine, and my Father is the vinedresser. Every branch of mine that bears no fruit, he takes away, and every branch that does bear fruit he prunes, that it may bear more fruit. You are already made clean by the word which I have spoken to you. Abide in me, and I in you. As the branch cannot bear fruit by itself, unless it abides in the vine, neither can you, unless you abide in me. I am the vine, you are the branches. He who abides in me, and I in him, he it is that bears much fruit, for *apart from me you can do nothing.* If a man does not abide in me, he is cast forth as a branch and withers; and the branches are gathered, thrown into the fire and burned. If you abide in me, and my words abide in you, ask whatever you will, and it shall be done for you. By this my Father is glorified, that you bear much fruit, and so prove to be my disciples (Jn. 15:1-8; "The Church," n. 6).

Explaining the metaphor of the vine   These words express Christ's image of the Church as an extension of himself. It is a comparison that pictures the total Christ. The metaphor has been employed extensively in the writings of the Fathers, in official declarations of the Church, and in papal documents. There is a powerful lesson to be drawn from this image of the union of Christ with his faithful. Pope Leo XIII wrote: "The Church is sustained and animated by the power which Jesus Christ communicates to it, almost as the vine nourishes and renders fruitful the branches that are united with it."

Several aspects of the influence of the vine on the branches can be noted:

1. *The faithful are in Christ and Christ is in them.* "I am the vine, you are the branches. He who abides in me, and I in him, he it is that bears much fruit . . ." (Jn. 15:5). A life-giving force flows from Christ to the faithful; he gives them a share of the Spirit dwelling within himself: "By this we know that we

165

abide in him and he in us, because he has given us of his own Spirit" (1 Jn. 4:13).

2. *The metaphor indicates that the very beginning of one's supernatural life is from Christ.* The branches presuppose the vine. This is begun through the sacrament of baptism: "We were buried therefore with him by baptism into death, so that as Christ was raised from the dead by the glory of the Father, we too might walk in newness of life" (Rom. 6:4).

3. *Union with the vine is the essential condition for life and productiveness.* St. Augustine said of this necessity:

> Lest anyone think that a branch can bear at least some small fruit of itself, since he said, "he bears much fruit," he does not say that without me you can do little; but "you can do nothing." Therefore, whether small or great, without him it cannot be done, without whom nothing can be done *(Treatise on the Gospel according to St. John)*.

Dependence on Christ for life is total. The imagery of vine and branches indicates the unity of action between Christ and those united to him.

4. *Outside the vine there is no salvation.* "If a man does not abide in me, he is cast forth as a branch and withers; and the branches are gathered, thrown into the fire and burned" (Jn. 15:6). "One of two things befits the branch," commented St. Augustine, "either the vine, or the fire; if it is not in the vine, it will be in the fire." The whole perfection of the Christian is found in his union with Christ.

5. *In the vine there are branches that are productive and others that are not productive.* Those that are nonproductive are the faithful who lack supernatural charity. They are not entirely lifeless because their faith, itself a supernatural grace, remains. This gives the branches a certain minimal life, but not enough for them to produce works that orientate them to salvation.

These five points concern the union of the individual soul with Christ. This aspect of the Church is more immediately and directly intended by this passage. Nevertheless, the social and communal aspect is not excluded. In fact, the context in which they are found in the Gospel of St. John, refers these points to the apostles' union with Christ. Vine and branches form one organic whole.

THE CHURCH: SPIRITUAL HOUSE

More often the Church has been called the house of God: "For we are fellow workers for God; you are God's field, *God's building*" (1 Cor. 3:9). Even Jesus compared himself to a stone which the builders rejected, but which became the cornerstone: "Jesus said to them, 'Have you never read in the scripture: The very stone which the builders rejected has become the head of the corner; this was the Lord's doing, and it is marvelous in our eyes?' " (Mt. 21:42). The Church is built by the apostles on this foundation: "For no other foundation can anyone lay than that which is laid, which is Jesus Christ" (1 Cor. 3:11), and from it the Church receives durability and unity. This house is described by many names: the house of God in which his family dwells: "I hope to come to you soon, but I am writing these instructions to you so that, if I am delayed, you may know how one ought to behave in the household of God, which is the Church of the living God . . ." (1 Tm. 3:14-15); the household of God in the Spirit:

> So then you are no longer strangers and sojourners, but you are fellow citizens with the saints and members of the household of God, built upon the foundation of the apostles and prophets, Christ Jesus himself being the cornerstone, in whom the whole structure is joined together and grows into a holy temple in the Lord; into whom you also are built for a dwelling place of God in the Spirit (Eph. 2:19-22);

God's dwelling place among men   "Behold, the dwelling of God is with men. He will dwell with them, and they shall be his people, and God himself will be with them" (Rev. 21:3); and, especially, the holy temple. This temple, symbolized by buildings for worship constructed of stone, is praised by the Fathers and is rightfully compared in the liturgy to the New Jerusalem. As living stones here on earth we are being built up along with this Holy City: ". . .. and like living stones be yourselves built into a spiritual house . . ." (1 Pt. 2:5). John sees this City descending from heaven and prepared like a bride adorned for her husband when God creates the world anew. "Then I saw a new heaven and a new earth; for the first heaven and the first earth had passed away, and the sea was no more. And I saw the holy city, the new Jerusalem, coming down out of heaven from God, prepared as a bride adorned for her husband" (Rev. 21:1-2; "The Church," n. 6).

Commentary on the Spiritual House This passage from the document on the Church shows how complex the image of the Church as Spiritual House is. The reason for the complexity, as can be seen from the scriptural verses quoted, is that several related metaphors are used by the Scriptures. Nevertheless, four practical conclusions can be drawn concerning this image:

1. *Christ is the cornerstone.* He sustains the building and joins the walls (Jews and Gentiles).

2. *The apostles and the prophets are the foundation stones.* This comparison differs slightly from 1 Cor. 3:11, where Paul refers to Christ as the foundation. Still, the reality that is taught is the same: the beginning is from Jesus.

3. *The faithful are built upon Christ, as living stones approaching the living stone who is Christ.* The faithful, affirms the apostle Peter, are living stones, living by the life of Christ.

4. *The communal aspect of the Church is clearly emphasized in the "temple" metaphor.* In this metaphor, the faithful are not only built upon Christ, but are built together with him. Aware of this imagery, St. Ignatius of Antioch wrote: "Hasten all of you together as to one temple of God, to one altar, to Jesus Christ alone, who came forth from one Father in whom he is and to whom he has returned" *(Ad Magnesios)*.

THE CHURCH: SPOUSE OF CHRIST

The Church, "that Jerusalem which is above," is frequently called our Mother (Gal. 4:26). She is described as the spotless spouse of the spotless Lamb: "Let us rejoice and exult and give glory, / for the marriage of the Lamb has come, / and his Bride has made herself ready /. . ." (Rev. 19:7). It was she whom Christ "loved and for whom he delivered himself up so that he might sanctify her" (Eph. 5:26), whom he unites to himself by an unbreakable covenant, and whom he unceasingly nourishes and cherishes. Once she has been purified, he willed that she be joined to himself, and be subject to his love and fidelity: "As the Church is subject to Christ, so let wives also be subject in everything to their husbands" (Eph. 5:24). Finally, he endowed her with eternal gifts so that we might recognize the love of God and of Christ for us, a love surpassing all knowledge. The Church on earth, journeying in a foreign land away from her Lord regards herself as an exile. Hence she seeks and experiences those things which are above, where Christ is seated at the right hand of God, where the life of the Church is hidden with Christ in God until she appears in glory with her Spouse:

> If then you have been raised with Christ, seek the things that are above, where Christ is seated at the right hand of God. Set your minds on things that are above, not on things that are on earth. For you have died, and your life is hidden with Christ in God (Col. 3:1-3; "The Church," n. 6).

Comments on the image   Writers on the spiritual life frequently use the image of a bridegroom and a bride to describe the spiritual relationship between the soul of the believer and Christ. In its New Testament use, however, the term "spouse" or "bride" is used to represent the Church instead of an individual soul. St. John speaks of the Church as a bride in his book of Revelation:

> And I saw the holy city, new Jerusalem, coming down out of heaven from God, prepared as a bride adorned for her husband; and I heard a great voice from the throne saying, "Behold, the dwelling of God is with men. He will dwell with them, and they shall be his people, and God himself will be with them; he will wipe away every tear from their eyes, and death shall be no more, neither shall there be mourning nor crying nor pain any more, for the former things have passed away."
>
> And he who sat upon the throne said, "Write this, for these words are trustworthy and true." And he said to me, "It is done! I am the Alpha and the Omega, the beginning and the end. To the thirsty I will give water without price from the fountain of the water of life. He who conquers shall have this heritage, and I will be his God and he shall be my son. But as for the cowardly, the faithless, the polluted, as for murderers, fornicators, sorcerers, idolaters, and all liars, their lot shall be in the lake that burns with fire and brimstone, which is the second death."
>
> Then came one of the seven angels who had the seven bowls full of the seven last plagues, and spoke to me, saying "Come, I will show you the Bride, the wife of the Lamb."
>
> —Rev. 21:2-9

Christ is called the bridegroom both by John the Baptist in the Gospel of St. John and by Christ himself in the Gospel of St. Matthew: "I am not the Christ, but I have been sent before him. He who has the bride is the bridegroom; the friend of the bridegroom who stands and hears him, rejoices greatly at the bridegroom's voice; therefore this joy of mine is now full" (Jn. 3:28-29). Jesus said to them, "Can the wedding guests mourn as long as the bridegroom is with them? The days will come, when the bridegroom is taken away from them, and then they will fast" (Mt. 9:15).

However, the principal text describing the union of Christ and the Church by the metaphor of marriage is found in the Epistle of St. Paul to the Ephesians:

> Wives, be subject to your husbands, as to the Lord. For the husband is the head of the wife as Christ is the head of the Church, his body, and is himself its Savior. As the Church is subject to Christ, so let wives also be subject in everything to their husbands. Husbands, love your wives, as Christ loved the Church and gave himself up for her, that he might sanctify her, having cleansed her by the washing of water with the word, that he might present the Church to himself in splendor, without spot or wrinkle or any such thing, that she might be holy and without blemish. Even so husbands should love their wives as their own bodies. He who loves his wife loves himself. For no man ever hates his own flesh, but nourishes and cherishes it, as Christ does the Church, because we are members of his body. "For this reason a man shall leave his father and mother and be joined to his wife, and the two shall become one." This is a great mystery, and I mean in reference to Christ and the Church; however, let each one of you love his wife as himself, and let the wife see that she respects her husband.
>
> –Eph. 5:22-33

Here St. Paul presents four key points about the relation of Christ and his Church:

1. *The love of Christ for the Church.* This love is explicitly indicated in verse 25 ("Husbands, love your wives, as Christ loved the Church and gave himself up for her"); it is held up as model for spouses to imitate. The love of charity is the most unifying of all loves; this love shows the closeness of the bond between Christ and the faithful. A powerful motive for love is indicated, for it is easier to return a love that has been given than merely to love in the first place. St. Augustine urged: "If we have been slow to love, at least let us hasten to love in return." Christ loves the Church as another self; his love is a model for husbands who are to love their wives as though they were their own bodies.

2. *Sanctification and incorporation into Christ.* The love of Christ is not cold and inactive. His love brings about a marvelous transformation of those whom it embraces.

171

Christ gave himself that he might sanctify the Church. Christ's works are the works of the faithful; all of the members share in his merits because of their incorporation into him. All are members of his body. The unity between Christ and the Church was prefigured in the nuptial union:

> Then the man said, "This at last is bone of my bones and flesh of my flesh; she shall be called Woman, because she was taken out of Man." Therefore a man leaves his father and his mother and cleaves to his wife, and they become one flesh (Gn. 2:23-24).

Thus marriage foreshadows and points to the union of Christ and the Church. Because of this union, the believer is part of Christ, in the same sense as a husband is to love his wife as himself (see above, Eph. 5:33). In this, the believer is following the example of Christ himself — Christ's love for the Church.

3. *The dependence of the Church on Christ.* In the opening verses of St. Paul's epistle to the Ephesians cited above, the subjection of the Church to Christ is compared to the loving subjection of a wife to her husband in those things that pertain to the duties of the husband. In the same way, because of his responsibilities as Messiah, Christ is the Head of the Church.

Christ loves the Church, not because the Church has already reached a perfection of holiness, but in order that it may become holy and glorious. God's love does not presuppose an already perfected goodness in the things he loves; rather, his love is the cause of that goodness. So great is the love Christ has for his spouse, the Church, that all of her beauty, all of her adornments, are gifts of the Bridegroom. This dependence underlines an important dogmatic point: the grace and perfection of the Church are dependent on, but distinct from, the perfection that belongs to Christ. He is the entire good of the Church.

4. *Perfection of the Church.* Ephesians 5:27 speaks of the glorious state of the Church in heaven; that is,

that the Church will be without wrinkle or blemish. This is the goal for which Christ gave himself and to which the life and being of the Church here below are ordered.

The Church, then, is a faithful bride of Christ because of Christ's loving presence to her and within her. Hence, the Church is ever teaching the truth, ever calling to holiness, and ever dispensing the sacraments of Christ. Formed from the side of Christ as he slept in death on the cross, the Church is the new Eve, faithful bride of the new Adam.

THE MARKS OF THE CHURCH

The most commonly known profession of faith to Catholics is called the "Nicene Creed." In the creed are found the words: "We believe in one holy catholic and apostolic Church." And down through the centuries the terms "one," "holy," "catholic," and "apostolic" have so characterized the Church that they have come to be known as the *marks* or *properties* of the Church. Of course, as properties of the Church, they are not metaphors or images of the Church. Nevertheless, because of their value in binding together the images projected in this chapter through metaphors and parables, they are fittingly included in this chapter as a kind of completion of the ideas offered.

The Church is One   The *unity* of the Church can be defined in this way: A property of the Church by which the Church is undivided in itself and divided from everything else in the profession of supernatural faith, in hierarchical rule, and in divine worship.

We have already seen that the Church of Christ must be uniquely one because the Mystical Body is a communication of the divine life, which is one and unique: "There is one body and one Spirit, just as you were called to the one hope that belongs to your call, one Lord, one faith, one baptism . . ." (Eph. 4:4-5). Therefore, this unity is *social,* for there is one jurisdiction, one government, and one obedience. Moreover, this unity is by *profession* of belief, since there is but one faith and one teaching to which all must assent. Finally, this unity is *liturgical,* for the essential form of worship and the means of salvation are common to all.

Thus all are united to the one saving sacrifice of the Lord Jesus in the Eucharist, and partake of the one Bread that united all in Christ. All receive the same sacraments. And there is also a unity in the communion with other parts of the Church throughout the world. Finally, there is a unity of confidence, because of Christ's promise: "And lo, I am with you always, to the close of the age" (Mt. 28:20).

The commentary of Vatican II   The unity of the Church is spoken of many times in the conciliar documents, but never more beautifully than in the following two quotations:

> After being lifted up on the cross and glorified, the Lord Jesus poured forth the Spirit whom he had promised, and through whom he has called and gathered together the people of the New Covenant, who comprise the Church, into a unity of faith, hope, and charity. For, as the apostle teaches, the Church is: "one body and one Spirit, even as you were called in one hope of your calling; one Lord, one faith, one baptism" (Eph. 4:4-5). For "all you who have been baptized into Christ, have put on Christ . . . for you are all one in Christ Jesus" (Gal. 3:27-28). It is the Holy Spirit dwelling in those who believe, pervading and ruling over the entire Church, who brings about that marvelous communion of the faithful and joins them together so intimately in Christ that he is the principle of the Church's unity. By distributing various kinds of spiritual gifts and ministries (1 Cor. 12:4-11), he enriches the Church of Jesus Christ with different functions "in order to perfect the saints for a work of ministry, for building up the body of Christ" (Eph. 4:12).
>
> In order to establish this holy Church of his everywhere in the world until the end of time, Christ entrusted to the College of the Twelve the task of teaching, ruling, and sanctifying. Among their number he chose Peter. After Peter's profession of faith, he decreed that on him he would build his Church; to Peter he promised the

keys of the kingdom of heaven (Mt. 16:19, in conjunction with Mt. 18:18). After Peter's profession of love, Christ entrusted all his sheep to him to be confirmed in faith (Lk. 22:32) and shepherded in perfect unity (Jn. 21:15-17). Meanwhile, Jesus himself forever remains the chief cornerstone (Eph. 2:20) and shepherd of our souls (1 Pt. 2:25; "Ecumenism," n. 2).

So it is that this messianic people, although it does not actually include everyone, and may more than once look like a small flock, is nonetheless a lasting and sure seed of unity, hope, and salvation for the whole human race. Established by Christ as a fellowship of life, charity, and truth, it is also used by him as an instrument for the redemption of all, and is sent forth into the whole world as the light of the world and the salt of the earth (Mt. 5:13-16).

–"The Church," n. 9

The Church is Holy Great mischief has been worked in the Church by those who have misunderstood the property called *holiness* which belongs to the Church, a property which must belong to the Church since she is the Mystical Body of Christ. The history of the Church is witness to the development of various errors based on the notion that personal virtue rather than sacramental ordination and apostolic commission give title to power and authority in the Church. Aside from being contrary to the plan of Christ, systems based on this notion have been completely unworkable and have invariably created such confusion among their adherents that the sects have disintegrated within a comparatively short time. Personal virtue cannot be assessed by natural means. An attempt at assessing virtue by natural means turns the curious into detectives, the gullible into slaves, and the self-righteous into hypocrites.

The property of holiness, then, does not mean that every member of the Church will be outstanding in personal virtue. Certainly, as has been shown in the parables, weeds will grow along with the wheat. *Holiness,* then, is that property which perfectly directs the Church's doctrine, sacraments, and members to the divine good. The Church's doctrine and sacra-

175

ments are holy in themselves and are productive of holiness. And there has always been a deep holiness in her members.

From Jesus and from his Holy Spirit comes all holiness. Because he is holy, his unchangeable doctrines as taught by the Church are holy; and the sacraments the Church ministers are holy, as is the worship of the Church. Thus, wherever the Catholic faith is lived, Christ brings forth fruits of holiness and repentance and confidence in the Holy One himself.

Vatican II comments

Faith teaches that the Church, whose mystery is being set forth by this sacred Synod, is holy in a way which can never fail. For Christ, the Son of God, who with the Father and the Spirit is praised as being "alone holy," loved the Church as his Bride, delivering himself up for her. This he did that he might sanctify her (Eph. 5:25-26). He united her to himself as his own body and crowned her with the gift of the Holy Spirit, for God's glory. Therefore in the Church everyone belonging to the hierarchy, or being cared for by it, is called to holiness, according to the saying of the Apostle: "For this is the will of God, your sanctification" (1 Th. 4:3; Eph. 1:4).

–"The Church," n. 39

The Church is Catholic   Because of the property of *Catholicity,* the Church is found essentially the same everywhere and in all ages. One day it will be completely diffused throughout the world and to all nations. St. Thomas Aquinas notes that Catholicity extends to more than just geographical boundaries. It includes people of all kinds and conditions; no one is left outside. Furthermore, the Church is universal in time, enduring from Abel to the end of the world, after which she will perdure in heaven.

Vatican II and Catholicity

It follows that among all the nations of earth there is but one People of God, which takes its citizens from every race, making them citizens of a kingdom which is of a heavenly and not an earthly nature. For all the faithful scattered throughout the world are in communion with each other in the Holy Spirit, so that "he who occupies the See of Rome knows the people of India are his members"

(St. John Chrysostom). Since the kingdom of Christ is not of this world the Church or People of God takes nothing away from the temporal welfare of any people. Rather does she foster and take to herself, insofar as they are good, the abilities, resources, and customs of each people. Taking them to herself she purifies, strengthens, and ennobles them. The Church in this is mindful that she must harvest with that King to whom the nations were given for an inheritance (Ps. 2:8) and into whose city they bring gifts and presents. This characteristic of universality which adorns the People of God is a gift from the Lord himself. By reason of it, the Catholic Church strives energetically and constantly to bring all humanity with all its riches back to Christ its Head in the unity of his Spirit. In virtue of this Catholicity each individual part of the Church contributes through its special gifts to the good of the other parts of the Church. Thus through the common sharing of gifts and through the common effort to attain fullness in unity, the whole and each of the parts receive increase ("The Church," n. 13).

The Church is Apostolic When the term *apostolic* is used to characterize the Church, it means the unbroken continuity of doctrine, worship, and government, from the time of the apostles in whom the Church was constituted, to our own era. Indeed, apostolicity is the power that gives birth to the Church. It signifies a mediation or a chain of dependence which begins with the power of the Trinity, passes first into the humanity of Christ, then into the sacramental and jurisdictional power of the apostolic body (which is uninterruptedly continued in the hierarchy), and finally into the Christian people. In this sense of the word, apostolicity would be the supernatural power which comes down from God, then from Christ, then from an apostolic body preserved by an uninterrupted succession, in order to form the Church.

Strictly speaking, then, *apostolicity* can be defined as that property of the Church by which she continues through a legitimate, public, and unbroken succession of pastors from the apostles, in a oneness of doctrine, sacraments, and government. History is witness to this mark of the Church. Yet, in a deeper sense, what is passed down is a mystery of faith pertaining to the uncreated soul of the Church. The sacramental powers, jurisdictional power, sacramental grace, as well as the divine truth entrusted to the apostles, remain in the Church.

Vatican II comments on Apostolicity

This is the unique Church of Christ which in the Creed we avow as one, holy, catholic, and apostolic. After his resurrection our savior handed her over to Peter to be shepherded (Jn. 21:17), commissioning him and the other apostles to propagate and govern her. He erected her for all ages as "the pillar and mainstay of the truth." This Church, constituted and organized in the world as a society, subsists in the Catholic Church, which is governed by the successor of Peter and by the bishops in union with that successor, although many elements of sanctification and of truth can be found outside of her visible structure. These elements, however, as gifts properly belonging to the Church of Christ, possess an inner dynamism toward Catholic unity.

—"The Church," n. 8

These final comments are the bridge which leads to the third chapter of this section, "The Mission of the Church."

Thinking it over • • •

1. Either define or describe the words "image" and "metaphor," relating these terms to the notion of "parable." What is the difference between a parable and a fable?

2. Why did Christ and the inspired writers find it necessary to explain the mystery of the Church in parables and images? In the New Testament, who is the most prolific author in the use of images to protray the Church?

3. Name the primary images used in the New Testament to illuminate the meaning of the kingdom of God. Which of these images are concerned with the exterior kingdom? Which show forth the interior kingdom?

4. Recall the content of the words of our Lord when he compares the Church to a sheepfold and himself to the door through which the sheep enter. What does this image mean as far as the relationship of Christ and his Church is concerned, and with regard to the relationship of Christ with an individual member of his Church?

5. Why does Christ call himself the Good Shepherd? What characteristics of the life and work of a shepherd pertain directly to the life and mission of Christ as Savior?

6. Name the central doctrine of the Church proposed by the image of the vine and the branches. According to the image as it is recorded by St. John in his gospel, what is the effect of those who "abide" in Christ? What is the punishment of those who sever themselves from the vine?

7. According to the document on "The Church" (n. 6), the Church has often been called "the edifice of God." Name some of the scriptural texts that expose and explain this image. Relate the terms "spiritual house" and "Temple of the Holy Spirit."

8. The Church is called "our Mother" as well as the spouse or bride of Christ. Is there a relationship between the two ideas? Why does Christ say that his disciples should rejoice while he is with them?

9. Reread the Epistle of St. Paul to the Ephesians, chapter 5, verses 22-33. Does St. Paul belittle the role of women here? If so, why? Is there another interpretation of this text based on Christ's insistence on the love of husbands for their wives?

10. Name the four marks or properties of the Church. Where can these marks be found as articles of Catholic belief?

11. What does the Second Vatican Council add to the teaching of the Church on its unity? Where is this oneness found and how does the history of the Church attest to it?

12. In what way do these marks of the Church complete the use of metaphors and images to explain the Church? Give examples from the definition of the holiness of the Church.

13. Can the notion of catholicity and universality as applied to the Church be proved both from the Scriptures and from history? Give scriptural texts to show this mark of the Church.

14. Why is the Church called apostolic? Show from the document on "The Church" that there is a continuity of doctrine from Abel to the present day.

Chapter 3

THE CHURCH'S REDEMPTIVE MISSION

At every moment the Church perdures as the fulfillment of Christ. In the previous two chapters it has been shown as the universal sacrament of salvation leading man to participation in the glorified life merited by Christ. Therefore, the Church is a living sacrament for the justification of the new People of God, the Mystical Body of Christ. Christ's redemptive action is carried on through the mission of the Holy Spirit—but in the Church. And in this redemptive mission is found the divine honor and glory. The document on "The Church" indicated the goal of the Church in this concise statement:

> When Jesus, who had undergone the death of the cross, had risen, he appeared as the one constituted Lord, Christ, and Eternal Priest, and he poured out on his disciples the Spirit promised by the Father. From this source the Church . . . receives . . . the mission to proclaim and to establish among all peoples the kingdom of Christ and of God and to be, on earth, the initial budding forth of that kingdom.

> —"The Church," n. 5

And, in another document from the Second Vatican Council, the decrees on the "Missionary Activity" of the Church, an even clearer teaching of the purpose and mission of the Church is set forth:

The Church has been divinely sent to all nations that she might be the "universal sacrament of salvation" ("The Church," n. 48). Acting out of the innermost requirements of her own catholicity and in obedience to her Founder's mandate (Mk. 16:16), she strives to proclaim the gospel to all men. For the Church was founded upon the apostles, who, following in the footsteps of Christ, "preached the message of truth and begot Churches" (St. Augustine, *Exposition on Psalm 44*). Upon their successors devolves the duty of perpetuating this work through the years. Thus "the word of God may run and be glorified" (2 Thes. 3:1) and God's kingdom can be everywhere proclaimed and established ("Missionary Activity," n. 1).

In obedience to the Father's will, therefore, Christ inaugurated the kingdom of God on earth. He revealed this kingdom to a sinful human race. This work of Christ must perdure until the end of time, so that his redemptive act may be applied to succeeding generations of men and women. Once more the Second Vatican Council gives voice to these truths:

Just as Christ was sent by the Father, so also he sent the apostles filled with the Holy Spirit. This he did that, by preaching the gospel to every creature, they might proclaim that the Son of God, by his death and resurrection, had freed us from the power of Satan and from death and brought us into the kingdom of his Father.

His purpose also was that they might accomplish the work of salvation which they had proclaimed, by means of sacrifice and sacraments . . . Thus by Baptism men are plunged into the paschal mystery of Christ: they die with him, are buried with him, and rise with him; they receive the spirit of adoption as sons "in which we cry: Abba, Father" (Rom. 8:15), and thus become true adorers whom the Father seeks.   —"The Liturgy," n. 6

Continuing Christ's mission on earth   Christ's mission of redemption must be carried on. After he rose from the dead, Christ ascended into heaven, and from there sent the Holy Spirit upon the apostles and through them upon the whole community of believers. Through this same Spirit he established his new People of God, the Mystical Body of Christ—the Church. It is for this reason that the Church must be seen as the universal sacrament of salvation. Through this sacrament, Christ remains continually active in the world to share his glorified life with us.

However, after Christ's death and exaltation, he no longer exercises any natural, ordinary contact with the Church. Rather, the Church is now the embodiment of Christ's presence in history. Christ alone is the Redeemer; only his death and glorification are meritorious and redemptive; he is the one mediator between God and man. Hence, Christ is present in the world today through his Church; and his death and exaltation touch the world through that same Church in which they are brought to fulfillment.

This means that the good news of the kingdom preached by Christ is an invitation to all people to "express in their lives, and manifest to others, the mystery of Christ and the real nature of the true Church" ("The Liturgy," n. 2). The Church is expressed in the personal union of its members with God through the faith and love he has infused into them. This union is effected by the members' giving themselves as an offering to God, by returning to him the same love he has given to them.

The continuing mission of Christ on earth must include the perspective that there are two aspects to the earthly phase of Christ's kingdom: 1) the Church is an institution, a visible, hierarchically constituted society embracing the means that are necessary for salvation; and 2) the Church is a community of the faithful, of individual believers who are intimately united to one another as each is vitally united to Christ. This dual aspect of the kingdom expresses the twofold relationship of Christ with his Church. First of all, Christ is related to the Church as *founder*, ruling and building up the Church by his power. Secondly, Christ is the *life* of the Church, animating the Church by his Spirit. This twofold relationship is beautifully united in St. Paul's concept of "head" and "body": "He is the Head of the Body, the Church" (Col. 1:18). This image has already been treated at length in the first chapter of this section.

The immediate conclusions that must be reached are these:

1. The Church founded by Christ is truly but not merely a spiritual and invisible union of believers.

2. In the synoptic gospels, Christ stresses the visible, the hierarchical, the monarchical, and the institutional side of his Church. But again, the Church has greater and more transcendent dimensions.

Christ's teachings on the Church, especially in the Gospel of St. Matthew, concern themselves with a reality which would be manifested in the future. St. John and St. Paul, however, speak of a Church which has already begun to show life and to grow. Both St. John and St. Paul were writing to those who understood well the apostles' concept of the Church. After all, the Church had been founded years before. Hence, the early Christians were certain of one important fact: *they were the Church.* The inspired images of the Church that were considered in the previous chapters — classical metaphors for the Church — were proposed by St. John and St. Paul about a Church which the faithful already knew they constituted. The faithful knew, even at that time, that they were the Body of which Christ was the Head; that they were the branches and he the vine; that they were the building blocks and he was the cornerstone; that they were the bride and he the bridegroom. Once again, they knew that they were the Church.

The door which opens into a deeper understanding of the redemptive mission Church has two keys. One of these keys is the realization that the Church is a *communion with God in Christ.* This doctrinal understanding of the Church as *communion* became the true heart of the Second Vatican Council's teaching on the Church. Communion is the one element which is new and yet, at the same time, still linked to the origins of the Church.

The other key is the realization that the Church is also *the visible means or instrument for attaining this fellowship, this communion.* The preceding two chapters considered the first key to an understanding of the Church in itself; this present chapter will focus on using the second key to obtain an understanding of the missionary activity of the Church. Central to this understanding will be an attempt to explain what it means to say that the Church is the *visible* means of attaining fellowship with God.

A VISIBLE SOCIETY

The setting for the emerging Church

The Last Supper of Jesus becomes recognizable as the true act of founding the Church; Jesus gives his disciples this Liturgy of his death and resurrection, and thus gives them the feast of life. At the Last Supper he repeats the Sinai Covenant; or better what had been only a foreshadowing in sign now fully becomes reality; the communion of blood and of life between God and man. In saying this, it is clear that the Last Supper anticipates the cross and resurrection and, at the same time, necessarily presupposes them, because otherwise everything would remain an empty gesture. For this reason the Fathers of the Church were able to say, using a very beautiful image, that the Church sprang forth from the pierced side of the Lord, from which blood and water flowed. When I say that the Last Supper is the beginning of the Church, in reality I say the same thing, although from another point of view. In fact, this formula, too, signifies that the Eucharist links men to one another, and not only to one another, but to Christ; and in this way it makes the Church. At the same time, the fundamental constitution of the Church is already given in this: the Church lives in Eucharistic community. Her Mass is her constitution, because she herself is, in her essence, Mass–service to God and thus service to men, *the service of the transformation of the world.*

The Mass is her form; this means that in her a completely unique relationship of multiplicity and unity, to be found nowhere else, is realized. In every celebration of the Eucharist, the Lord is really present. He is in fact risen, and dies no more; thus he can no longer even be divided into parts. He always gives himself entire and undivided. For this reason the Council says: "This Church of Christ is really present in all legitimately organized local groups of the faithful, which, insofar as they are united to their pastors, are also quite appropriately called Churches in the New Testament. For these are in fact, in their own localities, the new people called by God, in the power of the Holy Spirit and as the result of full conviction (1 Thes. 1:5) . . . in these communities, though they may often be small and poor, or existing in the diaspora, Christ is present through whose power and influence the One, Holy, Catholic, and Apostolic Church is constituted ("The Church," n. 26; Cardinal J. Ratzinger, "The Ecclesiology of Vatican II").

Spiritual origins   In its beginnings, Christ's mission seemed to be one of impressing on his hearers the spiritual nature of his kingdom. Aspirants to the kingdom should not parade their good works in public nor advertise their almsgiving to the poor, nor make a public display of fasting. They should strive to attain, not worldly treasures, but ". . . lay up for yourselves treasures in heaven, where neither moth nor rust consumes and where thieves do not break in and steal. For where your treasure is, there will your heart be also" (Mt. 6:20-21). Trust in God as Father was an essential disposition for salvation: "But seek first his kingdom and his righteousness, and all these things shall be yours as well" (Mt. 6:33). Hence, the primary aim of Jesus' early preaching was to state clearly that interior holiness is of the essence of the kingdom of heaven. The kingship of God is concerned chiefly with God's rule over the hearts and souls of the People of God. Thus, the Church is, in its foundations, a spiritual kingdom, with the interior relationship between the faithful and God as an essential element.

A visible society   But Jesus did not intend his kingdom to be simply invisible. From the outset, he was surely and consistently moving toward the formation of a *visible community*.

Certainly the most beautiful characteristic of his kingdom was to remain the interior, supernatural relationship between God and man. However, in order to safeguard this relationship—invisible and spiritual

–for future generations and to guarantee the preservation of the means by which this relationship would be established and strengthened, Jesus founded a visible society: his Church.

The purpose of this present chapter is to investigate in a detailed manner the *organization and structure* of this visible society. In doing this, distinctions must be made between the *essential and unchangeable elements* within the social organism of the Church, and those *elements that are variable and changeable*.

THE TWELVE AND THE FIRST MISSION

The formation of his Church was of primary concern to Christ. When he began his ministry he gathered a small band of followers who traveled with him and formed the nucleus of those who would listen to him. They stayed with him long after the crowds had dispersed. To this group of intimates Jesus interpreted many of the engaging parables he had spoken to the people; to them he revealed in greater detail the workings of his kingdom. On one historic occasion, calling these followers together, Christ chose twelve from among them; these would be known as his apostles. These twelve received special attention from Jesus. They received special instructions on the meaning of discipleship, because Jesus had special plans for them. They were to become "fishers of men"; they were to be the "salt of the earth"; their light was "to shine before men." In short, the apostles would be the laborers who would assist the Lord in bringing men and women to salvation.

The first mission   After giving them power over evil spirits and the power to cure every kind of disease and infirmity, Jesus dispatched the twelve with this command:

Go nowhere among the Gentiles, and enter no town of the
Samaritans, but go rather to the lost sheep of the house of Israel.
And preach as you go, saying, "The kingdom of heaven is at hand."
Heal the sick, raise the dead, cleanse lepers, cast out demons. You
received without pay, give without pay. Take no gold, nor silver,
nor copper in your belts, no bag for your journey, nor two tunics,
nor sandals, nor a staff; for the laborer deserves his food (Mt. 10:5-10).

These men were given the mission of carrying on the
work of Christ—in his name and by his power:
"Behold, I send you out . . . for it is not you who
speak, but the Spirit of your Father speaking
through you" (Mt. 10:16, 20). "He who receives you
receives me . . ." (Mt. 10:40). The preaching in which
they were to engage was repentance for the forgiveness of sins, and the imminence of the kingdom of
God. For this reason, and from that moment on,
Jesus took special care to teach the twelve concerning the kingdom. With great patience he guided
them in understanding the fundamental principles
of his doctrine concerning the kingdom. He realized
that they needed to be fortified by these teachings so
that they might be prepared for the task before
them: to take up, when the time came, the work
which he had begun.

Peter appointed leader   The work for which
Jesus prepared the apostles began to take shape
slowly. The complete picture would not emerge until
after the Lord had been crucified and had risen from
the dead. One of the principal elements of the emerging picture was indicated in the district of Caesarea
Philippi. Here on the northern frontier of Palestine
occurred the scene that was to prove so decisive in
the history of the Church. It was here that Peter is
set apart within the group of the apostles. He
receives confirmation of his belief in Jesus and is
awarded the leadership of the future community of
Christ's followers:

Now when Jesus came into the district of Caesarea Philippi, he
asked his disciples, "Who do men say that the Son of man is?" And
they said, "Some say John the Baptist, others say Elijah, and others

Jeremiah or one of the prophets." He said to them, "But who do you say that I am?" Simon Peter replied, "You are the Christ, the Son of the living God." And Jesus answered him, "Blessed are you, Simon Bar-Jonah! For flesh and blood has not revealed this to you, but my Father who is in heaven. *And I tell you, you are Peter, and on this rock I will build my church,* and the powers of death shall not prevail against it. I will give you the keys of the kingdom of heaven, and whatever you bind on earth shall be bound in heaven, and whatever you loose on earth shall be loosed in heaven."

–Mt. 16:13-19

In this passage, one may have expected to find the expression, "On this rock I will build my kingdom"; but "Church" is substituted for "kingdom of God." The word "church" means "an assembly of the people." In its classical use it signified a properly convoked civic assembly; in the Septuagint it designated the Israelites as a religious society especially chosen by God.

The word is used by Christ in both senses. First of all, the Church was to be a society of citizens *assembled* by God, having been *called forth* by him. Secondly, it was to be the new Israel, the society of believers in Christ. Israel, the kingdom of God of the Old Testament, enjoyed its special prerogatives because of its corporate faith in God and his promises. The new society formed by Christ out of his disciples, the kingdom of God of the New Testament, was henceforth to be the only true society of the faithful once Israel had rejected its Messiah-Redeemer.

One Church, not many   Today, the term "church" is applied to any religious society. Reference is made to the various non-Catholic "churches" and to the separated "oriental churches." The term "church" does not have such latitude of meaning in the New Testament. The Church is the one society founded by Christ, the one visible organization *in which* and *through which* men and women enter into association and fellowship with him. The Church is a unique reality, the one and only community of Christ's followers.

The Son of God was sent into this world by his heavenly Father in order to save the human race by his passion, death, and resurrection. Therefore, those to whom he had been sent had to be shown the *way*, taught the *truth*, and brought into contact with the *life* of Christ. In order that he might be accessible to all people in every age, Christ instituted his Church—a worldwide and imperishable society, which was to be the only authentic and infallible guide to, and source of, salvation until the end of time.

A visible, theocratic society   The kingship that Christ wished to exercise over people was principally a dominion over their hearts and minds. But the gospels show clearly that the kingdom is also a Church, an assembly. It appears under the guise of a visible and organized society. Christ's Kingdom-Church is closely linked with the Old Testament theocracy mentioned in the previous chapter. There, Yahweh's kingship was over a Chosen People, and its exercise was accomplished through visible representatives.

In the New Testament there is to be a new theocracy. Yahweh will continue to reign over his people, but a new period of the eternal kingship of God is inaugurated by the reign of the Son of God incarnate, Jesus Christ. The kingdom of Christ is the successor to Yahweh's ancient kingdom, Israel. This new kingdom and its king are the supernatural climax of a divine plan announced and developed for centuries in the history of Israel. The earlier state of God's kingdom as being under the Law is ended. The new society is completely identified with God's kingdom on earth. No other organization will ever replace the Church of Christ on earth. Truly, there will be another "coming" of Christ at the end of time, but the one society he founds will dwell forever in the presence of and in the possession of the living God, triumphant for all time.

Necessity of leaders   The public ministry of Jesus was too brief to reach everyone. He taught only a few, the twelve apostles whom he hand-picked. These in turn he sent forth to preach, first to the Jews, then to the world. Not only did he send these representatives whom he had personally trained to preach, but they were to *govern* also: to make laws, to pass judgment, to punish. To them Christ gave his own authority: "Go therefore and make disciples of all nations, baptizing them in the name of the Father and of the Son and of the Holy Spirit, teaching them to observe all that I have commanded you" (Mt. 28:19-20).

The kingdom that Christ came to establish would grow, expand, and cover the face of the earth. Christ intended his Church to be manifest to the world. Therefore, the Church had to be a human organization as well as a supernatural one. It was to have human beings for its leaders as well as its members.

The earthly phase of the kingdom, the New Testament Church, is a complex reality. To say that it is visible, however, is not to deny its invisible and spiritual elements. The Church of Christ embraces supernatural and invisible as well as institutional and visible elements. To deny one or the other aspect would be the same as denying the truth of Christ's visible, human nature, or his invisible, divine nature. Thus, just as Christ is one through the union of two natures in one person, so also the visible body, the members, are united to the invisible spiritual gifts and their source to form one Mystical Body of Christ—the Church.

"The Church" comments on this truth

Christ, the one Mediator, established and ceaselessly sustains here on earth his holy Church, the community of faith, hope, and charity, as a visible structure. Through her he communicates truth and grace to all. But the society furnished with hierarchical agencies and the Mystical Body of Christ are not to be considered as two realities, nor are the visible assembly and the spiritual community, nor the earthly Church and the Church enriched with heavenly things. Rather they form one interlocked reality which is comprised of a divine and a human element. For this reason, by an excellent analogy, this reality is compared to the mystery of the incarnate Word. Just as the assumed nature inseparably united to the divine Word serves him as a living instrument of salvation, so, in a similar way, does the communal structure of the Church serve Christ's Spirit, who verifies it by way of building up the body (Eph. 4:16).

This is the unique Church of Christ which in the Creed we avow as one, holy, catholic, and apostolic. After his Resurrection our Savior handed her over to Peter to be shepherded, commissioning him and the other apostles to propagate and govern her. He erected her for all ages as "the pillar and mainstay of the truth" (1 Tm. 3:15). This Church, constituted and organized in the world as a society, subsists in the Catholic Church, which is governed by the successor of Peter and by the bishops in union with that successor, although many elements of sanctification and of truth can be found outside of her visible structure. These elements, however, as gifts properly belonging to the Church of Christ, possess an inner dynamism toward Catholic unity.

–"The Church," n. 8

In the remainder of this chapter we will study the Church as it is a visible society. Remember that assisting the institutional or juridical Church is the Holy Spirit. This Spirit is continually active within the visible society as its dynamic and energizing life-principle.

A VISIBLE SOCIETY

Its characteristics   Christ united the members of the society he had founded under a common authority. He provided direction for the members' activities by setting a definite goal for them. Finally, he gave them common means or aids to assist them in achieving this goal. In summary, then, the characteristics of the Church of Christ insofar as it is a juridical institution are the following:

1. The agent or founder responsible for the constitution of this society, the one who has determined its particular goal and has provided the means for attaining that goal, is Christ himself.

2. The goal or purpose of this society is to be the embodiment of Christ's redemptive mystery on earth. The Church perpetuates Christ's worship of the Father and continually brings the fruits of redemption into the world.

3. Those who should belong to this society are men and women of all nations and of all times who are born after the founding of this Church.

4. Finally, what is it precisely that distinguishes the Church from any other society which might unite people in a common purpose? Clearly there are many unique features of this society: it is of divine institution; it is mystically identified with its glorified Founder, Christ; it is the temple of the Holy Spirit; and it is the perpetuator in history of the redemptive mystery of Christ worshipping the Father and communicating divine life to all.

All of these characteristics pertain uniquely to the Church founded by Christ. But the distinguishing note which identifies the Church as a *visible society* is that the Church shares in the mission of Christ to communicate divine life to men by making available to all the fruits of Christ's redemptive life, death, and resurrection. To share in the redemptive mission, the Church must share in his personal power to teach, to rule, and to sanctify. The possession of this threefold power is the determining feature of the structure or organization of Christ's Church. The specific structure of the Church, therefore, is determined by its authority or government. The form of government given to the Church by its participation in Christ's mission is traditionally referred to as its *hierarchical* and *monarchical* constitution.

Meaning of the terms   A society is *hierarchical* if it is ruled or governed by sacred power. The word "hierarchy" (*hieros,* sacred; *archein,* to rule) means sacred government. A hierarchy is a government whose authority is not from the people but from God. The Church is not a democracy (*demos,* people; *kratein,* to rule). That a hierarchical society is at the same time a monarchy simply implies that its supreme authority is vested in one individual (*mono,* alone; *archein,* to rule). A hierarchical-monarchical society is a society in which the ruling members derive their power and authority from God, with one person assuming a position of supreme authority among them.

It is a doctrine of faith that Christ instituted his Church as a hierarchical and monarchical society by giving his apostles the threefold power to *teach,* to *rule,* and to *sanctify* the faithful, and by conferring supreme authority on Peter.

The apostolic college   From the time that Christ sent his apostles, two by two, into the villages and towns to preach the gospel to the "lost sheep of the house of Israel," it was evident that they had been chosen to be the teachers of his doctrines. As has been pointed out earlier in this chapter, Christ singled out and specially instructed his twelve apostles and indicated that they were to be the first of a continuing line of laborers in the harvest. In his own lifetime on earth, Christ restricted his personal preaching, as well as that of the twelve, to the Chosen People. However, after his resurrection, their mission was extended to "all nations." Using a formula that has been called the "charter of the kingdom," Christ empowered the apostolic college to teach and to rule and to bring to sanctification *all* peoples.

> And Jesus came and said to them, "All authority in heaven and earth has been given to me. Go therefore and make disciples of *all nations,* baptizing them in the name of the Father and of the Son and of the Holy Spirit, teaching them to observe all that I have command you; and lo, I am with you always, to the close of the age."
>
> —Mt. 28:18-20

Everything that the gospels reveal of the thoughtful preparation of the apostles as a unique group with a special purpose in Christ's plan shows how carefully they were trained for this final commission given to them before his ascension into heaven. St. John solemnly records Jesus' mandate to them: "On the evening of that day, the first day of the week . . . Jesus came and stood among them and said to them: 'Peace be with you. As the Father sent me, even so I send you' " (Jn. 20:19-21).

Authority to teach   The apostles, then, were to be the official teachers of the doctrines of Christ. A number of scriptural texts attest this fact:

> All authority in heaven and earth has been given to me. Go therefore and make disciples of all nations . . . (Mt. 28:18-19).

> Go into all the world and preach the gospel to the whole creation (Mk. 16:15).

> But when the Counselor comes, whom I shall send to you from the Father, even the Spirit of truth, who proceeds from the Father, he will bear witness to me; and you also are witnesses, because you have been with me from the beginning (Jn. 15:26-27).

> As you have sent me into the world, so I have sent them into the world (Jn. 17:18).

> I do not pray for these only, but also for those who believe in me through their word . . . (Jn. 17:20).

> But you shall receive power when the Holy Spirit has come upon you; and you shall be my witnesses in Jerusalem and in all Judea and Samaria and to the end of the earth (Acts 1:8).

Clearly, the mission of the apostles is a continuation of Christ's own. They are his official teachers. To them he promises the Holy Spirit who will aid them in understanding and interpreting the life-giving message of the kingdom: "These things I have spoken to you, while I am still with you. But the Counselor, the Holy Spirit, whom the Father will send in my name, he will teach you all things, and bring to your remembrance all that I have said to you" (Jn. 14:25-26).

Authority to rule   The apostles were also to assume the jurisdictional control over Christ's kingdom until he returned again in glory on the last day. This jurisdictional power, the power to rule, is highlighted in a discourse of Christ to the apostles in which he uses the example of fraternal correction:

> If your brother sins against you, go and tell him his fault, between you and him alone. If he listens to you, you have gained your brother. But if he does not listen, take one or two others along with you, that every word may be confirmed by the evidence of two or three witnesses. If he refuses to listen to them, tell it to the Church; and if he refuses to listen even to the Church, let him be to you as a Gentile and a tax collector. Truly, I say to you, whatever you bind on earth shall be bound in heaven, and whatever you loose on earth shall be loosed in heaven.
>
> —Mt. 18:15-18

The last sentence of this passage from the gospel of St. Matthew is addressed directly to the apostolic leaders and their successors—not to the members of the Church at large. This is clear from the context of the passage. The nature of this extraordinary power to be conferred upon the apostles is found in the very wording of the text. The terms "bind" and "loose" were legal terms in Jewish law and were often used by the rabbis. Hence, when Christ uses these terms, familiar to his apostles, empowering them to "loose" and to "bind," he promises them the power of governing. A bond which is made or dissolved on earth and similarly treated in heaven can only refer to a law with moral force. To "bind" or to "loose" is to prohibit or permit; this is the equivalent of obliging to or dismissing from moral obligation.

Hence, Jesus promised, and before his ascension into heaven, conferred on his apostles the power of making laws and administering laws for people; this is a real power of jurisdiction over the members of the kingdom. Pope Leo XIII wrote: "Jesus Christ gave to his apostles the genuine and most true power of making laws, as also the twofold right of judging and punishing which flows from that power" *(Immortale Dei)*.

A denial of the authority of the Church to make and administer laws is contrary to the witness of the Scriptures and to the practice of the early Church. Indeed, the Church has declared such a denial to be heretical.

Authority to sanctify   The power to sanctify the members of the kingdom of God corresponds to the power to function as a minister of Christ's grace. Christ gave the twelve this power to sanctify when he empowered them to dispense his grace through the administration of the sacraments. For a further understanding of this power look ahead in this text to the sacrament of Holy Orders.

The authority to sanctify is especially clear in three events of Christ's life:

1. At the Last Supper the apostles were granted the power to carry out the central act of worship in the Church, the power to offer the Holy Sacrifice of the Mass—the renewal of the sacrifice of Calvary. The Mass provides the source of the sanctification of everyone. By bestowing this power, Christ constituted the apostles priests in the strict sense of the word. St. Paul records this solemn moment:

> For I received from the Lord what I also delivered to you, that the Lord Jesus on the night when he was betrayed took bread, and when he had given thanks, he broke it, and said, "This is my body which is for you. Do this in remembrance of me." In the same way also the cup, after supper, saying, "This cup is the new covenant in my blood. Do this, as often as you drink it, in remembrance of me." For as often as you eat this bread and drink this cup, you proclaim the Lord's death until he comes. Whoever, therefore, eats the bread or drinks the cup of the Lord in an unworthy manner will be guilty of profaning the body and blood of the Lord.
>
> —1 Cor. 11:23-27

2. The apostles were especially singled out and given divine power to forgive sins. This is clear from our Lord's words spoken to them on that first Easter Sunday:

On the evening of that day, the first day of the week, the doors being shut where the disciples were, for fear of the Jews, Jesus came and stood among them and said to them, "Peace be with you." When he had said this, he showed them his hands and his side. Then the disciples were glad when they saw the Lord. Jesus said to them again, "Peace be with you. As the Father has sent me, even so I send you." And when he had said this, he breathed on them, and said to them, "Receive the Holy Spirit. If you forgive the sins of any, they are forgiven; if you retain the sins of any, they are retained."

–Jn. 20:19-23

3. **The apostles were given the official charge to go forth baptizing all nations in the name of the Father, and of the Son, and of the Holy Spirit. To them, too, was given the power to confer the sacrament of Confirmation, as is evident from the Acts of the Apostles:**

And Peter said to them, "Repent, and be baptized every one of you in the name of Jesus Christ for the forgiveness of your sins; and you shall receive the gift of the Holy Spirit. For the promise is to you and to your children and to all that are far off, every one whom the Lord our God calls to him" (Acts 2:38-39).

The most recent Church document upholding the doctrine of the apostolic authority was produced by the Second Vatican Council:

This most sacred Synod, following in the footsteps of the First Vatican Council, teaches and declares with that Council that Jesus Christ, the eternal Shepherd, established his holy Church by sending forth the apostles as he himself had been sent by the Father. He willed that their successors, namely the bishops, should be shepherds in his Church even to the consummation of the world.

In order that the episcopate itself might be one and undivided, he placed blessed Peter over the other apostles, and instituted in him a permanent and visible source and foundation of unity of faith and fellowship. And all this teaching about the institution, the perpetuity, the force and reason for the sacred primacy of the Roman Pontiff, and of his infallible teaching authority, this sacred Synod again proposes to be firmly believed by all the faithful.

Continuing in this same task of clarification begun by Vatican I, the Council has decided to declare and proclaim before all men its teaching concerning bishops, the successors of the apostles, who together with the successor of Peter, the Vicar of Christ and the visible Head of the whole Church, govern the house of the living God ("The Church," n. 18).

198

COLLEGIALITY

The Lord Jesus, after praying to the Father and calling to himself those whom he desired, appointed twelve men who would stay in his company, and whom he would send to preach the kingdom of God. These apostles were formed after the manner of *a college or a fixed group,* over which he placed Peter, chosen from among them (Jn. 21:15-17). He sent them first to the children of Israel and then to all nations (Rom. 1:16), so that as sharers in his power they might make all people his disciples, sanctifying and governing them (Mt. 28:16-20). Thus they would spread his Church, and by ministering to it under the guidance of the Lord, would shepherd it all days even to the consummation of the world.

–"The Church," n. 19

Christ's salvific mission, which he had given to the apostles, was to last until the end of time according to the divine plan. This meant that the apostles necessarily had to appoint successors to themselves:

That divine mission, entrusted by Christ to the apostles, will last until the end of the world, since the gospel which was to be handed down by them is for all time the source of all life for the Church. For this reason the apostles took care to appoint successors in this hierarchically structured society.

For they not only had helpers in their ministry, but also, in order that the mission assigned to them might continue after their death, they passed on to their immediate cooperators, as a kind of testament, the duty of perfecting and consolidating the work begun by themselves, charging them to attend to the whole flock in which the Holy Spirit placed them to shepherd the Church of God (Acts 20:28). They therefore appointed such men, and authorized the arrangement that, when these men should have died, other approved men would take up their ministry.

Among those various ministries which, as tradition witnesses, were exercised in the Church from the earliest times, the chief place belongs to the office of those who, appointed to the episcopate in a sequence running back to the beginning, are the ones who pass on the apostolic seed. Thus, as St. Irenaeus testifies, through those who were appointed bishops by the apostles, and through their successors down to our own time, the apostolic tradition is manifested and preserved throughout the world.

–"The Church," n. 20

In order that the original college of apostles and their successors might be one and undivided, Christ placed Peter over the apostles and established him as a permanent and visible foundation of their unity.

Indeed, the Church is governed to this very day by those who have received a share in the sacred ruling power of Christ: the bishops, the successors of the apostles; the pope, successor of St. Peter and the Vicar of Christ on earth. The blending of episcopal and papal power in the Church is called *collegiality*.

Thus, central to the structure of the Church is the apostolic college with its head, the Vicar of Christ. The apostolic college is the visible and enduring focus of the power of the Holy Spirit dwelling in the Church. The Spirit continues to act through the apostolic college, particularly through the episcopal proclamation of the gospel and the ministry of the sacraments.

Apostles and bishops　　Although the bishops are the legitimate successors of the apostles, the continuation of the apostolic college, there is an important difference between the two. The apostles by their witness have been constituted as the irremovable foundations of the Church; they revealed to the Church what they had personally seen and heard. On the other hand, the bishops announce, explain, and protect the apostolic message handed down. By means of their government of the Body of Christ, God guarantees the identity between the Church of today and the Church of the apostles.

St. Peter's special role　　St. Peter held a special place in the apostolic college: "Christ placed . . . Peter over the other apostles and instituted in him a permanent and visible source and foundation of unity of faith and communion" ("The Church," n. 18). Since the Church is both a monarchical and hierarchical society, Peter holds not only a place of dignity within the apostolic college, but also the position of supreme jurisdictional authority. "Jurisdiction" simply means the "power to govern." Therefore, the primacy of Peter is precisely a primacy of authority. This sacred power of jurisdiction given him by Christ embraces the full and supreme power *to teach and to rule the universal Church*. Certainly the Scriptures manifest Christ's intention concerning Peter's place within the Church. The famous text singling out Peter as head of the Church—Mt. 16:13-19—was quoted fully earlier in this chapter. In that text, Christ said to Peter: ". . . you are Peter (Aramaic, *kepha;* Greek, *petros;* Latin, *petrus*), and on this rock (Aramaic, *kepha;* Greek, *petra;* Latin, *petram*) I will build my Church." Remembering that Aramaic was the language spoken by Jesus, we can see that the play on words in this passage makes unmistakable the real meaning he intended to convey. Peter is called the "rock" because he is the rock on which Christ's Church is to stand. He will be for the Church what a rock foundation is for a house.

Just as a building needs a solid and secure foundation, so also a society requires a guarantee of stability; and this guarantee is found in *authority*. The Church, Christ's newly-formed society, the new Israel, is to have Peter as its supreme source of authority. The very same hierarchical body that is to be governed by the apostolic college, will have one of this college vested with a primacy of jurisdictional authority.

The powers to teach and to rule the Church were promised to all of the apostles. These powers were not given to each individual independently of the others; rather, the powers were given to all insofar as they formed a single unit or college. This did not mean that the apostles as individuals did not receive powers. Each one was truly a legate or apostle commissioned by Christ to preach all of his revelation and to establish his Kingdom-Church among men. Furthermore, each was to be the true pastor over the particular Church which he was to form.

However, the authority of the apostles was inferior to that of Peter in three ways. A consideration of these differences points up the significance of Peter's primacy. In the first place, the authority of the other apostles was not universal in scope; consequently, it could not be exercised over all the Churches at once. Secondly, it did not extend to the other apostles individually or personally. Finally, it could not be exercised without reference to St. Peter as the ultimate, visible source of unity and stability.

The keys of the kingdom   Christ's words to Peter conclude with the bestowal of the keys of the kingdom upon this apostle as well as giving him the authority to bind and to loose: "I will give you the keys of the kingdom of heaven, and whatever you bind on earth shall be bound in heaven, and whatever you loose on earth shall be loosed in heaven" (Mt. 16:19). Christ used the metaphor of the keys *only* when speaking to Peter; others were given the power to bind and to loose, but Peter alone shall hold the keys. The one who has possession of and charge of keys has the power to lock and to unlock; and he has responsibility for that which is locked.

Jesus gave authority to all of the apostles, but Peter alone is the rock and to Peter alone did he give the keys. There is no uncertainty about the Lord's intention: to Peter alone is given supreme authority over Christ's kingdom; his authority is above that of the other apostles. Another confirmation of this intention can be found in Jesus' words to Peter at the Last Supper just before the prediction of Peter's threefold denial of the Lord: "Simon, Simon, behold, Satan demanded to have you, that he might sift you like wheat, but I have prayed for you that your faith may not fail; and *when you have turned again,* strengthen your brethren" (Lk. 22:31-32). Even a cursory examination of these words shows that they promise a primacy of authority for Peter; he alone is to have a special strengthening of faith, that his faith may not fail. Further, this faith is directed to a special goal, namely, that it be employed to "strengthen your brethren." Here, Peter is obliged to strengthen the faith of the apostles—and of all the faithful. Conversely, Christ's words oblige the apostles and all of the faithful to be obedient to the official teachings and commands of Peter. It would be impossible for Peter to strengthen his brethren if he were not given real authority over them and if they were not obliged to acknowledge his power over them.

After his resurrection from the dead, Jesus actually conferred on Peter the supreme power he had previously promised:

> When they had finished breakfast, Jesus said to Simon Peter, "Simon, son of John, do you love me more than these?" He said to him, "Yes, Lord; you know that I love you." He said to him, "Feed my lambs." A second time he said to him, "Simon, son of John, do you love me?" He said to him, "Yes, Lord; you know that I love you." He said to him, "Tend my sheep." He said to him the third time, "Simon, son of John, do you love me?" Peter was grieved because he said to him the third time, "Do you love me?" And he said to him, "Lord, you know everything; you know that I love you." Jesus said to him, "Feed my sheep."
>
> —Jn. 21:15-17

On more than one occasion Jesus speaks of himself as the Good Shepherd. Here he fulfills the promise to Peter. By his choice of words, repeated three times (adding a note of formality and solemnity), Jesus makes Peter the shepherd in his name, bestowing on him supreme jurisdiction. The phrase "to feed" is frequently used in the Scriptures to mean "to rule" or "to govern." Those who have the power of ruling are said to feed the people. Hence, the whole flock, the universal Church, is committed to Peter's care. He is given the sheep of the Good Shepherd to govern as the visible representative of Christ—who reigns invisibly at the right hand of the Father in heaven.

Primacy always within the college   The primacy of Peter and of his successors is always within the apostolic and episcopal college. Peter was not first established as primate, and then given the apostles as assistants or associates; rather, the New Testament indicates that the college was established first, and then Peter was given primacy. Peter received his primacy as a *member* of the college. This means that the members of the apostolic college were not, and are not today, mere agents of the Bishop of Rome. In the New Testament, responsibility always fell upon the group, and this is the implication of the term "collegiality."

The apostolic and episcopal college is a sacramentally constituted group. The pope differs from the other bishops only in the sphere of his authority to govern and to teach. Only the pope may exercise supreme, full, and universal authority in the Church. The bishops share in this universal government of the Church, but as members of the episcopal body, united to one another and to the pope.

Nevertheless, the bishops also have power that is personal and immediate. Each bishop is the source of unity, the preacher of the gospel, and the source of the sacramental life within his own flock. He constitutes them as a local Church within the Body of Christ. The bishops, then, are not representatives of the pope, but true vicars of Christ within the group committed to their care.

The unity within the episcopal college derives from the threefold sacred power that it has received from Christ. The external manifestation of this power is twofold: it may be embodied in the personal action of the pope, or it may find expression in the collegiate action of the entire body of bishops (Church councils, for example). In either case, the power is one. Within the college the keys to the use of the power are in the hands of the pope, the successor of Peter. He has the choice of using the power precisely as primate of the college, or he may use that power collectively with the bishops. In the first instance, all of the power is the pope's; in the second instance, all of the power is in the college of bishops.

Finally, no member of the Church—pope, bishop, priest, or layperson—must ever forget the mission in which he shares, the building up of the Body of Christ. The unity of the Church is not primarily derived by means of authority, but by a unity of the members with each other and with Christ, brought about by the Holy Spirit.

INFALLIBILITY

Jesus promised special assistance to his apostles as a group and to Peter personally, an assistance for teaching his gospel. This help was also intended for their successors, and consists in freedom from the possibility of error in matters of essential doctrine. Since Christ's truth includes both *things to be believed (faith)* and *things to be done (morality)*, his aid must be of a kind to preserve his teachers from error in matters of faith and morals. The special divine assistance given for this purpose is called *infallibility*.

Promised to the apostles   Christ promised such infallibility to the apostolic college when he said: "And I will pray to the Father, and he will give you another Counselor, to be with you forever, even the Spirit of Truth . . . whom the Father will send in my name, he will teach you all things" (Jn. 14:16-17, 26). "I have yet many things to say to you . . . When the Spirit of truth comes, he will guide you into all the truth" (Jn. 16:12-13). This promise clearly implies a special assistance of the Holy Spirit so that the apostles could teach Christ's doctrines with the assurance of freedom from error. Christ conferred this special divine aid when he gave the apostles (and their successors) "all power" to preach the gospel to the whole world.

Infallibility of Peter   Peter's unique role, both within the apostolic college and within the Church as a whole, required this special divine assistance of infallibility. That Christ conferred this on Peter directly and immediately (and on his successors) is a dogma of faith:

> This infallibility with which the divine Redeemer willed his Church to be endowed in defining a doctrine of faith and morals extends as far as the deposit of divine revelations, which must be religiously guarded and faithfully expounded. This is the infallibility which the Roman Pontiff, the head of the college of bishops, enjoys in virtue of his office when, as the supreme shepherd and teacher of all the faithful who confirms his brethren in their faith (Lk. 22:32), he proclaims by definitive act some doctrine of faith and morals . . . The infallibility promised to the Church resides also in the body of bishops when that body exercises supreme teaching authority with the successor of Peter. To the resultant definitions the assent of the Church can never be wanting, on account of the activity of that same Holy Spirit, whereby the whole flock of Christ is preserved and progresses in unity of faith.
>
> —"The Church," n. 25

The Pope and the bishops   Because the college of bishops, in union with the Pope, teaches, governs and sanctifies the Church, the doctrine of infallibility also extends to the college of bishops in union with the Pope. Infallibility is not guaranteed to any individual bishop, nor to any group of bishops, but to all the bishops when they teach collegially on matters of faith and morals. Furthermore, infallibility is not guaranteed to the college of bishops apart from the Pope, but when they teach in union with the Pope.

The Church that was born at Pentecost was born in the full vigor of life. She came forth completely armed with the armor and weapons of the Spirit. The Holy Spirit was not only her hidden strength, but was her executive power and force, an energy that permeated the apostles and continues to operate in her successors, the hierarchy of the Church. They speak, they make the pronouncements that everyone hears, but it is the Spirit of Truth that teaches and guides.

Priests with their bishops   No better description of the role of the priest in the mission of the Church can be found than that of the Second Vatican Council. In the document on "The Church," priests are called "prudent cooperators with the episcopal order, as well as its aid and instruments." A fuller explanation of the work of the priest follows:

> Associated with their bishops in a spirit of trust and generosity, priests make him present in a certain sense in the individual local congregations of the faithful, and take upon themselves, as far as they are able, his duties and concerns, discharging them with daily care. As they sanctify and govern under the bishop's authority that part of the Lord's flock entrusted to them, they make the universal Church visible in their own locality and lend powerful assistance to the upbuilding of the whole body of Christ (Eph. 4:12). Intent always upon the welfare of God's children, they must strive to lend their effort to the pastoral work of the whole diocese, and even of the entire Church . . . All priests, both diocesan and religious, by reason of orders and ministry, are associated with this body of bishops, and serve the good of the whole Church according to their vocation and the grace given to them.
>
> –"The Church," n. 28

In terms of humanity today, when social and economic unity seem more and more necessary, priests, under the leadership of their bishops and the Pope, must be united in concern and effort to remove divisions within mankind and bring the whole human race into the unity of Christ and the family of God.

Laypeople and their mission   Once more the Council speaks on the role of the laity in Christ's mission on earth:

> It is through the sacraments and the exercise of the virtues that the sacred nature and organic structure of the priestly community (the laity) is brought into operation. Incorporated into the Church through baptism, the faithful are consecrated by the baptismal character to the exercise of the cult of Christian religion. Reborn as sons of God, they must confess before men the faith which they have received from God through the Church. Bound more intimately to the Church by the sacrament of confirmation, they are endowed by the Holy Spirit with special strength. Hence they

are more strictly obliged to spread and defend the faith both by word and by deed as true witnesses of Christ.

–"The Church," n. 11

Even a share in the one priesthood of Christ is not denied to the faithful. Indeed, it is a necessary adjunct to their missionary activity as members of the Mystical Body of Christ:

> Though they differ from one another in essence and not only in degree, the common priesthood of the faithful and the ministerial or hierarchical priesthood are nonetheless interrelated. Each of them in its own special way is a participation in the one priesthood of Christ. The ministerial priest, by the sacred power he enjoys, molds and rules the priestly people. Acting in the person of Christ, he brings about the Eucharistic Sacrifice, and offers it to God in the name of the people. For their part, the faithful join in the offering of the Eucharist by virtue of their royal priesthood. They likewise exercise that priesthood by receiving the sacraments, by prayer and thanksgiving, by the witness of a holy life, and by self-denial and active charity.

–"The Church," n. 10

Religious life   Along with the ordained and lay members, a special group of people also serve the Church in Christ's work of redemption. These are the people we call "consecrated religious," who are members of the many religious communities active in the Church. More commonly, they are known as religious "brothers" and "sisters."

Many religious brothers are not ordained and do not exercise the rights and responsibilities of holy orders. They are, therefore, not to be mistaken as members of the clergy. They are, however, collaborators with the Pope and the bishops in fulfilling various needs of the Church under his guidance and direction. Religious, as we call them for short, provide many different services to the people of God, such as education, health care, social work, missionary apostolates, publication, and administrative services to name a few. Some of your own teachers in school may be religious brothers or sisters.

The religious take special vows by which they consecrate their lives to Christ and his Church. The vows common to all religious are known as the *evangelical counsels:* poverty, chastity and obedience. Each vow is intended to enable brothers or sisters to conform their lives more closely to the life of Christ and to totally devote themselves to service of the Church.

Religious brothers and sisters live in communities to support one another in observing their vows and accomplishing their mission. The vast majority of our Catholic schools, hospitals and other service institutions have been built and maintained by the efforts of the Church's religious.

Conclusion   The Church, despite its mysterious and mystical elements, is an organized, visible community, with a social structure. The Church has an essential framework of divine institution, but this is filled out with many variable and changing elements which fashion its historical embodiment in a particular time and place. Because the Church is this kind of reality existing in the world, Pope Paul VI wrote:

> In the pursuit of spiritual and moral perfection the Church receives an exterior stimulus from the conditions in which she lives. She cannot remain unaffected by or indifferent to the changes that take place in the world around.

> This world exerts its influence on the Church in a thousand ways and places conditions on her daily conduct. The Church, as everyone knows, is not separated from the world, but lives in it. Hence, the members of the Church are subject to its influence: they breathe its culture, accept its laws, and absorb its customs (*Ecclesiam Suam,* n. 44).

The Role of the Holy Spirit in the Church

When the Holy Spirit had descended on the Apostles on Pentecost, their timidity and fear was changed to boldness and courage. They came out of hiding and showed themselves to the public. They were no longer silent, but began to preach in tongues so the people of many different nations and languages all understood their words. They gave public witness to their faith that Jesus Christ is the Risen Lord. They called their neighbors to repentance and began to baptize them as Jesus had commanded them before his Ascension. Note that only *after* the descent of the Holy Spirit were they able to do these things. Thus the Church was born only through the power of the Holy Spirit, and every Pentecost we celebrate the "birthday of the Church."

The Holy Spirit works in the life of the Church today as it has from the day of the first Pentecost. No essential element of the Mystical Body's life falls outside the influence of the life-giving Spirit of Christ. This divine outpouring may be summarized in the works of the Spirit within the Church.

1. *The work of indefectibility.* The work of the Spirit of Christ in preserving the Mystical Body unchanged throughout its earthly course—in faith, sacraments, form of government, and all other essential matters—is called *indefectibility.* The presence within the Church of the Holy Spirit assures the Church of permanence and an identity and unchangeableness in all the essential characteristics determined by Christ when he inaugurated his kingdom. The various vocations of Christ's members and the graces of state given them by the Spirit guarantee this work of indefectibility.

2. *The work of infallibility.* This work of the Holy Spirit consists in his divine assistance to the teaching Church that it may inviolably keep and faithfully expound the revelation delivered to it by Christ and the apostles. In this work, the Holy Spirit helps the Church more by positive graces of light and strength than by negative interventions.

3. *The work of inspiration.* The work of inspiration should not be confused with scriptural inspiration. The latter is an impulse of the Holy Spirit which is

limited to the author's recording the word of God in the Sacred Scriptures. The work of inspiration in the Church is an impulse of the Holy Spirit by which he may move any member of the Church to the performance of an act beneficial to the common good of the Mystical Body. For example, the Spirit could, by a special actual grace, move an individual to instigate a reform movement within the Church. These graces have been found in abundance among the great shepherds of Christ's flock, as history abundantly bears witness.

4. *The work of sanctification.* Sanctification, or justification, of individual souls is especially attributed to the Holy Spirit. This justification involves not only the forgiveness of sins, but the supernatural animation of the soul through sanctifying grace, the healing of the intellect and will by means of the infused moral virtues, as well as the elevation of these same faculties by theological virtues, with the special help of the gifts of the Holy Spirit. Included in this work are the many and varied actual graces suited to the recipient's particular state of life, and received from the Holy Spirit for the performance of supernatural works. Each member receives his own holiness according to the measure imparted to each one (1 Cor. 12:11), and according to the disposition and cooperation of each individual.

5. *The work of conversion.* The Holy Spirit is especially associated with the missionary apostolate of the conversion of all people. The Spirit that descended upon the Church on Pentecost was the Spirit of whom Christ had said: "It is not for you to know times or seasons which the Father has fixed by his own authority. But you shall receive power when the Holy Spirit has come upon you; and you shall be my witnesses in Jerusalem and in all Judea and Samaria and to the ends of the earth" (Acts 1:8). The mission entrusted to Christ's Church was to convert

all nations, all mankind; for this was the Holy Spirit sent at Pentecost.

Thus, the redemptive mission of the Church is always guided and assisted by the Holy Spirit, enabling the Church to perform actions which, while outwardly human, are filled with divine power. Such is the indwelling soul of the Church, as it animates and is enshrined in the entire Body of Christ, and in each individual member of that Body. The mission of the Church, then, can be found everywhere and in everyone; it acts in the hierarchy and in the priesthood and in the members, because the whole Church is united to the Spirit of love within the Trinity of Persons.

Thinking it over • • •

1. What is the goal of the Church? Can you quote from the document on "The Church" and from the document on the Church's "Missionary Activity" to substantiate your answer?

2. What does it mean to say that only Christ is Redeemer; that only his death and resurrection are meritorious? Relate your answer to the meaning of Christ as the one mediator between God and ourselves.

3. Name the two principal aspects of the earthly phase of Christ's kingdom. What are the two main expressions showing Christ's special relationship with the Church as the Mystical Body of Christ?

4. If someone were to say to you, "I am the Church," what would the meaning of such a declaration be? St. John and St. Paul are the two inspired writers who propose this point of view. On what do they base these original thoughts?

5. Discuss the setting for the emerging Church in terms of the new Covenant that Christ establishes. Include an explanation of the image of the blood and water flowing from the pierced side of Christ.

6. The Church is both an invisible and a visible society. Explain. Why did Christ think it necessary for him to found a visible society?

7. Discuss the choosing of the twelve apostles. Can you find in their being named by Christ evidence of the grace of a vocation? What are some of the images Christ used to describe the nature of their discipleship?

8. Christ sent his disciples first to Israel. Why? Was there any indication in the teaching of Christ that the apostles would have a mission that would go beyond the borders of Israel?

9. Quote the scriptural text from the gospel of St. Matthew wherein St. Peter is awarded the leadership of the Church. Once more give the etymological definition of the word "church" and apply it in the way it was used by Christ. Is the Church one or many? Explain.

10. What does the word "juridical" mean? Name the characteristics of the Church that prove it to be a juridical institution.

11. Give the etymological definitions of the words "hierarchical" and "monarchical." Apply the terms and compare them to the meaning of the word "democracy." Is the Church a democracy? Is it an hierarchical and/or a monarchical society? Explain.

12. Discuss the apostolic college in terms of the authority given by Christ to the apostles. Quote three passages from the New Testament that bear witness to the right of the apostles to teach.

13. The apostles were also given the authority to rule and to sanctify. What do these two powers mean in relation to the redemptive mission of the Church?

14. What does collegiality mean? Discuss collegiality insofar as it applies to the apostolic succession. How does collegiality affect the bishops' power and the power of the pope?

15. St. Peter's authority went beyond the authority of the other apostles. Name the scriptural texts to prove this fact; explain the meaning of primacy.

16. Discuss the role of priests in relation to their bishops and to the pope. Compare the role of laypeople in the Church with that of the priest.

UNIT III

Chapter 1

THE CHRISTIAN SACRAMENTS

INTRODUCTION

As we begin the section on sacramental economy St. Augustine's statement referring to the side of Christ as he slept the sleep on the Cross as that from which came forth the wondrous sacrament of the whole Church, we must pause. In its liturgy the Paschal mystery is that toward which the Church is directed. Through its liturgy the Church, itself a sacrament, celebrates the sacraments of the Church. What then is liturgy? For Christians, liturgy means a participation of God's people in his work. It is the work of Christ's life, prayer, salvation and action in his Church as he communicates himself to his people "until he comes again in glory."

The liturgy, of course, is Trinitarian. The Father is blessed and adored in the Church as the source of all blessings in creation. Through his Son these blessings which include salvation are communicated to the Church and to us by the mission of the Holy Spirit who teaches us all truth. The Holy Spirit also prepares the people to encounter Christ in the splendor of his transforming power.

We must emphasize the fact that the complete liturgical life of the Church revolves around the Eucharistic sacrifice and the sacraments. But this section will be confined to those elements common to the seven sacraments.

The seven sacraments of the Church were instituted by Christ. Protestants differ in the number they recognize. Jesus' words and actions in his public life were salvific and they anticipated the power of his Paschal mystery. The Spirit guides the Church into all truth and gives us the Spirit of filial adoption. Christ's Body, the Church, is like a sacrament in which the Holy Spirit dispenses the mystery of salvation.

When the Church celebrates the sacraments she really confesses the faith received from the apostles, and the liturgy is the forming element of a holy and living Tradition. So the law of prayer is the law of faith: the Church believes as she prays.

Christ was aware of the fact that humans cannot see spiritual realities with bodily eyes. So in the sacraments he entrusted to the Church he gave us efficacious signs of grace through which his divine life is dispensed to us. These visible rites are signs which make present the graces proper to each sacrament. These signs are efficacious because Christ is at work in the sacraments. The Spirit graces and transforms those who receive him properly in the sacraments by conforming them to the Son of God.

THE WHO, HOW, WHEN AND WHERE THE LITURGIES ARE CELEBRATED

Who Celebrates?   Liturgy is the action of the whole Christ. It is an eternal liturgy, consequently, the Holy Spirit and the Church enable us to participate whenever we celebrate the mysteries. It is the whole Community, the Body of Christ united with its Head.

So basically and sacramentally liturgical services are not private. This is the common priesthood of Christ in which all his members participate, but all do not have the same function. For example those consecrated by the sacrament of Holy Orders act in the person of Christ as the head for the service of all the members. And the members each have their particular ministry in Christ.

How is Liturgy Celebrated?   Liturgical celebration involves signs and symbols of creation, human life, and the history of salvation. These cosmic elements, rituals, and remembrances of God become the bearers of the saving and sanctifying action of Christ. Liturgical signs from the Old Covenant such as circumcision and the Passover prefigure the sacraments of the New Covenant. Christ himself is the meaning of all these signs. The harmony of song, music, words and actions is even more fruitful when expressed in the cultural richness of the people of God who celebrate. Christian images frequently express the same Gospel message that Holy Scripture tells us in words. The catholicity of the Church is also enhanced by legitimate diverse liturgical traditions and rites which signify and communicate the same mystery of Christ. Fidelity to apostolic Tradition is the key which insures unity amid diversity of liturgical traditions. We speak of communion in faith and the sacraments that is both signified and assured by apostolic succession.

When is Liturgy Celebrated?   Sunday is the principal day of celebration. Through his Resurrection on Sunday Christ conquered sin, suffering and death. He made it a family day of great joy and rest and the foundation of the liturgical year. During each year various facets of the one Paschal mystery gradually unfold. The same holds for the cycle of feasts which surround Incarnation's mystery. The memorials of the saints such as Mary, the mother of God, the apostles, martyrs, and others are fixed through the liturgical year which shows the unity of the Church on earth with the saints in heaven. The celebration of the divine office is arranged so that the whole day and night are made holy, as Christ continues his priestly work through his Church.

Where is Liturgy Celebrated?　　Worship is not tied exclusively to a particular place because it is celebrated in the spirit and truth of the New Covenant—built with spiritual stones. However, while we are still human we need places where the community can gather. The house of God should show good taste and decorum where Christ is especially present and active. We must always bear in mind that the Liturgy of the Word is an integral part of the celebration.

Historical background　　One of the key differences separating the Christian churches today concerns the sacraments: their existence, their effect on the recipient, the appropriate minister of the sacraments, and their number. The Catholic and Orthodox churches acknowledge the existence of seven sacraments, agree as to their effects on the recipients, and are in accord on the question of who can minister the sacraments to others. The Anglican church makes certain distinctions about the sacraments which are not customarily made by the Catholic and Orthodox communions, but is in basic agreement.

The Protestant churches have widely differing views about these sacred rites. Usually the Protestant churches avoid the word "sacrament," for reasons that we shall see later. In general, Protestants acknowledge baptism and "The Lord's Supper," these observances being quite clearly commanded by Jesus in the New Testament. The remaining five rites or sacraments, which are not so clearly mentioned in the New Testament, are not usually employed in Protestant church services.

This great difference within the Christian churches originated at the time of the Protestant Reformation, which began in 1517, the year when Martin Luther nailed his ninety-five theses to the door of the church at Wittenberg in Germany. That event was the opening salvo in a major confrontation between those European Christians who rejected not only the grave abuses that were practiced by some officials of the Catholic Church but also the Church itself, and those who sought to defend the Church. This led to adoption by protesting leaders of a fundamental feature of Protestantism: Sacred Scripture is the sole rule of faith. Believing that to be so, the existence of many observances or rites in the Christian Church were questioned. The questioning led to a denial that Jesus had given the Christians such rites. And so five of the seven rites which had come to be called "sacraments" were discontinued in the church observances of Protestants.

At the time Catholics noted that there had never been a serious misunderstanding about the sacraments until the rise of Protestantism. Because this was so, there were no *ex cathedra* statements by the Church prior to that time. When the Protestant churches rose with vigor, however, Catholics summoned an ecumenical council, the Council of Trent, to clarify and to solemnly define the Church's views concerning matters disputed by the Protestant communions. Solemn definitions dealing with the sacraments were published by this great council. As a result, the differences between Catholics and Protestants were clearly spelled out; that is, these differences were, from the Catholic point of view, solemnly defined. Today, serious discussions are taking place between carefully chosen delegates from the Catholic Church and from different Protestant churches, who seek to clarify and overcome misunderstandings among the churches.

In Catholic teaching the seven principal rites of worship are appropriately called "sacraments." This word does not appear in the New Testament. It first came to be used by a brilliant Catholic thinker, Tertullian (c. 230 A.D.). When Tertullian employed the word, *sacramentum*, used by Roman soldiers to describe the tatoo which identified the legion to which they belonged, he was writing about the rite and the effect of baptism. Probably, *sacramentum* implies a calling to mind of something that is sacred (Latin: *sacris*, meaning "holy" or "sacred," and *mens*, meaning "mind"). In any event, Tertullian used the word in his discussion of baptism. Later writers enlarged on Tertullian's use of the word. St. Augustine (c. 430 A.D.) spoke of sacraments, meaning the rites of Christian worship. But it was not until many centuries had passed that the Church came to realize that of the many observances or sacred rites that were employed, only seven are properly called "sacraments." At one time, Christian writers described as many as eleven "sacraments"; for example, the consecration of a monarch, the vows of a religious, and the ceremony that gave widows a special place in the Christian community were called "sacraments."

By the time of St. Thomas Aquinas (1225-1274 A.D.) the theological question had become quite clear. To a large extent his writings were based on the work of Peter Lombard, a great Christian teacher who had gathered and organized the opinions and the teachings of the important Christian thinkers who had lived before. Lombard's writings restrict the word "sacrament" to those seven ceremonies with which we associate the word today. In writing his great *Summa Theologiae*, Thomas sets out to discuss the general notions of a sacrament and then to write a tract on each of the seven sacraments. (Unfortunately, he died before he completed work on all of the sacraments, though we learn a great deal about his views from earlier writings.)

Thomas begins his consideration by stating that a sacrament is a "sign" He gives this definition: "a sacrament is a sign of some sacred thing which makes us holy." This definition is quite general and for a surprising reason. St. Thomas believed that there were sacraments in the ancient Jewish religion, but these differed notably from the sacraments of the Christian faith. The key idea, however, is that both religions were given sacred ceremonies through which those participating could become more holy, more acceptable in God's eyes. All of the great ceremonies that were celebrated in the Jewish Temple at Jerusalem, the morning and evening sacrifices, the ceremonies required at certain great moments in life, such as circumcision and the buying back from God of a first-born male, were "sacraments," that is, sacred rites that expressed a person's source of holiness. Christianity had its own sacred observances. Eventually, these came to be known as "sacraments."

The definition of a sacrament in the Christian community differs, however, from the general definition of a sacrament with which Thomas Aquinas begins his discussion. For the Christians, the sacred rites of worship are not only "signs" of something that is sanctifying them, but they are also *causes* of that very sanctification. This is so because Christians believe that the salvation of every man and every woman, from Adam to the present, is brought about by the life, death, and resurrection of Jesus. Therefore, if I am to be forgiven for my sins and to be found acceptable in God's eyes, I can only achieve these blessings in and through Jesus Christ. To be more precise, I can do this only by being united with him in his passion, death, and resurrection. Whereas the Jews who lived before Jesus Christ were moved interiorly through the celebration of their Temple rites to accept God and his promises to them, the Christian has an even greater blessing. What does this mean?

The Church teaches us that the "sacraments effect what they signify" This is an absolutely fundamental, key expression. We must be sure we understand it. But in seeking a clear understanding of this basic truth, we must first be sure that it does not mean certain things. For example, a Christian sacrament does not produce any effect in the person who does not have the correct dispositions. If I attempt to receive the sacrament of marriage, for example, but have no intention of observing those basic requirements which oblige a husband or wife, I am not truly married and I do not receive this sacrament. If I am committed to a life of grievous sin, I cannot receive the sacrament of reconciliation even if I try. Each of us has a free will. We can obtain the grace of the sacraments only if we freely submit ourselves to the work within us which Jesus seeks to accomplish through these sacred rites.

Accordingly, we should enlarge somewhat the statement with which we began the previous paragraph. To be complete, the statement should declare: "The sacraments effect what they signify *in those who place no obstacles to them.*" This statement is not as difficult as it may sound at first. Jesus Christ works in us through the sacraments. But we have to cooperate with him. For example, Jesus will wipe away all of our sins in the sacrament of reconciliation, but only if we are sorry for our wrongs, and only if we promise ourselves and promise him that we shall strive as best we can to conquer future temptations. In other words, if we do our part, Jesus will, through the sacraments, do more than his part for us.

But, if a sacrament is basically a "sign," what does this mean? The answer is really not so difficult. We live in a world of signs, though we hardly notice this fact. Try to attend to this rather basic truth: a sign tells us about something other than itself. You see an octagon which is red and which has four letters written on it: STOP. Usually, it is on a post at a street intersection. Probably, you barely look at this device. You do not tell yourself or the person with whom you are riding in a car that it is attractive. You do not count the eight sides of the panel, nor ask yourself what shade of red is used, nor even bother to comment to yourself that the four letters are white. Think carefully, then, that this sign, *as every sign,* points to something other than itself.

When you wash someone in the waters of baptism, there is a symbol of refreshment, of cooling, and of cleansing. What you actually observe is one thing; the reality is another. Men and women perform the rite of washing. But Jesus Christ, who is symbolized by their presence and by their visible actions, takes away the sins of the person being baptized. A priest in celebrating the Eucharist, says: "This is my body" and "This is my blood," but he is only a sign or a symbol of Jesus Christ who changes bread and wine into his body and blood. Every sacrament has a tangible, visible ceremony which expresses something beyond itself. Every sacrament is a *sign.*

Every Christian sacrament signifies Jesus Christ working in our souls. In fact, every sacrament signifies three things: the cause of our holiness which is the passion, death, and resurrection of Jesus; the giving of that holiness here and now when I receive a sacrament worthily, usually called "sanctifying grace"; and the pledge or promise of Jesus that I shall, so long as I am faithful, come to eternal happiness.

Each of the sacraments is said to have "matter" and "form" The *matter* of a sacrament is that which is seen or heard or felt, some real thing which is experienced by our external senses. The pouring of water in baptism, the anointing with oil in the sacrament of the sick, the imposition of hands by a bishop during the ordination of a deacon, a priest, or another bishop, are the matter of those sacraments.

The *form* of sacraments is the words that are uttered by him who administers the sacraments. "I baptize you in the name of the Father . . .," for example, is the form of baptism. The matter and form of a sacrament must both be employed and in such a way that they are understood to go together. A person is not baptized if I pour water over his head and several days later supply the words, "I baptize you . . ." which I neglected to say at the time when the water was employed.

Special effects   Three of the sacraments achieve a special effect within the recipient which is called a *character*. The word "character," originally a Greek term, meant a brand used to mark cattle. Later, the Greeks also applied the word to the branding of a soldier. Christianity borrowed the term to express the effect of three sacraments, baptism, confirmation, and holy orders, which cannot be repeated. The earliest Christians understood that these three sacraments so changed a man or a woman that the change was irreversible. If you are baptized, if you are confirmed, if you are ordained, the effect lasts forever. In the last third of the second century, an outstanding bishop in North Africa, St. Cyprian, made an error in this matter. He said that those who had denied their Christianity to avoid persecution and death should be forgiven if they repented. But he wanted them baptized again. The bishop of Rome, Saint Stephen, informed him that no one could be re-baptized, because this idea "has not been handed down to us [by the apostles] from the beginning." The Church has always believed that the three sacraments, baptism, confirmation, and holy orders cannot be given to the same person a second time, because there is a marking of the soul, a "character," which is ineradicable.

This character entitles the person who possesses it to engage in the other rites of Christian worship. During the first three centuries, those who had not yet been baptized had to leave the place where the Christians were worshipping God, after the early part of the ceremonies. Once baptized, a man or woman could then engage actively in the worship of God according to the Christian religion. Specifically, they could participate in the Holy Eucharist. But they could also join in other sacramental rites. Eventually, the restriction which applied to catechumens was removed. But it remains the teaching of the Church that no one can receive another of the sacraments until baptism has been undergone.

Sacraments as given by Christ   Catholics believe that Jesus Christ established the seven sacraments in order to give those who receive them a share in the grace which he won for each of us. Although Jesus established all seven sacraments, the Church understands that he was less concerned with the concrete way in which the sacraments are administered and much more concerned with their observance and their meaning. We know from the New Testament that Jesus was quite explicit about baptism and the Eucharist. The words to be employed when these sacraments are administered are expressly stated by Jesus. The New Testament is not so specific about the other five sacraments, though St. Paul urges Timothy not to "neglect the gift you received when, as a result of prophecy, the presbyters laid their hands on you" (I Tim. 5:14). The specifics of the rites of confirmation, holy orders, penance, the anointing of the sick, and matrimony are not given in the New Testament. The Christian churches have always employed the laying on of hands by a bishop as the matter in the sacrament of holy orders. Apart from that exception, the symbols used vary in the Eastern and Western churches. This is acceptable as long as the basic meaning of the words and symbols used does not change.

Ministers of sacraments   The minister of a sacrament, with the exception of one who baptizes and of one who distributes the Holy Eucharist, must be ordained. An ordained deacon can administer baptism solemnly and he can preside at a communion service solemnly. A deacon can also be the Church's formal witness in a rite of marriage (in which the ministers of the sacrament are the bride and groom). Only a priest can administer the sacraments of the Holy Eucharist (that is, only a priest can consecrate bread and wine into the body and blood of Christ), penance, and the anointing of the sick. A specially designated priest can administer the sacrament of confirmation. Only a bishop can administer the sacrament of holy orders and, under normal circumstances, the sacrament of confirmation.

Everyone who receives a sacrament expects the minister of the sacrament to be worthy of the sacred duty which that minister performs. But what if the minister is unworthy? In such a case, is the sacrament that is received *valid*? And is the sacrament administered *licitly*? To answer these questions, one must have a clear understanding of the words "valid" and "licit."

If the sacrament is invalid or, in other words, if a sacrament is administered invalidly, this means that, in fact, there was no sacrament. To be sure, the ceremony of administering the sacrament takes place, but none of the effects of the sacrament occur. For example, if I was baptized as an infant, yet grew up in ignorance of my baptism, I cannot receive the sacrament a second time. I may come to that stage when I ask to be baptized a Christian and actually receive the sacrament from a person who shares my belief that the sacrament can be received only once. In fact, however, I do not receive baptism on that occasion, even though the rite is performed prayerfully and worthily. The sacrament, in other words, is administered *invalidly*.

On the other hand, if I receive the sacrament of baptism from a minister who is in the state of grievous sin, the sacrament is given *validly* but *illicitly*. The person in the state of grievous sin administers the sacrament sinfully. This has no effect on me, the recipient of the sacrament, because every valid minister of a sacrament is taking the place, then and there, of Jesus Christ, who is the principal minister of every sacrament that is conferred. Accordingly, to receive a sacrament illicitly is to receive the sacrament in such a way that a personal sin is involved in administering the sacrament.

To enlarge on this point, two additional facts must be noted First, in a state of emergency, a sinful minister can offer a sacrament without committing sin. If I am a layman and am in the state of serious sin, I should not hesitate to baptize an adult who has a serious heart attack and asks me for baptism because of a fear of death. If I am a priest in the state of serious sin and must say Mass on Sunday for those who have to fulfill their Sunday obligation, I may offer that Mass without sin, if there is no other priest at hand who could hear my confession or, even, who could offer the Mass that is required. Because the sacraments are for the faithful, in an emergency, a sinful minister can still perform the necessary sacraments without committing additional sin.

Secondly, it is possible for the recipient of a sacrament to receive the sacrament validly but illicitly. That is, a person may be baptized, confirmed, ordained, or may marry and obtain the title to the grace that the sacrament offers, without actually receiving grace itself at that moment. If I am in the state of serious sin when I marry, the marriage takes place, but I not only do not receive the grace which the sacrament offers, I also commit another grievous sin. Once I sincerely confess all of my grievous sins in the sacrament of reconciliation the grace of the sacrament of marriage is then given to me. The same is true of an adult who receives the sacrament of baptism without renouncing his commitment to mortal sins that he has been committing. Once the newly baptized confesses this previous attachment to sins (that is, confesses that he was not *sorry* for his past sins, and that he had not promised himself that he would strive to overcome them in the future), he is forgiven and the grace of the sacrament of baptism flows into his soul.

The Church's greatest benefit, in a way, is that it offers us continuously a share in the grace of Jesus Christ. We obtain this by a reverent reception of the sacraments. Knowing that we are sinners, we come to the sacraments with sorrow for our past sins, with a promise to ourselves and to God that we shall work at overcoming the temptations that are constantly with us, and that we shall place our special confidence in Jesus Christ. We believe that if we seek Jesus' help through the seven rites of worship that we call "sacraments," he will bestow that help on us. Even though we must return often to the sacraments of penance and the Holy Eucharist, and though we may have to receive the sacrament of the anointing of the sick on many occasions, we consider it a humble privilege to join ourselves through these sacred rites, these sacred signs, to the work which Jesus Christ accomplished for all of us once and for all.

Thinking it over • • •

1. With what other churches does the Catholic Church agree as to the number, effects, and proper minister of the sacraments?

2. Which two Christian rites or ceremonies do the Protestant churches accept?

3. What is the fundamental feature of Protestant belief?

4. What was the name of the ecumenical council which clarified the Church's views concerning the sacraments?

5. Who was the first to use the word "sacrament" to describe a Christian rite of religion?

6. Who was the great thinker upon whose writing St. Thomas Aquinas based his treatment of the sacraments?

7. Give examples of "sacraments" which were celebrated in the Jewish religion.

8. What is the basic difference, according to St. Thomas Aquinas, between sacraments of the Old Law and sacraments of the New Law?

9. The sacraments effect what they signify. Does this mean that anyone who receives a sacrament obtains the effect intended by that sacrament? Explain. Give examples.

10. What is the principal characteristic of a sign?

11. Of what is every Christian sacrament a sign?

12. What do we mean by the "matter" of a sacrament? What do we mean by the "form" of a sacrament?

13. What is a sacramental "character"? To what does it entitle us?

14. Must the valid minister of a sacrament be ordained? Explain.

15. Explain the difference between the terms "valid" and "licit" when these are applied to the seven sacraments.

16. What does it mean to say that a sacrament is administered invalidly?

17. Is it possible for a person to receive a sacrament validly but illicitly? Explain and give examples.

Chapter 2

BAPTISM AND CONFIRMATION

The Sacraments of Initiation   Initiation into the Church is accomplished by three sacraments: Baptism, Confirmation and the Holy Eucharist. For this reason, these three sacraments together are called "the sacraments of initiation." Baptism is the beginning of new life in Christ. It is the first sacrament the Christian receives, and opens to him the door to the other sacraments. Confirmation strengthens and perfects baptismal grace. By the reception of Confirmation the Christian, configured more deeply to Christ, becomes more perfectly bound to the Church and is enriched with the gifts of the Holy Spirit. Holy Eucharist completes Christian initiation, uniting the believer to Christ himself and to his Body, the Church, through the food of eternal life, the Body and Blood of Christ himself. The Eucharist nourishes the believer throughout his Christian life. For this reason, unlike Baptism and Confirmation, the Holy Eucharist may be received more than once in a lifetime. Indeed, the Church encourages daily reception of Holy Communion. Full and complete membership in the Church is accomplished by the reception of Baptism, Confirmation and the Holy Eucharist.

Are you not aware that we who were baptized into Christ Jesus were baptized into his death? Through baptism into his death we were buried with him, so that, just as Christ was raised from the dead by the glory of the Father, we too might live a new life. (Rom. 6:3-4 NAB)

Baptism The sacrament of baptism is the beginning of the Christian life, the "new life" of which St. Paul speaks in the quotation above, taken from his letter to the Romans. Baptism is for each of us who receives the sacrament, a second birth, a new beginning. St. John's gospel relates the conversation that Jesus had with Nicodemus, an admirer of Jesus who came to the Savior secretly because of fear that he would be ostracized by his fellow Pharisees if they knew that he respected Jesus. "I solemnly assure you," Jesus said, "no one can enter into God's kingdom without being begotten of water and Spirit" (Jn. 3:5). St. John wrote his gospel two or three decades after the other three gospels were composed. Since some of the Christian rites were being abused by those who were not truly Christian, St. John does not speak directly about the rites of the sacraments. So, in the passage cited, he speaks of baptism in a way that differs from the statements recorded by Saints Matthew, Mark, and Luke.

The early Church did not allow outsiders to attend its sacred rites of worship. Baptism, of course, is the first of the seven sacred signs which the Church celebrates for those who seek to lead the Christian life. When St. John was writing his gospel, probably about the year 100, even baptism was a "secret," that is, a celebration which only those who were baptized and in good standing could attend, while those who were to receive the sacrament had been prepared through careful instruction. Despite St. John's silence about the way that the Christian rites were celebrated, we learn from him something of their deeper meaning. What is the deeper meaning of baptism?

The rite or external ceremony of baptism is performed in different ways The early Church baptized adults by taking them to a river, a stream, a lake, a pond, or an artificial pool constructed for this purpose. The person to be baptized was lowered into the water so that his whole body was covered by it. This is known as *immersion*. Some Christian groups still administer baptism in this way. But from earliest times other forms of "baptizing" were used. The Church did not require those who were physically incapable of descending into a pool of water to do so in order to be baptized. A person who was dying or could hardly move was baptized by *sprinkling* with water or by the *pouring* of water. The symbolism had to be one of washing the individual, for baptism washes away the filth of our sins. But baptism also symbolizes that we die to ourselves and rise to new life in Jesus Christ. This is why the early Church preferred to baptize by immersion and why some Christian churches still choose this form. In any event the use of water is the basic matter of this sacrament.

Together with the use of water, the person administering the sacrament must recite the words: "I baptize you in the name of the Father and of the Son and of the Holy Spirit." (As long as the meaning is not changed, some alterations in this statement can be made. The Greek Church uses a slightly different formula: "The servant of God [the name of the one baptized is here inserted] is baptized in the name of the Father and of the Son and of the Holy Spirit.") This *form* of the sacrament is essential. If the correct *form* is not employed, no sacrament is administered.

The matter and the form of baptism, the use of water and the recitation of the formula must complement one another. What does this mean? First, the two actions, the use of water and the recitation of the formula, must be performed by one and the same person. Second, the use of water and the recitation of the proper words must be employed at the same time. A person who is baptizing another does not have to pour water continually while saying the Trinitarian formula. But it must be obvious to the minister, the recipient, and to those in attendance that the words used apply to the action being performed. The Church asks that water be poured three times on the head of the one being baptized or that one be immersed three times in water while the baptismal formula is being recited. But this is not absolutely required; that is, the sacrament can still be validly administered and received without the triple washing. In an emergency, the triple action can readily be set aside.

The Church's use of the Trinitarian formula and the triple pouring of water in Baptism emphasizes the Trinitarian nature of this sacrament. Each baptized person becomes an adoptive child of God the *Father*, a member of *Christ's* Body, and a temple of the *Holy Spirit*. It was Jesus himself who commanded to the apostles before his Ascension: "Go, therefore, and make disciples of all nations. Baptize them in the name 'of the Father and of the Son and of the Holy Spirit' " [Matthew 28:19]. The Trinitarian formula used at Baptism underscores the indivisible co-operation of the Father, Son and Holy Spirit in God's redemptive work with man.

The Church surrounds the actual administration of the sacrament with many ceremonies; some of these precede the actual giving of baptism, some follow. These ceremonies are lovely and should be carefully studied by the parents of an infant to be baptized, by the sponsors (or "godparents"), or by the one who is to be baptized after reaching the use of reason. These ceremonies are, in fact, instructions. They are teaching devices that attempt to give us a better appreciation of the meaning of the rite and of the effects in us that this sacrament produces. The ceremonies remind us that we are not only carnal but also spiritual beings. Especially, they teach us that we are not created by God for this life only. If we are faithful to the baptism that we receive, we have eternal happiness awaiting us.

Is baptism necessary?   Jesus teaches us that without baptism no one can be saved. Or does he? Read the appropriate passages in the New Testament and it is difficult to draw the conclusion that only those who are actually baptized can be saved. For example, St. Mark reports the words of Jesus in this way:

> Go into the whole world and proclaim the good news [the gospel] to all creation. The man who believes in it and accepts baptism will be saved; the man who refuses to believe in it will be condemned (Mk. 16:15-16 NAB).

St. Matthew gives the familiar words of Jesus, which words are the very conclusion of his gospel:

> Full authority has been given to me / both in heaven and on earth;/ go, therefore, and make disciples of all the nations. / Baptize them in the name / of the Father, / and of the Son, / and of the Holy Spirit. / Teach them to carry out everything I have commanded you. / And know that I am with you always, until the end of the world (28:18-20 NAB).

St. Luke does not record the Lord's command to baptize. Toward the very end of his gospel, he quotes Jesus as saying to the apostles:

> Thus it is written that the Messiah must suffer and rise from the dead on the third day. In his name, penance for the remission of sins is to be preached to all the nations, beginning at Jerusalem (Lk. 24:46-47 NAB).

The proper interpretation of these texts bothered the early Church. St. Augustine, who lived four centuries after Christ, was saddened when a young man whom he was instructing for baptism died before the sacrament was received. St. Augustine finally reasoned that there is such a thing as "baptism of desire." Someone who wants to be baptized and who is prevented from receiving baptism through no fault of his own, will not be held accountable by Almighty God. St. Augustine reminded his readers of the argument made by an earlier bishop, St. Cyprian of Carthage. Reflecting on the gospel report concerning the good thief who died with Christ, and to whom Jesus said, "This day, you will be with me in paradise," St. Cyprian concluded that actual baptism with water was not absolutely necessary. Thinking on this, St. Augustine went further; he said: ". . . not only can suffering for the name of Christ supply for what was lacking in baptism, but even faith and conversion of heart can do so when it is impossible, owing to the difficulties of the times, to celebrate the mystery of baptism" (*The One Baptism of Children.* 4). So the Church came to recognize three forms of baptism: the sacrament of baptism, sometimes called "baptism of water"; martyrdom for the love of Jesus, called "baptism of blood"; and the mature search for what is good and correct in human life, called "baptism of desire."

Catholic teaching authority   Catholic authority does not hesitate to say that those who know that Jesus calls everyone to the sacrament of baptism and who reject that call cannot be saved. But the same Catholic authority is quick to add that there are millions of men and women who do not receive baptism through no fault of their own. To such individuals, God offers adequate opportunity to save their souls, even if innocently they do not come to know Jesus Christ. Such people can readily be saved through a "baptism of desire." Moreover, there are millions of adults who hear about the sacrament of baptism, who read what Christianity teaches about the necessity of this sacrament, but who do not believe. One should not say that such individuals are guilty of rejecting baptism. One can come to baptism only through faith. But faith is God's gift, a free act of generosity. We do not know why he offers this supernatural gift to some and withholds it from others. Not knowing, we ought not say of any individual that he or she has rejected the sacrament of baptism which we perceive as necessary for salvation. God will judge each of us according to the gifts he has freely offered us. Many are not offered the sacrament of baptism. Many are not given the faith by which they could accept the necessity of this holy rite. God, then, will judge them according to the other opportunities that he has afforded them.

Martyrs   In the long history of Christianity there are many who died because they believed in Jesus, though they had not been baptized. The children who were slaughtered by Herod, who was seeking to destroy the Infant Jesus, have always been reverenced by the Church as saints, the Holy Innocents. But anyone who sheds his blood in testimony to Jesus Christ, even if the sacrament of baptism has not been received, receives the most excellent form of baptism. The words of Jesus certify this truth:

> This is my commandment: / love one another / as I have loved you. There is no greater love than this: / to lay down one's life for one's friends" (Jn. 15:12-13 NAB).

To shed one's blood generously for the love of others and in recognition of Jesus' example and teaching is the highest form of baptism.

Gifts of baptism   The person who is baptized receives four marvelous gifts: 1) the washing away of all sin; 2) the enrichment of the soul with divine grace; 3) incorporation into the Body of Christ; and 4) an outpouring of the Holy Spirit and his gifts. Consider these effects of baptism, one by one. On the day when a person is baptized he is cleansed of all sin and of all the penalties that arise from sin. This means that original sin is removed, replaced with the grace of Jesus Christ and the gifts of the Holy Spirit. There is a difficulty here, to be sure. When we speak of original *sin,* we use a word that has a meaning which is different from the use of that same word when we speak of personal *sin.* Actually, original sin is the absence of the supernatural life which Adam and Eve possessed from the first moment of their creation. They lost this free gift by personal sin, thus falling from grace. God restored them to grace; but as a consequence of their sin they and their children were deprived of God's superabundant gifts. Moreover, not only was supernatural life lost by Adam's sin but nature itself was wounded: the mind was darkened, the will weakened, and the appetites or passions became disordered. This is a great mystery. But that mystery is matched by another: to free us from the sin of Adam and Eve, Almighty God chose to do something out of love for us which we can scarcely comprehend. He chose to come to earth himself, to be one with us, to be like us in everything except the actual commission of personal sins. And he chose to redeem us, that is, to restore us to the gifts which Adam and Eve had lost. What is stunning about this incredible fact is that if Adam and Eve had not sinned, God would not have become man. How do we know this? We know it because the only reason that is given in Sacred Scripture for the Incarnation—God becoming man—is to save us from our sins. When each of us is born, we lack that supernatural gift which was first given to Adam and Eve. Lacking this, we have no title to heaven. But, as St. John testifies, "God is love" (I John 4:8). And God who is love, does for us what only true love can do: he gives himself for us. Through baptism, the love of God is poured into our souls. In other words, the absence of that love—sometimes we call this the absence of grace— which is "original sin," ceases. And this is the first effect of the sacrament of baptism.

Once a person comes to the use of reason, personal sins are committed. All of us are guilty of committing sins, personal sins for which we are responsible. Now if a person has committed sins and then is converted to Christianity, it follows that he will seek baptism. In receiving the sacrament, all personal sins are wiped away. Even grievous or mortal sins are cleansed from the soul of such a person. Baptism fills the soul with grace; sin is destroyed; there is the total absence of any kind of sin. Moreover, the penalties owing to sin are totally destroyed. They are no more. From earliest history the Church has understood that the person who dies immediately after baptism goes directly into the eternal joy of heaven. Of course, this belief presumes that the person who is baptized has given up affection for, or attachment to, sins committed in the past. Given that, the gates of heaven open immediately to the soul of one who is baptized just before dying.

Infant Baptism   Because of its understanding that all human beings are born with original sin, the Church has long held the practice of infant Baptism. From the earliest days of the Church until the present time, Catholic parents have traditionally presented their infant children to the Church for Baptism. This is because they recognize not only the presence of original sin, but, more importantly, the power of God's grace to eradicate sin and restore us to life with himself. The grace of Baptism does not presuppose human merit; infant children are baptized into the Church community. The *Catechism of the Catholic Church* eloquently teaches us this truth.

But what of infants who die without baptism?

On this matter the Catholic Church has always been officially silent. Some great theologians have believed in *limbo,* a place of perfect peace, happiness, and contentment, where the souls of those who die without personal sin on their souls, but who have not been given the supernatural grace of baptism, live without the ultimate joy for which we were made: the vision and enjoyment of God who is seen face to face. But Catholics are not obliged to believe in limbo. Indeed, many Catholics who are faithful to the teachings of the Church believe that infants who die without the sacrament of baptism still go straight into the presence of God. Why? Because, as they argue, God is not restricted to the sacraments. That is, God who saves us through our reverent use of the sacraments can also save us when we have, *through no fault of our own,* failed to use them. Because the Church maintains an official silence on this issue, loyal Catholics are free to believe that infants and those who never achieve the use of reason who die without baptism are given the eternal joys of heaven through the grace of Jesus Christ.

Sacramental character   The Church has always believed and taught that the sacrament of baptism can be received only once. There can be no re-baptism. Recall what was said in the previous chapter [section about the error of St. Cyprian of Carthage]. He called for the re-baptism of those who had been baptized by heretics and of those who had denied their baptism during persecution. The Bishop of Rome ruled against St. Cyprian, however, saying that from the beginning the Church has never re-baptized anyone. St. Cyprian relented and accepted the teaching of the successor of St. Peter.

As the Church's understanding of this great sacrament grew, so did the language which it uses to explain this and other mysteries. One of the words which began to be applied to baptism and two other sacraments was "character." Originally, as we saw in the previous chapter, the word was used by Tertullian to describe the marking of the soul of those who are baptized. This marking is ineradicable; so no one can receive baptism a second time. Indelibly branded with this marking of Jesus' priesthood, the baptized are forever dedicated to a share in the work of Jesus. Some fail grievously, that is, they sin mortally, and lose the grace or divine life that is given with baptism. Because they have been ineradicably marked with the sacramental character of baptism, they do not need to be baptized again in order to return to the life of grace.

They can regain the state of grace through one of the other sacraments to which they are entitled by the baptismal character.

Who can baptize another? The answer to this question is revealing. That is, it manifests God's abundant love for each of us. For anyone can baptize. Anyone! Validly to administer this sacrament, the one baptizing must employ water in the proper way, recite the proper words of baptism, and intend to do what the Church intends. One does not have to be baptized in order to baptize another. One does not have to believe in the Christian faith or to believe in the power of baptism in order to baptize validly. One does not have to be a man or a woman, a youngster or an adult, a Christian or a non-Christian. As the longstanding expression says, one has only "to do what the Church does," that is, to perform this rite in the way that is required by Christianity and for the purpose which is intended by Christianity.

To make this clear, we Catholics distinguish between simple and solemn baptism. A nurse, for example, who knows that a newborn infant is dying should baptize the infant, pouring water on its head and reciting the Trinitarian formula. This is simple baptism. Solemn baptism is administered by a deacon, a priest, or a bishop of the Church. All of the solemnities with which the Church surrounds the actual baptism of a candidate can be performed only by one of these ordained ministers. These ceremonies are so important that the Church asks those who have been simply baptized in an emergency, should they recover from extreme illness and danger of death, to undergo these ceremonies but without the actual performance of the baptismal rite.

Baptismal sponsors When one is baptized solemnly, baptismal sponsors should present the one to be baptized. Usually, we refer to these sponsors as "godparents." Sponsors must be Catholics in good standing. They must have been confirmed. And they must be at least sixteen years of age. Actually only one sponsor is required by the common law of the Church, though in the United States two sponsors, one male and one female, are usually invited to accept the role of sponsor. The parents of a child who is to be baptized choose the sponsors, though an adult who is to be baptized chooses sponsors directly. In general, these "godparents" accept responsibility for the one to be baptized, promising that they will do what they can to be of assistance to the newly baptized in the life of faith.

CONFIRMATION

Probably because the second of the sacraments was traditionally celebrated in conjunction with baptism, it remained for so many centuries the least well-known theologically of the seven sacraments. This is not to say that Christians were ignorant of this great rite; rather, Christian theologians wrote less about this sacrament than about any of the others. In the first several centuries, when one was baptized, even as an infant, one was immediately confirmed, all in the same ceremony. We find some grounds for this practice in the Acts of the Apostles. St. Luke writes in that book that Paul came to the city of Ephesus where he found a dozen Christians. Meeting them, St. Paul asked the question: "Did you receive the Holy Spirit when you became believers?" Learning that they had not even heard of the Holy Spirit, Paul asked them: "Well, how were you baptized?" When they replied that they had received the baptism of St. John the Baptist, Paul immediately baptized them "in the name of the Lord Jesus." Then, the narrative continues:

> As Paul laid his hands on them, the Holy Spirit came down on them and they began to speak in tongues and to utter prophecies (Acts 19:6 NAB).

Today, Catholics in the Oriental churches, that is, the churches which originated in the eastern Mediterranean, still confirm infants and adults immediately after they have been baptized. Furthermore, each newly-baptized and confirmed person in the Eastern churches receives Holy Communion. This practice underscores the unity of the three sacraments of initiation: Baptism, Confirmation, and the Eucharist. In the Western or "Latin" church, confirmation is not given to infants. But when an adult is baptized, the priest who performs the baptism immediately confirms the one who has been baptized.

What is the meaning or purpose of confirmation? Quite simply, the sacrament is given to strengthen the recipient against the spirit of worldliness which allures us all. As everyone will admit, the world is powerfully attractive, especially to the young. Christians are called upon to fight against the temptations of the world. Because these temptations can be so alluring, at times so overpowering, Jesus gave us a special sacrament to strengthen us against worldly attractions.

Confirmation, then, is the sacrament of spiritual strength. The purpose of the sacrament is to give the recipient an added strength against the many worldly temptations that arise, to offer the ability to profess the Christian faith especially when it is difficult to do so, and to provide that special grace which is needed from time to time to stand up to oppression and to identify oneself with Christ in the presence of those who reject him or, especially, in the presence of those who hate him. While each of us too readily follows the crowd in almost any social matter, there are times when the true Christian will refuse. This refusal, made humbly but firmly in the name of Jesus, is possible only to the mature. And such maturity is given to us through the sacrament of confirmation.

"Matter" of confirmation   In confirmation, the matter of the sacrament is the anointing of the person being confirmed with sacred chrism. Chrism is a pure oil to which another element that gives off a pleasant odor, usually called "balm" or "balsam," has been added. Chrism is consecrated by a bishop during the special ceremonies that are held each year in Holy Week at the cathedral of the diocese. Small vessels containing this chrism are then distributed to all the priests of the diocese. (Chrism is also used toward the end of the rite of baptism.)

This anointing of the forehead with chrism is done together with the simultaneous laying of the minister's hand on the head of the person receiving the sacrament. The imposition of the hand is important in this sacrament, for the earliest testimony, that of the apostles themselves as recorded in the New Testament, affirms that the sacrament was given in this way. Later on, the Church added the anointing with chrism. Accordingly, the laying on of the right hand together with the anointing with chrism is the *matter* of this sacrament.

The "form" of the sacrament is the phrase, "Receive the seal of the Gift of the Holy Spirit"
This implies that the person who is confirmed receives the same effect as did the apostles on the day of Pentecost. On that day God the Holy Spirit filled the hearts and minds—indeed, the very souls—of the apostles. Immediately their faith in Jesus was strengthened. Immediately they understood the work to which Jesus had called them. Immediately they began that work.

Like baptism this sacrament imprints a character on the soul of the recipient   But, where the sacramental character obtained through baptism designates one as privileged to worship God according to the rites of the Christian religion, confirmation impresses a character, a marking of the soul, that does more. The character of confirmation is Jesus' pledge that we shall receive, if we cooperate with him, the strengthening graces that are needed for the active, public profession of our faith. Moreover, the character is a pledge that we shall have the strong, spiritual help that we need to bear witness by words and deeds that will inspire others. If the power of good example is, in fact, the power to be a teacher, then the sacrament of confirmation offers us the grace to inspire others, that is, to teach them, in what we say and do. This power flows into our words and deeds through the character of this sacrament.

The sacramental character of confirmation, like the sacramental character of baptism, is indelible. Unfortunately, many who are confirmed fall into serious sin, thus losing the grace of the sacraments of baptism and confirmation. Because character remains forever indelibly marked in their souls they can regain the grace of baptism and confirmation through true sorrow for sin and the sacrament of penance. But confirmation may be received only once and for the same reasons that were discussed above in our study of baptism.

Who can be a minister of this sacrament? In the Western Church the sacrament of confirmation is administered to people who were baptized as infants by a bishop or by a priest who has been specially designated by the bishop to administer the sacrament. In the Eastern Church, confirmation is always administered immediately after baptism and in the same ceremony, whether the recipient of baptism is an infant, a child, a young person, or an adult. And, as we noted earlier in the section on Baptism, Eastern Rite Catholics also receive their First Holy Communion along with Baptism and Confirmation. This ancient practice of the Eastern Church demonstrates the unity of the three sacraments of initiation. In the Latin Rite (the

Western Church) the priest who baptizes a young person or an adult confirms the newly baptized in the same ceremony. Also, in the Latin Church, the pastor of a parish can confirm a member of his parish who is gravely ill. Otherwise, the importance of this sacrament is proclaimed in the Latin Church by its administration at the hands of a bishop. When a bishop is the minister of confirmation, the importance of this sacrament is stressed, particularly the fact that those who receive it are through the sacrament given the grace to practice their faith maturely, as adults.

Who may receive this sacrament?   "Every baptized person not yet confirmed can and should receive the sacrament of Confirmation" [*Code of Canon Law,* can. 889, #1]. More completely put, since Baptism, Confirmation, and Holy Eucharist together form complete initiation into the Catholic Church, it follows that Confirmation should be received by all baptized Catholics early in their lives. It is, therefore, important for us to understand the prerequisites for a person to be confirmed in the Church.

First of all, to be confirmed, the candidate *must have been baptized.* Since Confirmation completes or perfects Baptism and increases Baptismal grace, it follows that one must be baptized prior to being confirmed.

Additionally, the candidate for Confirmation in the Latin tradition should have *attained the "age of reason."* Traditionally, the Church has considered the age of reason to be about seven years old. However, the practice in our country at present puts the age of Confirmation closer to about twelve to fourteen years of age.

Another important requirement for Confirmation is that the candidate must *profess the faith.* This profession of faith is made solemnly during the Rite of Confirmation in the form of questions asked by the bishop and answered by the candidate. Studying and learning about the teachings of one's faith helps him to understand more fully the creed he professes and seeks to live out.

Also, every candidate for Confirmation must also have the *free intention* of receiving this sacrament. While God offers us his grace, he does not force it upon us.

Also, the candidate for Confirmation must be in the *state of grace*. This requirement means that a candidate must be free of mortal or grievous sin in order to be cleansed and properly disposed for the gift of the Holy Spirit. Intensified prayer is also encouraged as part of one's preparation for the reception of Confirmation.

Part of the proper frame of mind for the reception of Confirmation is that the candidate is prepared and willing to assume responsibility for the apostolic mission of the Church. An active Catholic participates in the Mass and the Sacraments, performs corporal and spiritual works of mercy for other people, continuously studies the teachings of the Church, and generally strives to live his daily life according to the moral values of the Gospel. The Twelve Apostles moved from passive to active faith when they received the Holy Spirit at Pentecost. Similarly, the outpouring of the Holy Spirit upon the christian at Confirmation moves him to mature, active faith.

Eligible sponsors   When the sacrament is administered solemnly, that is, apart from those instances when one is confirmed at baptism or when in danger of death, a sponsor should present the person to be confirmed. This sponsor should be a practicing Catholic who has been confirmed. And the sponsor should be capable of offering mature example and even instruction to the one being presented. When an adult is baptized and confirmed in the same ceremony, the same sponsors may fulfill the role of sponsor for both sacraments. Too often a sponsor assumes only a ceremonial role. In fact, the sponsor is responsible for the newly confirmed and should generously, patiently provide good example and prayers for the one confirmed.

Confirmation is a summons to active work on behalf of others in the name of Jesus Christ. Often, today, any such work is called "ministry." Those who engage in full or part-time teaching efforts at the elementary, secondary, or the collegiate level; those who give of their time to instruct young people who are students in public schools in the foundations of their religion; those who bring the Eucharist to shut-ins; those who offer their time to do much of the paper work that must be performed when adults are seeking favors from diocesan courts; those who assist deacons and priests in so many other ways are all seen as performing the works of mature Catholics, that is, of the confirmed. Since Christianity is essentially a missionary religion, calling on all its members to turn outward from themselves toward others, the sacrament of confirmation cannot be overemphasized. Each of us who is confirmed is sent to others. Each of us who is confirmed agrees to be a missionary, to pursue a ministry, on behalf of others.

Thinking it over • • •

1. In his gospel, St. John does not speak directly about the rites of the Christian religion. Why?

2. Baptism can be administered in three ways. Name these and briefly describe each way.

3. What are the words or *form* which the person who is baptizing must recite?

4. Does Jesus say that only those who are actually baptized can be saved? What does the New Testament quote him as saying?

5. When a person is baptized, he receives three gifts. What are these?

6. What, actually, is original sin?

7. What does the Church teach officially concerning limbo?

8. What do we mean when we say that baptism imprints a "character" on the soul?

9. Who can baptize another? What conditions must the one who baptizes fulfill?

10. Who can administer solemn baptism?

11. What conditions must one fulfill in order to be a sponsor at another's baptism?

12. How many baptismal sponsors are actually required by the Church?

13. When should one be confirmed if one's baptism takes place later in life?

14. Why did Jesus give us the sacrament of confirmation?

15. What is the *matter* of the sacrament of confirmation? What is the *form* of this sacrament?

16. If you are asked to be a sponsor at someone's confirmation, what conditions must you fulfill before you can accept the invitation?

17. What are some of the works or "ministries" that the confirmed Catholic may be asked to do?

Chapter 3

THE HOLY EUCHARIST

That which is most sacred in the Catholic religion is the sacrament of the Eucharist. Traditionally this gift has been called "the Most Blessed Sacrament," "the Most Holy Eucharist," and "the Sacred Banquet." Through almost twenty centuries true Christians have reverenced this sacrament as the centerpiece of their religion. Among the seven great rites of the Christian faith, by which we worship Almighty God and simultaneously receive his gifts, this sacrament is the principal one. Every other sacrament must be understood in its relationship to the Holy Eucharist. "The other sacraments and all the apostolic works of Christ are bound up with, and directed to, the blessed Eucharist" (Code of Canon Law, Can. 897).

251

Sacred Scripture is quite clear that the Holy Eucharist was given to us by Jesus at the Last Supper Because it has become customary to begin a new day at midnight, Christians customarily say that Jesus celebrated the Last Supper "on the night before he died." But Jesus was a Jew. According to Jewish practice, which still continues, a new day begins at sundown. Jesus took his twelve apostles for the observance of the Passover meal; they began this celebration after the sun had set. During this celebration, Jesus established the sacrament of the Holy Eucharist. On the same day, by Jewish reckoning, Jesus died on the cross. These two great moments in the history of the world took place on the same day! Their relationship is so important that this fact must ever be kept in mind.

Signs and symbols Since every sacrament is a sign of something other than itself, we begin our study of the Holy Eucharist by asking: what are the signs or symbols that make up this sacrament? And we ask: of what are these the sacred signs? The answer to the first question is rather easy. The answer is agreed to by all Christians. Why? Because the New Testament gives clear testimony:

> During the meal, Jesus took bread, blessed it, broke it, and gave it to his disciples. "Take this and eat it," he said, "this is my body." Then he took a cup, gave thanks, and gave it to them. "All of you must drink from it," he said, "for this is my blood, the blood of the covenant, to be poured out in behalf of many for the forgiveness of sins. I tell you I will not drink this fruit of the vine from now until I drink it new with you in my father's reign" (Mt. 26:26-29 NAB).

> Then, taking bread and giving thanks, he broke it and gave it to them, saying: "This is my body to be given for you. Do this as a remembrance of me." He did the same with the cup after eating, saying as he did so: "This cup is the new covenant in my blood, which will be shed for you" (Lk. 22:19-20 NAB).

> I received from the Lord what I handed on to you, namely, that the Lord Jesus on the night in which he was betrayed took bread, and after he had given thanks, broke it and said: "This is my body, which is for you. Do this in remembrance of me." In the same way, after the supper, he took the cup saying, "This cup is the new cove-

nant in my blood. Do this, whenever you drink it, in remembrance of me." Every time, then, you eat this bread and drink this cup, you proclaim the death of the Lord until he comes! This means that whoever eats the bread or drinks the cup unworthily sins against the body and blood of the Lord" (I Cor. 11:23-27 NAB).

Other historical facts These testimonies to something so sacred seem brief, slightly different in each account, and of lesser importance than the Catholic Church proclaims. But one must reflect that the early Church was hesitant to publicize the full meaning of its sacred ceremonies or the way in which they were celebrated. St. John's gospel gives no account of the institution of the Eucharist. However, it must again be emphasized that St. John wrote two, or perhaps almost three, decades after the other evangelists, and about fifty years after St. Paul wrote his First Letter to the Corinthians. By the time that St. John was composing his gospel, many religious groups were trying to borrow the Christian rites and to profane them. At the same time, Christians were being persecuted here and there because of their religion. The writers of that period did not want to reveal the way in which the Christians gathered or the observances which they kept in their meetings.

From several other sources, however, we know many details of the way in which the first and second century Christians celebrated the Eucharist. *The Doctrine of the Twelve Apostles,* written about the year 80 A.D., gives several reports about the importance to the first Christian assemblies of the Blessed Sacrament. St. Justin Martyr, who was born about the same time as St. John was composing his gospel, and who died about sixty-five years later (100 A.D. to about 165 A.D.), tells of the way in which deacons ministered the Eucharist to other participants in the Christian gathering and of the way that some present were permitted to carry the Eucharist to those who were absent. St. Justin testifies to the Christians' belief that in the

Eucharist we have both the flesh and the blood of Jesus. St. Justin says quite clearly that only those who have been baptized, who have been properly instructed, and who live according to the truths taught by Christ, should participate in the Holy Eucharist.

There is fascinating testimony from modern archeologists concerning the places where the Christians of the first three and a half centuries celebrated the Eucharist. This was during the period of persecutions, which flared up in many places from time to time, and which caused the Christians to celebrate the Eucharist and their other rites in secret. For example, a recent study shows that the Christians of Rome celebrated the Eucharist at the tomb of St. Peter, yet in such a way as not to broadcast either that St. Peter was buried there or to publicize that the place was popular among Christians. Baptism and the Eucharist were customarily celebrated at St. Peter's tomb, yet secretly, or at least quietly, with provisions made to conceal the purpose for the baptismal pool or for the altar where the Eucharist was offered.

The New Testament, as we have seen, testifies to the establishment by Jesus of the Eucharist Christians generally accept this testimony, and almost every Christian church observes this rite in some way and at least from time to time. The Catholic tradition, of course, does not rely solely on the Sacred Scriptures for its understanding of what Jesus taught or of what the earliest Church authorized in his name. Catholics believe that sacred tradition—enlightening us concerning those things revealed but not written down clearly in the New Testament—is an integral source of what we believe. This is especially important when one reflects upon the meaning and purpose of that which Catholics hold as most sacred: the sacrament of the Most Holy Eucharist.

Matter and form of the Eucharist　　As with each sacrament, Catholic thinkers approach the study of each of the seven sacred rites of the Church by asking, "What is the *matter* of this sacrament? What is the *form* of this sacrament?" In a way, this is not a difficult question when we deal with the Eucharist. Yet there is an issue of special importance in this sacrament which does not apply to the other six. For in the Eucharist, there is a double matter and form, though there is only one sacrament. What does this mean? The Eucharist is both a "sacrament" and a "sacrifice." We must be quite careful in making this statement. To say that the Eucharist is a "sacrament" is to say that it is a sacred sign, which is *received* by those who eat this bread and drink this cup. To say that it is a "sacrifice" means that it is *under sacramental signs* the offering of Jesus' sacrifice of himself. In other words, when we speak of receiving communion, we think of the Eucharist as a "sacrament." When we speak of the celebration of Mass, we think of the Eucharist as a "sacrifice." In fact, there is only one sacrament, a rite which is both a sacrifice as offered and a sacrament as received.

The *matter* of this sacrament is bread and wine. The bread should be made from wheaten flour. This flour is mixed with water and without leaven (though some of the Eastern rites require that leavened bread be used). The bread used in the Eucharist should have been recently made or otherwise protected from corruption. The wine that is used must be natural, made from grapes of the vine, and not corrupt. To the wine a small quantity of water is added as a symbol of our union with Christ. The consecration of both bread and wine is required for this sacrament. A priest is never permitted, no matter what the circumstances, to consecrate only bread or wine. He must intend to consecrate both, and both bread and wine must have been prepared for this purpose.

The Eucharist may not be celebrated outside of the large ritual which is usually called "the Mass" This is composed of four principal sections: the introductory rite; the liturgy of the word; the liturgy of the Eucharist; and the concluding rite. The first two parts are designed to prepare our hearts and minds for the great mystery which we gather to celebrate. The introductory rite and the liturgy of the word are based on the Jewish synagogue service, the principal elements being the public reading of Sacred Scripture, reflections on these, and a sermon or homily based on the texts which have been read. The homily can be given by a bishop, a priest, or a deacon. Those who have not been ordained to one of these holy orders are not permitted to preach a homily. On Sundays and great feasts, the profession of faith, using an ancient formula, is made by all who participate. This part of the rite concludes with public prayers for the Church and those who govern it, for the people who are gathered, for their particular intentions, and for other general intentions for which we should implore Almighty God.

The third part of the Mass, the liturgy of the Eucharist, begins with the preparation of the gifts which we offer to God, bread and wine. A tiny quantity of water is added to the wine in order to symbolize our unity with the body and blood of Jesus into which our gifts will be changed. With brief prayers, the priest offers these gifts to God, asking that he accept them, while acknowledging that we have these gifts to offer only through the goodness of God. Symbolically, the priest then washes his hands, saying a prayer which asks that the Father wash away his sins as he prepares for the moment when he will perform the highest action that a priest can perform. Inviting the congregation to join their intentions to his, he then says the prayer that concludes these preparations.

Solemnly now, the priest sings or recites the Preface or beginning of the central part of this most holy rite. The congregation responds to this inaugural prayer by singing or reciting the "Holy, holy, holy Lord . . ." that is so familiar to all Christians. Then, when the assembly has become silent, the priest recites the great Eucharistic Prayer. Actually, there are several versions of this prayer so the priest selects the one that seems the most appropriate for the season or for the particular congregation that is assembled. In the middle of this prayer the priest discontinues reciting this prayer in his own name. At the consecration, that is, at that moment when the bread which has been offered becomes the body of Christ and the wine becomes Christ's blood, the priest says the words of consecration as though Jesus himself were present and reciting them. For at this moment the priest who stands visibly at the altar is taking the place of Jesus sacramentally. In other words, it is Jesus who recites the formula of consecration, using the visible human priest as the sacred sign of his presence. To appreciate the sacrament of the Holy Eucharist, one must reflect carefully on this marvelous fact. The human, visible priest is the sacred sign of the presence of Jesus at the altar.

Transubstantiation   When the priest has completed the words of consecration by which bread is changed into Christ's body and wine into his blood, the sacrifice of the Mass is essentially complete. Where before there was bread and wine on the altar, now there is the body and the blood of Jesus Christ. The Church refers to the mysterious change as *transubstantiation*. The word, which was a medieval addition to Catholic language, is rejected by Protestants. In the face of the misunderstanding which arose, the Council of Trent said that the word was most appropriate and should be used. What does transubstantiation mean? Quite simply, it implies that the whole substance of the bread that is on the altar is changed into the whole substance of the body of Jesus Christ and the whole substance of wine is changed into the whole substance of the blood of Jesus Christ, the "accidents" of bread and of wine alone remaining. The accidents are the appearances. What the priest now holds in his hands, and what the faithful receive in communion, has the taste, the odor, the feel, the color of bread and wine. These features are unchanged. But the substance that supports or underlies these appearances has been totally changed. No longer bread and wine, these substances are now, truly, actually, verily the substance of the body and the blood of Jesus.

Because the two substances are separated on the altar, they signify the death of Jesus, who died on the cross in the shedding of his blood. Gathered around the Christian altar, then, we are present at Calvary. We are there because the priest who utters the words of consecration is taking the place of Jesus who first did this at the Last Supper. We are also there in very fact because sacraments become the realities which they express. Although offered under signs, the sacrifice of Jesus Christ on the cross of Calvary is given to us in every time and place, not only symbolically, but in very truth. This is the great marvel of this sacred rite. The one moment in human history that is indispensable for all of us is given to us by God's unbelievable generosity. In the Mass, when bread and wine have been consecrated, those who participate are present at Jesus' sacrifice on Calvary, not only through belief but in fact.

The prayers that follow immediately after the consecration proclaim this in various ways. And they profess our unity with Christians of all ages, especially those who are alive at the present time. But these prayers also proclaim our oneness with the great saints of Christianity, most especially with Mary, the Mother of God.

Holy Communion   The priest who celebrates the Eucharist asks all to rise at the conclusion of the Eucharistic Prayer. Those who have been baptized, who are practicing Catholics, and who are in good standing, are invited to communion, "to eat the flesh of the Son of Man and drink his blood." Too often, individuals approach the communion table who should not do so, either because they are not baptized, or because they are not one in faith with the Catholic Church, or because they are in the state of grievous sin, or because they have not observed the Church's requirements that they be fasting from food and drink for at least an hour. Many Protestants object that the Church unduly denies the reception of communion to them, even though they are baptized, practicing Christians who believe many of the truths which Catholics believe. Yet the Catholic view is that the reception of the body and blood of Jesus Christ in the sacrament of the Eucharist requires that one have faith in Jesus, in his truth as proclaimed by the Church which he established for this purpose, and that one be prepared to receive this most sacred gift through active belief and, when necessary, following the sacrament of reconciliation. By our reception of Christ in Holy Communion we actually and truly become one with Christ, which means that we also become one with his body, the Church. Christ brings us into communion with our fellow Catholics on earth, the communion of saints in heaven, and our beloved faithful departed who await their full communion with the Lord. St. Paul warns: "Every time, then, you eat this bread and drink this cup, you proclaim the death of the Lord until he comes! This means that whoever eats the bread or drinks the cup of the Lord unworthily sins against the body and blood of the Lord. A man should examine himself first; only then should he eat of the bread and drink of the cup" (I Cor. 11:26-28 NAB).

After communion has been distributed, there should follow a moment of silence which allows all who participate to meditate on the great saving action in which they have been involved. The communion service, this third part of the Eucharist, concludes with the postcommunion prayer that is recited by the priest.

Dismissal rite   The Eucharist, or Mass, ends with the final blessing and the encouragement that is offered to all: go in peace.

The Eucharist strengthens the Church's bond of unity   The Church is the Mystical Body of Christ, and the person who receives Holy Communion receives the Body of Christ. It stands to reason that one who receives the Body of Christ within himself becomes one with the Body of Christ. There is a colloquial saying, "You are what you eat." Simply put, when we partake of the Body of Christ in the Eucharist, we are the Body of Christ. This is one of the most beautiful truths of the Eucharist: no matter how we are separated by time and space, Catholics are one by reception of the Eucharist. The Church exists through the Eucharist.

> The cup which we bless, is it not a participation in the Blood of Christ? The bread which we break, is it not a participation in the Body of Christ? Because there is one bread, we who are many are one Body, for we all partake of the one bread (1 Cor. 10:16-17).

Because Holy Communion incorporates the members into the Mystical Body of Christ, the Eucharist is a sacrament of initiation. Through the Eucharist, Christ unites each individual, all the faithful in his Body, the Church. That is why the Eucharist is celebrated daily in churches throughout the world. Holy Communion renews, strengthens and deepens our incorporation into the Church begun at Baptism and ratified in Confirmation. In fact, the Eucharist is so important a sacrament that the Church allows persons to begin receiving Communion at the age of reason even when they haven't been confirmed.

Since the Eucharist intimately unites the believer to the Church, the Body of Christ, it follows that only those people who are members of the Church should receive Holy Communion. For this reason, the Church has traditionally forbidden inter-communion, or reception of Communion by non-Catholics, even non-Catholic Christians. Such inter-communion would imply a unity that does not exist. Furthermore, because mortal sin separates the believer from the Body of Christ, the Church also traditionally instructs Catholics who are in a state of mortal sin not to receive Holy Communion. "Anyone conscious of a grave sin must receive the sacrament of Reconciliation before coming to communion" (CCC #1385). People of good will should pray unceasingly for a restoration of unity of all separated Christians to the one body of Christ and the one Eucharist.

Catholics believe that the Eucharist is required for salvation But this statement must be carefully interpreted. Those who through no fault of their own do not accept the Christian faith, especially those who have not heard of the Christian faith, are not asked by Almighty God to do the impossible. Traditionally the Catholic Church has taught that all must have the *implicit desire* to receive this sacrament if they wish to be saved. Consider carefully the meaning of this statement. "Implicit" means that one does not have *explicit* understanding of the sacrament, yet one wants to do whatever is necessary to achieve the goal of human life. Jews, Moslems, Hindus, Confucians, and others to whom Christianity has not been carefully explained or who do not have the ability (the divine faith which God gives) to understand the Christian religion, are not held accountable by God. They are said to have the faith "implicitly." Those to whom God has freely offered the faith, the supernatural ability to believe in his revelation and in Jesus Christ, are bound by that faith to reverence the Eucharist and to receive this sacrament often during their lifetimes. This spiritual food offers strength, refreshment, and nourishment, without which one cannot be faithful to Christ or to what he has taught.

The Catholic Church also teaches that the faithful must receive this sacrament when they are seriously in danger of death. When death is near, one especially needs all of the spiritual strength that is possible. The greatest source of that strength is Jesus himself, with whom we are united really in the sacrament of the Holy Eucharist. Perhaps this is best summed up in the prayer which Thomas Aquinas wrote for the Church's annual celebration of the Feast of Corpus Christi:

"O Sacred Banquet in which Christ becomes our food, the memory of his passion is celebrated, the soul is filled with grace, and a pledge of future glory is given to us!"

Thinking it over · · ·

1. Why do we say that the Holy Eucharist is the principal sacrament?

2. Why is it important to reflect, when one thinks of the Eucharist, that a Jewish day begins at sundown?

3. Why does St. John's gospel give no explicit account of the institution of the Holy Eucharist?

4. What are two early sources that tell us about the way in which the first Christians celebrated the Eucharist?

5. What are the two sources for Catholics that tell us what Jesus taught and that inform us of what the early Church believed?

6. The Eucharist is both a sacrament and a sacrifice. Briefly explain the difference between these two.

7. Describe the qualities which the bread and wine used in the Eucharist should possess. Are there any differences in the qualities of the bread used in the Latin rite and in the Eastern rites?

8. When Mass is offered, there are four principal parts. What are these?

9. What is meant by "transubstantiation"?

10. In speaking of the Holy Eucharist, what do we mean by "accidents"? Give examples.

11. In what sense may I say that those who participate in the Mass are present at Calvary?

12. Some individuals should not receive holy communion. Describe those who should not receive the Eucharist.

13. What do Catholics mean when they say that to be saved everyone should have at least the implicit desire to receive the Eucharist?

Chapter 4

RECONCILIATION AND ANOINTING

One of the most sobering facts about our human lives is that we are all sinners. All of us know of outstanding men and women who are totally dedicated to the welfare of others. They give themselves tirelessly, patiently, and with extreme generosity to assist those who need care and loving concern from others. On a rare occasion you may meet such a person, who is perhaps surrounded by men and women who crowd in to shake hands and to say a few words. If you have such an opportunity, you are filled with joy. Sometimes we refer to such outstanding people as "holy." And we know that the Church at times proclaims, after the death of such a person, that he or she is a saint. Does this mean that the saint was not a sinner?

With the exception of Mary, the Mother of God, we are all sinners If you admit this to yourself with sincerity, a number of changes will take place in you and in your dealings with others. If I am a sinner, what right do I have unduly to criticize others for their sins or failures? To recognize one's own weaknesses, to acknowledge one's own temptations to selfishness and to self-satisfaction, is in practice the beginning of the Christian life. One who can say with sincerity, "I am a sinner," has taken the first step on the road to Christian maturity.

Jesus loved sinners One of the most evident features of Jesus' life is that he loved those who were sinners. In the third gospel, written by St. Luke, a Gentile, who was keenly aware that Jesus came to call sinners, there are many stories about Jesus and his loving relations with sinful men and women. What is startling about God becoming a man is that he did this to deliver you and me from our sins. All four of the gospels make this clear. But it is St. Luke who wrote his gospel to impress this truth upon his readers. When the paralyzed man was let down from the roof of the house where Jesus was speaking to a room filled with listeners, Jesus said to the cripple, "My friend, your sins are forgiven you" (Lk. 5:20 NAB). It is also St. Luke who recounts Jesus' story about the prodigal son, the rich man and Lazarus, and the Pharisee and the tax collector, and who tells us of Jesus' encounter with Zacchaeus and with the good thief who died next to Jesus on the cross.

Jesus forgave sins Sorrow for sin, the sincere intention to repair evils which we have caused, the promise made to ourselves and to God to fight against temptations that will arise in the future, all of these are clearly an essential part of the gospel or message which Jesus preached. All Christians who read the New Testament piously, reverently, acknowledge this truth. The Catholic Church, the Orthodox church, and

266

the Anglican church believe that Jesus not only forgave the sins of his contemporaries but also forgives
our sins through a sacred rite or sacrament which is
called the sacrament of reconciliation or the sacrament of penance.

The sacrament of penance   We have already
seen that a sacrament is a sacred sign which Jesus
established to give grace to the humble recipient. Of
the seven such signs, one of the most frequently employed is reconciliation. Its sign or sacred rite is a com-
bination of the external acts of a penitent and of the
priest who is the minister of this rite. From these
external symbols, one understands that the sinner's
sincere repentance and the forgiveness of those sins by
the priest are indispensable ingredients of this sacrament. As with the other sacraments, the effect of this
rite is achieved because Jesus Christ is the actual
priest who, working through the human minister,
forgives the sins of the contrite penitent.

Matter and form of reconciliation   Since every
sacrament is composed of *matter* and *form,* we must
immediately ask: what are the matter and the form of
reconciliation? This is not a difficult question to
answer so long as we understand that the matter of
this sacrament is not a concrete substance such as one
finds in the sacraments of baptism, where water is
employed, or confirmation, which uses oil and the
imposition of the minister's hand on the recipient's
head, or in the Eucharist, where bread and wine are
employed. In the sacrament of reconciliation, the matter of the sacrament is the acts of the penitent who
acknowledges the sins committed after baptism, who
is sorry for these sins, and who promises to make satisfaction. The form of the sacrament is the words of the
priest, who says:

> God the Father of mercies, through the death and resurrection of
> his Son has reconciled the world to himself and sent the Holy
> Spirit among us for the forgiveness of sins. Through the ministry
> of the Church may God grant you pardon and peace. And I absolve
> you from your sins in the name of the Father and of the Son and
> of the Holy Spirit.

Is this sacrament necessary for eternal salvation? It should be obvious that a person can be saved without receiving this sacrament. An adult can be baptized just before the moment of death. Such a person has no need of the sacrament of reconciliation, for baptism wipes away every stain of sin, every penalty owing to sin, and destines the newly baptized to immediate glory in heaven. Little children who have been baptized but who have not reached the use of reason cannot be guilty of sin, at least not of serious sin, and have no need of this sacrament. And, at least theoretically, an adult who has never fallen into grievous or mortal sin, does not have to approach the sacrament of reconciliation. But all who have reached the age of discretion are bound by the law of the Church to confess their grievous sins at least once a year (Canon 989). This law of the Church, however, must be understood as a minimum requirement. The Catholic faithful are certainly encouraged to confess any grievous sins into which they may have fallen as soon as possible and as often as their consciences tell them that they have sinned.

This sacrament is usually referred to as "a second plank after baptism." The early Latin writer, Tertullian, who was the first to use the term "sacrament" (in reference to baptism), coined this phrase. The metaphor was used by other early writers and became a popular description of the rite of forgiveness. The Council of Trent employed this simile when writing about the sacrament of penance or reconciliation. The meaning should be clear. Baptism is a spiritual birth and one can only be born once. But reconciliation is comparable to medicine which one takes who, having been born, becomes sick. Just as medications can be taken as often as they are necessary for good health, so the sacrament of reconciliation can be employed as often as one senses a personal weakness because of sin. St. Peter once asked Jesus, "Lord, when my brother wrongs me, how often must I forgive him? Seven times?" Jesus' answer was immediate: "No . . . not seven times; I say, seventy times seven times" (Mt. 18:21-22 NAB). Jesus is using a Semitic expression in answering Peter. And the meaning of that expression is quite simply, "without limit." Through the sacrament of reconciliation, Jesus will forgive me my sins as often as I am sorry for them and seek forgiveness. Perhaps this sacred rite should be called the "sacrament of compassion," for Jesus instructed his apostles: "Be compassionate, as your Father is compassionate" (Lk. 6:36 NAB).

But reconciliation or penance is more than a sacrament It is one of the basic virtues of the Christian life. Indeed, none of us can approach the sacrament of reconciliation unless we are sincerely penitential. This means that we must be moved inwardly by God to those actions which are indispensable if one is to be forgiven for personal sins. One must reflect very carefully on this profound truth. If I have sinned grievously, I have lost the ability to be sorry for my sins. Only the unbelievable generosity of God restores that ability; that is, only by God's gracious, gentle motion can I find within myself the ability to be penitential. The virtue of penance, which I have as a permanent possession as long as I do not commit serious sin, is restored to me by God and through this interior restoration I can sincerely repent of my sins and obtain forgiveness for them. This means a number of things: 1) that God has turned my heart from sin and called me back to his grace and love; 2) that I make an act of faith in his willingness to forgive me for the evil I have done; 3) that at least I fear the punishment which will be mine eternally unless I obtain forgiveness; 4) that I humbly hope for forgiveness; and 5) that as a necessary condition for my forgiveness I promise to make amends to God and to others against whom I may have sinned.

The sacrament of reconciliation is especially intended for those who sin grievously   Grievous sin is a turning away from God in order to find happiness in some pleasure or to seek satisfaction in some way that leaves God out of the picture. In other words, the goal of the sinner cannot coexist with the goal of loving God. Choose one of these goals and the other is automatically canceled out. When, therefore, I sin mortally, I turn completely away from God. In fact, this may not be my explicit intention. Often when a person sins mortally that individual would like to have both: the enjoyment of something sinful and the possession of God. The fact about grievous sin is that you cannot have both. It is one or the other. Either I do God's will or I do my own will in opposition to God's will. If, after sinning grievously, I see that the "perfect good" which I was substituting for God is not so perfect after all, and if I am remorseful and sorry for the mistake and the evil I have done, I can turn again to God as my only perfect good. This is repentance. And if I am truly penitent, truly contrite, I can be forgiven by a God who always loves me, even when I have failed to love him.

Why this sacrament?   This is why Jesus gave his Church the sacrament of reconciliation. Once a sinner has been moved inwardly to sorrow for sins, the sacrament of reconciliation can be approached and God's forgiveness obtained. One must do this with true faith, with sincerity, with humility, and with integrity. I must believe that God wants to forgive me for my sins. I must sincerely seek that forgiveness. I must frankly acknowledge that I am weak and sinful, in need of the support which only God can give me. And I must confess my sins carefully, acknowledging what I have done, the number of times, and any important conditions that existed at the time. Then, I must listen carefully to the priest to whom I am confessing my sins, answer any questions he may ask which can clarify my state of soul, accept the symbolic penance which he imposes, and be attentive to the words of absolution which he recites over me. Leaving the place where my confession has taken place, I am humbly aware that my sins have been forgiven. They are no more. With gratitude I recite the prayers that have been imposed as a sign of my penance or depart to undertake the works which have been given me by the confessor.

As long as I live, there is no sin that I can commit which cannot be pardoned in the sacrament of reconciliation. But here one must be careful to understand that grievous sins which one repeatedly commits after receiving forgiveness in the sacrament of reconciliation can become a sign of one's ingratitude to God. If I promise myself and promise God that I will strive mightily to overcome temptations that will surely arise again, yet quickly fail when the first opportunity presents itself, how can I say that I was truly sorry for grievously offending God? Contempt for sacred things is a great evil. If, then, I quickly turn from the God who has forgiven me and steep myself again in sin, I am probably guilty of contempt. This is especially the case when I soon regret that I have repented of past sins, or if I reject an earlier promise to God to confess my sins. It is also a sign of contempt if I persist in my hatred of others, refusing to grant them forgiveness for wrongs done against me. Everyone sins from carnal weakness. But persistent hatred of others is not a sin of fleshly weakness. It is a deep-rooted evil concerning which we must be constantly on guard.

In the sacrament of reconciliation, God wipes away our sins altogether   But God does not take away our past history. This sacrament cannot destroy the memory of sin. And when I do wrong, even when I am unaware that I am doing wrong, there is a penalty which must be paid. Obviously, if I mistakenly take your textbook and discover that a five dollar bill has been used for a bookmark, I may honestly ask myself: who placed this money in my textbook? If I cannot find out whose money is in my book (since I am still unaware that the book is not mine), I spend the five dollars. Only afterwards do I learn that the book and the five dollars which it contained belong to another student. I must make restitution for the book and for the money. One can give many such examples. The important truth which such examples reveal is that when I do wrong, especially when I recognize that I am doing wrong, but also when I do not recognize this fact, I have to pay a penalty. And here, one comes face to face with one of the deepest mysteries of human life. God can bring good out of evil. If I repent of my sins, I must make amends for them. By doing so I can become better than I would have been otherwise.

St. Gregory the Great, who was bishop of Rome from 590 to 604, once said that "those who have strayed from God may recover their previous losses by subsequent gains," adding that "a general in battle regards more highly that soldier who, after deserting, returns to attack the enemy more bravely, than some other who never turned his back but who never did anything courageously" (Homily XXXIV on the Gospels). The Church has always reverenced St. Mary Magdalene as among its truly outstanding saints for the simple reason that she was a grievous sinner who was forgiven by Jesus, and who became for all of us the perfect model of a sinner who, having been forgiven, falls in love with the God who forgave her.

Venial sins   Besides grievous sin, we are all frequently guilty of venial sin or, as it is sometimes called, "light" sin. Venial sins are failures, usually out of weakness or inattention, which do not substitute some created good for the uncreated good, God.

It is a wearisome fact of life that we are weak and disposed to evil, even to those evils which do not redirect our lives from God to creatures. Even the most generous teacher has moments of weakness and can say things to students which are offensive. All of us have times when we are tired, disappointed, or so concerned with one matter that we neglect others. In such moments, we can fail to perform tasks which are required of us, or we can overlook some kindness that we should perform for another, or we can omit saying prayers which we should recite. Human weakness is so obvious, so universal a fact, that we sin venially almost without thinking about it.

We need constantly to arouse in ourselves the frank desire to do God's will rather than our own. This means that we promise ourselves that we shall take careful, positive steps, to overcome the habits of venial sins into which we so easily fall. One needs to be honest about his or her own weakness. To overcome habits of venial sin, one must address such habits one at a time. Daily self-examination, daily prayer for strength and assistance, daily efforts to do the opposite of that to which one is inclined by a habit of sin, must be the pattern. Especially, one must acknowledge that even to overcome a habit of venial sin is far from easy.

The sacrament of reconciliation is not necessary for those who have committed only venial sins. Devout prayers, the generous assistance to others out of love for God, the fruitful reception of the Eucharist can absolve one of venial sins and, often, of any punishment owing to venial sin. But the sacrament of reconciliation should not be neglected by those who have committed no grievous sins. For in this sacrament, as in all of the sacraments, we come face to face with Jesus Christ who is the source of our forgiveness. To approach this sacrament with humility in the desire to encounter Jesus is a marvelous strengthening against the temptations that constantly arise.

Contrition   When I approach the sacrament of reconciliation, there are three actions which I must perform. We have already seen that these constitute the *matter* of the sacrament. Consider each of them more closely. The first, *contrition,* is internal sorrow for sin, sorrow which is truly expressed to myself, sorrow which is sincere. It implies that I detest the sins which I have committed and that I resolve to do what is necessary to avoid committing them again. In the sacrament of reconciliation, my sorrow or contrition must be supernatural. This contrition, then, must arise from a supernatural motive. If that motive is perfect, I regret having sinned because my sins are offenses against God's love for me and because they block my responding love for God. Sometimes, my contrition is supernatural but imperfect. I have what is properly called "attrition," that is sorrow for sin because I fear the loss of heaven or the sufferings of hell. God's generosity to us is so immeasurable that he does not demand that we have perfect contrition when we receive the sacrament of reconciliation. Imperfect contrition, or "attrition," will suffice.

Confession   The second of the three acts that constitute the *matter* of the sacrament of reconciliation is *confession.* I must tell my personal sins (those committed after baptism and not previously confessed) to a priest. This telling of one's sins is usually done in a "confessional," though it may be done in any convenient place where the confidentiality of the sacrament can be protected. In some critical situations, one is prevented from actually telling his sins to a priest because privacy is impossible, as might be the case when one has been seriously injured in an automobile accident; because of the medical personnel or others attending, one would be unable to recite his sins confidentially. In such cases, one does not have to state his sins but only to indicate that he seeks forgiveness for his sins and is contrite. Should such a penitent

274

recover from the injuries sustained, he is required by the law of the Church to reveal the sins for which he has already been forgiven on the next occasion when he approaches the sacrament of reconciliation.

In confessing sins, one has a critical obligation to inform the priest of grievous sins committed since one's last confession, of the specific evil deeds which one has performed, of the number of times in which one has engaged in these actions, and of any circumstances which might alter the deed that one is confessing. To be specific one must not only confess, for example, that a sin of impurity has been committed; one must confess that the sin was one of self-abuse, fornication, adultery, or homosexuality. While at times it may be difficult to remember the exact number of times that one has committed the same grievous sin, at least an estimate of the number of times must be given: "Through my own fault, I failed to attend Mass on Sundays about four times." And one must admit to circumstances which change the gravity of the action performed: "I stole a large sum of money *from a lady who is poor.*" While a confessor does not want to hear unnecessary details, he is obligated to know precisely what one is confessing in matters of mortal sin.

We are not, however, bound to be so specific when we confess venial sins. It is sufficient that we confess the venial sins which we have committed. There is no need to describe such failures in detail, and it is not required that we enumerate the times when such actions have been performed. Sorrow for all such sins and the humble confession of these failures in general, that is, without enumerating the number of times, is all that is required. Of course, when one is seeking the grace to overcome habits of venial sin, it is well to confess to the priest that the sin is habitual or often committed.

Satisfaction   The *third* of the three actions which comprise the *matter* of this sacrament is *satisfaction.* Christians who understand what the gospels tell us know that the satisfaction for all of our sins was performed by Jesus Christ when he voluntarily, freely gave his life for our sins. Still, we must unite ourselves with Jesus in his passion and death. We do that in each of the seven sacraments, but the awareness of this truth is of special importance to those who approach the sacrament of reconciliation. For in this sacrament, we seek to be associated with Jesus in his suffering for our sins. In fact, we cannot, of ourselves, make adequate satisfaction for the grievous sins which we commit. Through this sacrament, though, we unite ourselves with the satisfaction that Jesus has achieved. When the confessor imposes a penance, we are to accept this small task, whether it is one of saying prayers that are imposed or of doing good deeds that are asked, and unite these works in our hearts and minds with the suffering of Christ. Sometimes, no penance is assigned because the penitent is close to death. Sometimes, too, the priest will impose a token penance and voluntarily undertake to do all or most of the penance himself. This can happen when the penitent is very ill or quite elderly.

Another practice by which a penitent can make satisfaction for the temporal punishment due to personal sin is found in the doctrine of *indulgences.* An indulgence is a remission before God of the temporal punishment due to personal sins that have already been forgiven in the sacrament of Penance. While the personal guilt and eternal punishment of sin is wiped away in sacramental confession, the penitent is bound to the temporal punishment of his sins. For example, a man who murders the father of three children may receive forgiveness for his sin, but in justice he may be bound to support the children. Satisfaction or penances are positive acts the penitent must complete to satisfy for temporal punishment. The Church, by her Christ-given power to bind and loose sins, attaches indulgences to certain positive acts to relieve all or part of temporal punishment. A *partial* indulgence satisfies for a part of the temporal punishment while a *plenary* indulgence satisfies for all of the temporal punishment.

The Church applies indulgences to "major prayers and devotional, penitential, and charitable works" [*The Handbook of Indulgences*, p. 15]. These works, as well as the type of indulgence attached to them, are specified by the Church.

Indulgences are not some sort of magical formula nor a kind of vengeance inflicted by God. Rather, they are among the treasury of gifts and graces that God bestows on his people through the authority and ministry of the Church as a means to salvation. They are effective due to the merits of Christ and the saints who intercede on our behalf with our merciful Father. Additionally, indulgences are not the sum total of the means of satisfaction and reconciliation with God, but part of a greater and uncountable treasury by which satisfaction and reconciliation is achieved. This treasury is linked to the merits of Christ himself, who alone earned our salvation by his Paschal Mystery.

Indulgences may be applied to the living and the dead. Those still living can merit indulgences for themselves by performing positive acts to which indulgences are attached. Those who have died and await their purification in purgatory, however, can no longer perform these positive acts. Still, they can gain the merit of indulgences by those of us living who intentionally apply the merits of our good works to their purification.

When considering indulgences, we must keep in mind the total picture of our reconciliation to God. Our ultimate goal is perfect communion with him, and all our positive acts work together to make us an acceptable sacrifice to him [*Catechism of the Catholic Church*, #1473].

A priest's power to forgive sins   When a priest is ordained, he receives the power to forgive sins through the sacrament of reconciliation. Only a priest (or, of course, a bishop) can administer this sacrament. Because the sacrament is administered in the form of a trial, with the penitent being both the accuser and the accused, while the priest functions as judge, a priest must be authorized to hear confessions. If he has no such authorization, no "faculties," as this authorization is commonly called, he cannot validly administer the sacrament of reconciliation. The law of the Church, however, allows any priest, even one who has given up the priestly ministry, to hear confessions of someone who is in danger of death.

When a priest receives in writing from the bishop of a diocese the authorization to hear confessions, he may exercise the office of confessor anywhere. Of course, for unusual and serious reasons, the priest can be restricted by the bishop, but normally this is not done. Commonly, priests have general faculties. If the priest does not belong to a diocese but instead is a member of a religious order, he also must have in writing the authorization to hear confessions from the bishop of a diocese. Of course, another bishop may forbid a priest to hear confessions within the territory of his diocese. In such a case, the attempt to hear confessions would be invalid. Religious superiors can give "faculties" to priests of their orders or congregations to hear confessions in any houses of their orders. But, like the bishop of a diocese, they can restrict this right for serious reasons.

Confessional seal   The "seal" of confession is an ancient practice of the Church, officially dating back more than seven hundred years. The recent revision of the universal law of the Church did not change this most sacred, extraordinarily serious legislation. The law of the Church says:

> The sacramental seal is inviolable. Accordingly, it is absolutely wrong for a confessor in any way to betray the penitent, for any reason whatsoever, whether by word or in any other fashion.
>
> An interpreter, if there is one, is also obliged to observe this secret, as are all others who in any way whatever have come to a knowledge of sins from a confession (Canon 983).

So serious is this law of the Church that one who knowingly violates the seal of confession is severely penalized. A priest who breaks the seal of confession is by that very fact excommunicated. He may not celebrate any of the sacraments and he may not receive the sacraments, unless he is in danger of death, until his case has been heard by the Holy See. If a priest violates the seal indirectly or accidentally, he is to be punished with a penalty that is determined by the gravity of his offense. Others who violate the seal of the confessional "are to be punished with a just penalty, not excluding excommunication" (Canon 1388). If, then, I have accidentally heard another person's confession of sins and I reveal this to a third person, I must confess this grievous violation of a most sacred law of the Church. The penance I receive will be severe and, if I have done serious injury to another, I can be excommunicated. In fact, no practice of the Church is more carefully observed, more diligently guarded, or more obediently observed by priests than the law of the sacred seal of the confessional.

ANOINTING THE SICK

The anointing of the sick, in earlier days called "extreme unction," is the fifth of the seven sacraments. This sacrament can be administered to those who are seriously ill, whether or not their illness is terminal. Because the purpose of this sacred rite is to strengthen a sick person during the trial which sickness brings, and, at times, to restore the sick person to good health, the sacrament is one of the great treasures of the Church.

Protestants agree that the Church has a special ministry to those who are ill. But, because in their view the New Testament does not have clear, undeniable texts that speak of this sacrament, they do not believe that there is such a sacred rite. Prayers for those who are ill, however, and the demonstration of unselfish Christian love and concern are paramount features of the Protestant ministry.

New Testament verifications   Catholics believe that St. Mark's gospel has a kind of reference to the ritual or sacrament of anointing. When Jesus sends his twelve apostles to preach and heal the sick, St. Mark adds: "With that [the Twelve] went off, preaching the need of repentance. They expelled many demons, anointed the sick with oil, and worked many cures" (Mk. 6:12-13 NAB). This report occurs in an early passage of St. Mark's gospel, before Jesus had established the Eucharist and before he had ordained the apostles as priests. But the passage certainly foreshadows one of the important ministries which will be given to the apostles and their successors. In any event, there is a very clear reference to the use of this sacrament in the Letter of James (which many Protestants do not accept as part of the inspired writings of the New Testament). "Is there anyone sick among you? He should ask for the presbyters of the church. They in turn are to pray over him, anointing him with oil in the Name of the Lord. This prayer uttered in faith will reclaim the one who is ill, and the Lord will restore him to health. If he has committed any sins, forgiveness will be his" (Jas. 5:14-15 NAB).

Essential parts of the sacrament   Because every sacrament is an outward sign, we again ask the question, "What is the *matter* and what is the *form* of this sacrament?" The matter of the anointing of the sick is the imposition of oil on the forehead and on the hands. The oil that is used is customarily olive oil, but any suitable oil taken from a plant which produces an oil that is similar to the oil of the olive plant may be used. Tracing the form of a cross on the forehead and upon the hands, the priest follows the unbroken custom, as we see in the citation from St. James, of imposing pure oil on the person who is sick. The oil used is called the "Oil of the Infirm," and it is blessed for the purpose of anointing the sick. Usually the diocesan bishop blesses it when he blesses the oils of the Church at the Chrism Mass on Holy Thursday. When necessary, however, the priest himself blesses the oil as part of the Rite of Anointing.

The *form* of the sacrament is the words recited by the priest as he is anointing the forehead and the hands of a sick person: "Through this holy anointing may the Lord in his love and mercy help you with the grace of the Holy Spirit. Amen. May the Lord who frees you from sin save you and raise you up. Amen." Part of the effect of this sacrament is conditional. While the inner or spiritual effects surely take place in anyone who receives the sacrament worthily, the physical healing that can occur depends on the will of God for the person receiving the sacrament. The possible effects of this sacrament greatly strengthen the ill person. Usually the loved ones present at the anointing receive comfort and consolation, too.

Recipients of anointing   As the very name implies, this sacrament should be administered to those who are ill. The illness from which one suffers should be serious. This is not to say that one's illness must be critical or that one must be in proximate danger of death. If I have a mild case of the flu or a common cold or a broken leg, I cannot receive this sacrament. The Church teaches that one's condition must be serious. Accordingly, one who is to undergo surgery because of a dangerous condition should be anointed. If there is doubt about the patient's condition, the doubt should be resolved in favor of the patient, though consultation with a knowledgeable doctor is surely warranted.

The Church teaches that there is one clear exception to this general understanding about the proper recipient of the sacrament of the anointing of the sick. "Anointing can be performed on the elderly who are greatly weakened in strength, even though no dangerous illness is apparent." Those who suffer from debility because of their advancing years may validly receive this sacrament often. Obviously, those who are quite elderly are coming close to the end of their lives. While it is true that some may live for ten, or fifteen, or even twenty more years, the majority will not. To strengthen them spiritually, and perhaps even physically, the Church asks that they receive the sacrament from time to time.

Even children who are dangerously ill may receive the sacrament of anointing validly. However, the recipient must have reached the age of reason. Even if a child has committed no grievous sins, in dire illness the child should be anointed. Through this sacrament, God can strengthen the child spiritually for the ordeal through which the child must pass. And, if God chooses to do so, the child can be restored to health through this holy rite.

At times, a priest is asked to anoint someone who has fallen into unconsciousness. He may readily do this if it is presumed that the person would have asked for the sacrament had the seriousness of the illness been manifest. And if the unconscious person has the right dispositions, the sacrament will absolve him from all sins. Moreover, God may use this opportunity to restore the person to consciousness and even to good health. But what of a person who has just died? If it is clear and certain that a person is dead, he may not be anointed, since all of the sacraments are for the living. But if there is doubt whether the sick person has actually died, the priest should administer the sacrament of anointing conditionally, that is, the priest says, in one way or another, "If you are still alive, then through this holy anointing . . ."

Sacramental strength   The administration of every sacrament, even the sacraments of reconciliation and of anointing, are occasions of joy for those who receive the sacraments, for those who administer them, and for those who assist. Accordingly, the Church prefers that the sacrament of anointing be solemnized. This does not mean that the priest or others participating should overlook the attitude or the preferences of the sick person who is to be anointed. Often, the person who is ill will want to receive this sacrament quietly, with only a few people in attendance. But at times, the sick person will accept the invitation to solemnize the sacrament, that is, to administer the rite during the celebration of the Eucharist. When so performed, the anointing of the sick is administered following the reading of the gospel and the homily. In this way, the sick person can also receive Viaticum, and should receive the body and blood of Jesus under the forms of both bread and wine.

All of God's gifts to us are gracious   All of them draw us toward eternity, toward an endless life of absolute happiness in his presence. Each of the sacraments is a gentle, marvelous blessing by which God tries to draw us away from the allurements of sin and toward himself. Clearly, that is the purpose of the lovely sacrament which we call the anointing of the sick. When we are suffering, those among our friends and neighbors who are gentle of heart and who are generous reach out to assist us. We are forever grateful to those who are so selfless in assisting us in time of need. Yet Almighty God is our closest friend, our most selfless, most generous lover. When we think carefully about his gifts, we are especially moved by the generosity of his gift which we call the anointing of the sick.

Thinking it over • • •

1. What good does it do for me to admit that I am a sinner?

2. What was Jesus' attitude toward sinners? Which of the four gospels gives the best evidence for your answer?

3. Do all Christians accept the sacrament of reconciliation or, as it is also called, the sacrament of penance? Explain.

4. What is the *matter* of the sacrament of reconciliation? What is the *form*?

5. Are there individuals who can be saved without the sacrament of reconciliation? Who are they?

6. Explain what is meant by grievous sin.

7. What are some of the indications that one has in gratitude to God?

8. What must I do to overcome the habits of venial sin?

9. What are the three actions which comprise the matter of the sacrament of reconciliation? Briefly explain each.

10. What is "attrition"?

11. If I have grievous or mortal sins to confess, I must be specific. What does this mean?

12. What is the purpose of the satisfaction which we must make for the sins that we confess in the sacrament of reconciliation?

13. What is meant by the "seal" of confession? How seriously is this practice to be taken?

14. To whom can the sacrament of the anointing of the sick be validly administered?

15. Why do Protestants deny that there is such a rite as the anointing of the sick?

16. In what two books of the New Testament do we find texts which imply that there is such a rite as the anointing of the sick? Which of these is the more important? Why?

17. One should be seriously ill to receive this sacrament. But there is one notable exception to that understanding. What is it?

18. May a priest administer the sacrament of anointing to someone who is unconscious?

Chapter 5

HOLY ORDERS AND MATRIMONY

While all of the sacraments except the sacrament of reconciliation are publicly and joyously celebrated, the last two of the seven Christian rites of worship are called "social" because they directly affect the society which is the Church. We shall consider the sacrament of marriage, one of these two sacraments, after studying the other, the sacrament of holy orders.

Priesthood–Old Testament   Jesus Christ is now and will forever be the only true and perfect priest. There were priests in the Jewish religion, to be sure. Aaron, brother of Moses, and his sons were ordained priests at the command of God:

> Aaron and his sons you shall also bring to the entrance of the meeting tent, and there wash them with water. Take the vestments and clothe Aaron with the tunic, the robe of ephod, the ephod itself, and the breastpiece, fastening the embroidered belt of the ephod around him. Put the miter on his head, the sacred diadem on the miter. Then take the anointing oil and anoint him with it, pouring it on his head. Bring forward his sons also and clothe them with the tunics, gird them with the sashes, and tie the turbans on them. Thus shall the priesthood be theirs by perpetual law, and thus shall you ordain Aaron and his sons.
>
> –Exodus 29:4-9 NAB

The priestly class has disappeared from the Jewish religion largely because of the destruction of the Temple at Jerusalem in 70 A.D. Since the Jews were allowed to worship God with sacrifice only in the Temple, and because sacrifice could be offered there only by the descendants of Aaron, the ritual of sacrifice and the Jewish priesthood no longer exist in Jewish observances.

Priesthood–New Testament   Christians believe that the Jewish religion was a foreshadowing and a preparation for the coming of the Messiah, Jesus Christ. He is the perfect priest and his priesthood fulfills and brings to perfection the priesthood of Aaron and his descendants. Because of the absolute perfection of his priesthood, Jesus is the one and only mediator between God and the human race. Being truly God and truly man, he alone can perfectly represent the Godhead and humanity and so restore what Adam lost: our supernatural living with God. This truth is a key to everything that Christians believe. With Adam's fall from the intimate, loving relationship that he had with God, we are all born as Adam's sons and daughters without the title to friendship with God. The absence of this friendship is original sin. Because the title, the claim to friendly, loving relationship with God is supernatural, it is above and beyond human nature to reclaim. In other words, it is *beyond the natural,* super-natural; that is, there is nothing in the human nature with which we were born that is capable of going beyond itself, beyond the natural, beyond the nature that we have. If Jesus were only a man, he could not reach to the supernatural because he has the same nature that you and I have. But because he is also God, he is able to do what you and I cannot do by ourselves.

We must insist on this truth. Jesus is not a human person. He is in very truth a man because he has a human nature as each of us does. Because the human nature that is his is united with his divine personality, he cannot also be a human person. Were he to be both a divine person and a human person, he would be two persons, not one. Now, since he is a man like us in everything but sin, he perfectly represents us. Since he is a divine person, he perfectly represents God. This is why all Christians understand that only Jesus Christ is the perfect mediator, the perfect priest, standing between God and mankind. Perfectly, he belongs to both, to the Godhead and to mankind.

Other priests?   Catholics, Orthodox, and Anglicans differ from other Christians on the issue of whether there are other priests. Largely because of grievous abuses by some Catholic bishops and priests, Martin Luther dismissed the priesthood as an element in the Christian religion. For the same reason he argued that the Eucharistic sacrifice, the Mass, was a Roman development without foundation in Sacred Scripture. He claimed that since Jesus died once for all of us, the Mass is unnecessary, and if the Mass is unnecessary, so is the priesthood. Jesus Christ, Luther argued, is our only priest through whom we worship God the Father and through whom we obtain redemption for our sins.

But the Catholics, Orthodox, and Anglicans believed that Martin Luther went too far in his attempts to remedy the Church of its excesses and serious defects. Consequently, when the Council of Trent considered the sacrament of holy orders, it made a number of *ex cathedra* pronouncements to correct the mistakes which had been made by Protestant leaders. It taught the following:

> There is a visible, external priesthood in the New Testament which has the power of consecrating and offering the body and blood of the Lord and of remitting and retaining sins (Denzinger 961).
>
> Orders or holy ordination is truly and properly a sacrament instituted by Christ the Lord; it is more than a kind of rite for the choosing of ministers of the word of God and the sacraments (Denz. 963).

In the sacrament of holy orders a character is imprinted so that once a man is ordained he can never truly become a layman again (Denz. 964).

In the Catholic Church there is a divinely instituted hierarchy which consists of bishops, priests, and ministers [deacons] (Denz. 966).

Even as Jesus Christ came not to be served but to serve others, the sacrament of holy orders is given to certain individuals to emulate Christ and to be of service to others. The Christian priesthood, fundamentally, is a work of serving the members of the Church. In the late Middle Ages and at the time of the Protestant Reformation, Catholic bishops and priests in large numbers had lost sight of this fundamental truth. Bishops had become lordly, many of them leading the lives of the extremely wealthy. They did not see their office as roles of service; rather, they expected to be served; and their princely lives were supported through an egregious system of taxes which the ordinary citizen was expected to pay. So outlandish were the lives of some Catholic leaders that one wonders why a critical rupture did not occur before the time of Martin Luther.

Calling bishops and priests back to a way of life more in keeping with the clear teaching of the New Testament, the Council of Trent also stigmatized those who went too far in the opposite direction. In the view of the Council, it is one thing to correct abuses; it is another to destroy altogether that which is being abused. The priesthood of Christ is shared by certain men who are summoned to a life of simplicity and of dedicated service. In a special manner, the ministers of the Church are asked to imitate Jesus in their lives and in their work.

Three degrees of Holy Orders   By virtue of Baptism, all the faithful share in the priesthood of Jesus Christ. The faithful exercise their baptismal priesthood by sharing in the mission of Christ according to their various states in life. This participation is called the "common priesthood of the faithful." Distinct from the common priesthood of the faithful is the ministerial or hierarchical priesthood of Holy Orders. Ordained priesthood differs from the common priesthood in that Holy Orders sets men apart by the laying on of hands to build up and serve the Church. Ordained men are singled out to teach, govern, and sanctify the faithful. From ancient times, ordained ministry in the Church has been exercised in three degrees: bishops, priests, and deacons. Bishops and priests participate in the ministerial priesthood of Christ, while deacons help and serve them in the exercise of their priesthood.

Bishops receive the fullness of Holy Orders. They are the successors of the Apostles and members of the episcopal college. Acting collegially under the authority and leadership of the Pope, the bishops teach, govern, and sanctify the Church universal. Each bishop is also the visible head of the particular diocese entrusted to him. With the fullness of Holy Orders, bishops administer *all* of the Seven Sacraments.

Priests are ordained to be co-workers of the bishops. They are entrusted, in varying degrees, with the apostolic mission of the Church under the direction of their bishops. Priests are the extension of their bishops' authority and ministry into the various parishes and institutions of their dioceses. As co-workers of the bishops, priests are also concerned with the universal mission of preaching the Gospel, celebrating the Eucharist, and saving souls. Priests do not participate in the fullness of Holy Orders and are, therefore, regular ministers of only five of the sacraments. They may not administer the sacrament of Confirmation, except in emergency situations, and they can never validly administer the sacrament of Holy Orders.

Deacons are ordained not to the priesthood, but to the ministry of service to the Church. Deacons are ordained in order to serve the other members of the

Church in imitation of the humble service of Christ. They are singled out by the laying on of hands. Deacons are responsible to participate and lead the faithful in performing the corporal and spiritual works of mercy. They exercise and direct the charitable and social ministries of the Church. Sacramentally, deacons assist bishops and priests during the Mass, distribute Holy Communion, proclaim and preach the Gospel, witness and bless marriages, and preside over funerals.

The unique vocation of priests So special a calling as the priesthood requires a special strengthening because it is given to a man for life. This is why the Church teaches that this sacrament imprints a character on the soul of the man who is ordained. Through this sacred marking, which is indelible, the deacon, or priest, or bishop, receives God's pledge of the special grace that is necessary to discharge worthily his service to others. Because the sacramental character in this sacrament, as in baptism and confirmation, is ineradicable, a man can only be ordained once to the diaconate or the priesthood or the episcopacy. Of course, an individual who has been ordained can sin grievously and so fall from God's grace, but even in the state of mortal sin the sacramental character of holy orders remains. Through the sacrament of reconciliation, the sinful deacon, priest, bishop can return to God's grace. When he does so, the special graces of the sacrament of holy orders are restored to the sinner because of his sacramental character.

Unlike the other sacraments which are intended for all of the faithful according to their needs, the sacrament of holy orders is not offered to everyone. Only those who are called to this sacrament may receive it licitly. How is one called? Interiorly, a man is attracted to the priestly office in ways that are impossible to define. One young man's interest may be sparked by a priest whom he admires and who offers him encouragement. Another may be asked directly to consider the possibility of studying for the priesthood by a more mature Catholic or by a priest. A man whose wife has died and whose children are grown and independent may want to spend the remainder of his life in priestly service to others. In each of these instances, and in countless others, God works quietly, almost secretly, in those whom he calls. After long, careful preparation, the candidate for the diaconate or the priesthood stands before a bishop in the ceremony of ordination. Early in the ceremony, the bishop interrogates the candidates, asks those assembled whether anyone objects to the ordination of the candidate (or candidates), and then formally *calls* the candidate to ordination. This is why we speak of "vocations," which is the English version of the Latin term *vocatio,* a calling. The sacrament of holy orders is bestowed on those who are called. The sacrament is not offered to all.

An unbroken teaching of the Catholic Church is that only those who are male can be ordained

Any attempt to administer this sacrament to a woman would be invalid. Jesus called only males to leadership in the ministry which he established. Until the contemporary period, there was hardly any disagreement about this fact or its meaning. With the increasing concern of society's leaders that the oppression and subservience of women be discontinued and that serious inequities in society be corrected, it is not surprising that many men and women believe that the restriction of the sacrament of holy orders to males is old fashioned and out of keeping with the rising disapproval of the oppression of women. To restrict the sacrament of holy orders to men seems to some a continuation of male chauvinism. The Church sanctions those movements which oppose the unjust oppression of anyone, especially of women. At the same time, the Church affirms repeatedly, consistently, that the sacrament of holy orders cannot be validly received by a woman.

Just as the sacrament of the anointing of the sick cannot validly be received by one who is not ill, so the sacrament of holy orders cannot validly be received by one who is not a male. This is not, the Church affirms, misogyny or antifeminism. It is rather a recognition that God has assigned different roles, different functions for men and women in society. God establishes a profound difference between the sexes for the building up of the Mystical Body of Christ. Men and women have distinctive contributions to make and everyone is asked to make a contribution in keeping with God's plan. The principal contribution of women is motherhood, not only in the giving of birth but especially in the nourishing of others. No one exemplifies this better than Mary, the mother of Jesus, whom Jesus gave to us as a mother. The kind of maternal love which she exemplifies is her mission. Women especially are asked by God to pattern their lives and works on the life of Mary. The service of all in the position of leadership, however, is a mission that God offers to some men.

But not to all   Only a few, a very few, are called to serve the rest. To be called, one must not only be a baptized male but must have other qualities which are required for the lawful (licit) reception of this sacrament. First, he must be in the state of grace. Of course, one can be validly ordained while in the state of serious sin. In such a case, the sacramental character is imprinted on the soul, but one does not receive sanctifying grace. Indeed, one commits a sin of sacrilege by knowingly receiving the sacrament while already in the state of sin. At so sacred a moment as one's ordination, nothing could be more important in the individual's preparation than the supernatural gifts which fill the soul of him who is in the state of grace.

Right intention   Second, the candidate for holy orders must have the right intention. This means that one should not present himself for ordination out of the desire for personal gain, the assurance of financial support, the social esteem among those with whom he lives and works, or any such worldly consideration. To be a deacon or priest one gives himself selflessly, most generously to the spiritual welfare of those to whom he is sent.

3. As worthy as possible   The third condition, then, follows on the second. One called to priestly service must intend to be as worthy as a sinner can be. The candidate must have succeeded in the practice of virtue. He must be chaste. He must have proven to himself that he can lead a life of chastity, overcoming the temptations against this virtue which constantly arise, especially in the lives of younger men. He must have proven to himself that he can accept the directions of others in a spirit of obedience which he aspires to model on the obedience of Jesus. Most especially, he must be a man of charity, a generous person who commits himself without self-seeking to the welfare of others.

4. Called by God   The fourth condition is that he must have assured himself and others that he has a vocation, a calling, from Almighty God. The Letter to the Hebrews speaks of this qualification:

> Every high priest is taken from among men and made their representative before God, to offer gifts and sacrifices for sins. He is able to deal patiently with erring sinners, for he himself is beset by weakness and so must make sin offerings for himself as well as for the people. One does not take this honor on his own initiative, but only when called by God as Aaron was (Heb. 5:1-4 NAB).

How does one know that he is called by God? Interiorly, God moves each of us gently toward his purposes. One first finds an interest in priestly service, begins to pray about it, does a bit of quiet reading, and eventually seeks the counsel of a close friend, perhaps of a priest, a religious brother, a religious sister on whose advice or counsel he has come to rely. Eventually, he discusses the possibility with parents and other family members. If he is encouraged, or even sometimes when he is not, he continues to reflect and to pray. To be sure, there is no exact pattern, for God works in each of us differently. One who is convinced that he should pursue the matter further, however, should apply to the diocese or the religious order in which he has become interested. These organizations have programs that are offered to those who apply. They offer wise counsel, step-by-step leading the candidate to those decisions which he alone must make. Sometimes, a diocese or order will advise a candidate that he should not pursue the priestly vocation. In the end, the prayer of the candidate, if humble and sincere, will lead him to a clearer understanding of the work and form of life to which God is gently calling him.

Other Church requirements   Besides these four conditions for the lawful reception of holy orders, which can easily be seen as God's loving law for each of us, the Church has added several requirements. Besides the need for suitable letters of recommendation from responsible men and women, and beyond the requirement that one have medical examinations of both physical and psychological matters, the Church requires that the candidate for the diaconate who also wants to be ordained to the priesthood (the so-called "transitional" diaconate) must be twenty-three years of age. A man to be ordained to the priesthood must be at least twenty-five years old.

Before ordination, the candidate must have completed university studies and received a bachelor's degree, and then he must spend additional years in the graduate study of philosophy, theology, and allied fields. Almost every diocese or religious order requires a candidate to work full-time as a deacon in a Catholic parish or in a similar Catholic setting for an extended period of time, usually six months to a year. At the conclusion of this assignment, the deacon must make a retreat for at least five days preparatory to receiving ordination to the priesthood.

Impediments to holy orders The Church has established certain "impediments" which bar a man from receiving holy orders. Some of these are quite technical and require a careful study of the Church's law. In general, however, those may not be ordained who:

1) suffer from serious mental illness;
2) have apostasized, been guilty of public heresy, or joined a schismatic church;
3) have committed a homicide or been intimately involved in an abortion;
4) attempted suicide or maliciously mutilated himself or another; or
5) pretended publicly to be a bishop, priest, or deacon.

Moreover, those who are married (unless they seek the permanent diaconate), those who hold civil office, and those who are responsible for the civil administration of the good of another, may not be accepted as candidates for the priesthood. Should a man's wife die, however, or should he set aside the administrative duties which bind him in civil law, he can then be considered as an applicant for the priesthood. The Church also bans those who are new converts to the Catholic faith from acceptance into a seminary or religious order, though occasionally a bishop or major religious superior can grant a dispensation from this prohibition.

Only an ordained bishop can validly administer the sacrament of holy orders This is the only sacrament where no exception is possible. We have seen that a bishop is the normal or usual minister in the solemn celebration of confirmation and in the consecration of the holy oils used in the sacraments.

Under certain conditions, a priest can be allowed to confirm or to bless the holy oils. But no exceptions are made in the sacrament of holy orders. For validity, an ordained bishop must be the minister of the sacrament. Attend the rite of ordination and you will notice that after the bishop all priests who are present, one by one, impose their hands on the head of the newly ordained. This is not essential to the rite of ordination but is rather a symbol of the unity of the priesthood, since all who are ordained priests share the one priesthood of Jesus. The bishop alone, however, confers the sacrament of holy orders.

The absolute and unbroken practice of ordination by a bishop underscores a special relationship that priests share with their bishops. On the one hand, priests share with the bishops in the dignity of ordained priesthood. At the same time, the bishops alone exercise the fullness of priestly dignity, and the ordained priests depend on their bishops in the exercise of the sacerdotal ministry. Ordained priests are co-workers with their bishops, caring for and ministering to the faithful under the direction and leadership of the bishop.

The matter and form of Holy Orders   Holy Orders is conferred by the laying on of hands by a validly ordained bishop. In each degree of orders, deacon, priest or bishop, the bishop imposes his hands on the head of the candidate being ordained. This imposition of hands is the essential act of ordination, thus comprising the matter of this sacrament.

The form of Holy Orders is a solemn prayer of consecration that a bishop says over the candidate being ordained. There is a different prayer of consecration for the deacon, priest and bishop. Each prayer invokes the Holy Spirit to bestow upon the candidate those special gifts and graces necessary for the exercise of that particular office.

Prerequisite ministries   The Church requires that all who present themselves for the order of diaconate or priesthood must first have been installed in two offices of ministry that are stepping stones to the sacrament itself. These offices are bestowed by a bishop or by a major superior of a religious order on those who belong to his community. The offices of reader (or lector) and acolyte are closely associated with the celebration of the Eucharist, the principal ministry of both deacon and priest. Those installed as readers should be well-trained in the public proclamation of the Sacred Scriptures and should be prepared to undertake this ministry with great respect and in a spirit of service to others. Men who are installed as acolytes must have demonstrated a great reverence for the Holy Eucharist. By this office, they are allowed to administer communion to others when a priest or deacon is not available. They can readily be delegated to bring communion to those who are unable to join a congregation in the celebration of the Eucharistic mysteries.

"Once a priest, always a priest"   Due to the sacramental character of holy orders, one can never be ordained a second time because one can never lose the spiritual change which has occurred in him. Everyone is a sinner, of course, and a priest is no exception. Yet the priest is accorded specific graces by Almighty God through the sacrament of holy orders so that, being assisted in a special manner to overcome the temptations that face all of us, he can be of humble assistance to others. Truly, this sacrament is social. It is given only to some but it fortifies them with God's unique assistance for the welfare of others. Seeking the benefits of God for other men and women, a priest must give himself without qualification to this often difficult, arduous task. Surely it is for this reason, only one among many, that God sanctifies a deacon, a priest, and especially a bishop with an indelible mark, a character that strengthens him through his own cooperation for his work among others.

MATRIMONY

Even those who do not believe that Jesus Christ is the promised Messiah and that he is God are impressed with the story that St. John relates early in his gospel. The marriage feast at Cana, if one reflects carefully on the details given by St. John, reveals important elements about Jesus and what he taught. For a moment think about a few of the facts in this story. Jesus goes to a very human and joyous celebration. After the Jewish celebration of marriage, one of the loveliest rituals of religion, he joins others in human festivities. Jesus' mother is also there. St. John does not say this but it is obvious that she is helping with the observance, trying to see that everyone is having a good time, enjoying food and drink, warmed by the presence of friends. But Mary discovers that the groom and his bride are about to be embarrassed. The wine used in the celebration is almost gone. What should she do? Since Mary is a poor woman, and because we presume that St. Joseph was dead, she could only turn to her Son. She does this, and she does it quietly.

One can hear her whispering to him, whispering because she does not want to upset others, whispering because she does not want to compromise Jesus. He whispers back: "Woman, how does this concern of yours involve me? My hour has not yet come" (Jn. 2:4 NAB). Certainly, Jesus does his best to suppress the smile that is playing at the corners of his mouth. Obviously, he makes this remark to his mother with eyes twinkling. So Mary goes to the waiters and says simply, "Do whatever he tells you" (Jn. 2:5 NAB). Immediately, Jesus moves quietly into action. To the waiters he says, "Fill those jars with water" (Jn. 2:7 NAB). Each of the jars held up to twenty-five gallons.

St. John offers little explanation of the waiters' response. Perhaps grum-bling, yet urged by Jesus' quiet but commanding presence, they do as he tells them. "Now," he said, "draw some out and take it to the waiter in charge" (Jn. 2:8 NAB). Obliging Jesus, they bring a sample to the chief steward. Mystified, he samples what has been brought to him, though St. John is careful to note that he did not know what it was or where it had come from. Delighted with the wine he had tasted, he still reproached the groom: why would anyone save the finest wine until lesser wine had been exhausted?

Reflection on Cana   We reflect on this narrative at length because marriage is in the Christian view a marvelous rite, a very social sacrament. Catholics enter marriage in a sacred rite, whether it is celebrated simply or with solemnity, and then joyously celebrate the sacramental union of a man and a woman with their relatives and friends. Just as the sacrament of holy orders is a social sacrament that is celebrated for the good of him who is ordained but also, and especially, for the good of others, so marriage is a public, societal celebration, a rite of joy. Few celebrations are of greater importance to the Church than the joyous observance of marriage, both in the sacred ceremonies themselves and in the Cana-like observances that follow immediately.

Why is this observance so sacred and so joyous to the Christian faithful? The best answer to that question is given by St. Paul:

"For this reason a man shall leave his father and mother, / and shall cling to his wife, / and the two shall be made into one" This a great foreshadowing; I mean that it refers to Christ and the Church. (Eph. 5:31-32 NAB)

Marriage is at once a human celebration and a sacred observance   After the solemnities and the reception are concluded, the bride and groom are thenceforward united to one another in the most intimate union that is possible in this life. And in this most personal union, the bride and groom live a life that is a sign, a symbol of the union which Christ has with each of us.

The nature of conjugal love   The bond of love shared by husband and wife is called *conjugal* love. Conjugal love involves the giving of the total person, body, mind, soul and emotion, to the spouse. Conjugal love is not merely a contract whereby each party gives a certain percentage to the other. Rather, it is a total giving of oneself to the spouse without regard to percentages or cost. The key elements of conjugal love are *unity, indissolubility, fidelity,* and openness to *procreation.*

Unity   In teaching the Pharisees on marriage, Jesus declared:

> Have you not read that at the beginning the Creator made them male and female and declared, 'For this reason a man shall leave his father and mother and cling to his wife, and the two shall become as one'? Thus they are no longer two but one flesh. (Matthew 19: 4-6 NAB)

By these words Jesus teaches us that the union of husband and wife is the deepest relationship between two human beings on earth. It is two people becoming "one flesh," coming together as two bodies of water merging into one. This union involves a lifelong process of the spouses sharing their lives through mutual self-giving. Furthermore, it is a union willed by God himself, and brought about through the grace of Jesus Christ, who is the third partner in every Christian marriage. Sacramentally, the union of husband and wife is solemn because it is a sign of Christ's union with his Mystical Body, the Church.

Indissolubility   Indissolubility means that the marriage bond is permanent. Most of us are familiar with the words, "till death do you part" which refer to matrimony. They mean simply that the bond of

Christian marriage is permanent until the death of one of the spouses. No human authority can change that, since Christian marriage is willed and brought about by God. The teaching of Jesus is very clear on this point:

> Therefore let no man separate what God has joined . . . Whoever divorces his wife and marries another commits adultery against her; and the woman who divorces her husband and marries another commits adultery (Mk. 10: 9-12 NAB).

There is no equivocation in our Lord's words. Marriage is intended by God to be indissoluble, so much so that divorce and remarriage lead to adultery. This precept is for the good not only of the spouses and their children, but also of the Church. If Christian marriage is a sign of Christ's love for and union with the Church, then spouses can no more leave each other than Christ can leave his Church. Thus it is a lifelong commitment and responsibility of the spouses to continually work together to maintain and develop their marital union.

But what of the prevalence of divorce and remarriage in our society today? As the Church teaches, in fidelity to the words of Christ we studied above, Christian marriage is a lifelong union. Therefore, the Church does not recognize civil divorce of a valid Christian marriage. Rather, the Church encourages married couples to use the many resources available to couples in distress to help them maintain a healthy marriage bond.

In some cases a husband and wife living together becomes impractical for a variety of reasons. In these situations, the Church permits physical separation of the couple, recognizing that they are still married before God. While the couple is living apart, neither party is free to relinquish the marriage bond and pursue a sexual or marital relationship with another party.

Despite the teaching of the Church, many couples validly married in the eyes of the Church still obtain a civil divorce. In these cases the Church again is very clear. While they may have been divorced in the eyes of *civil* law, they are still validly married in the Church and are not free to pursue another marriage, even civilly. Those couple who divorce and remarry after being validly married in the Church place themselves in a situation that objectively contravenes Divine law. In such cases, the Catholic parties, while not totally separated from the Church, are nevertheless unable to receive Holy Communion. They are encouraged to reconcile themselves to God and the Church morally and sacramentally with the help of a priest. In the case of those Catholics who were validly married then civilly divorced but not remarried, the Catholic parties are still free to receive Holy Eucharist.

Fidelity Along with indissolubility, fidelity is another important element of marriage. If spouses are to become "one flesh" and remain so until death, it follows that they must be faithful to each other to achieve so intimate a union. In marriage, the spouses open themselves to each other in the deepest way humanly possible. For two people to give themselves over to each other completely as demanded in marriage, unwavering trust is essential. Nothing shatters that trust more than infidelity or adultery. Nothing shatters the communion of family life more than spousal infidelity or adultery. And, adultery is not limited to physical act of unlawful sexual union. Jesus said, "You have heard the commandment, 'You shall not commit adultery.' What I say to you is: anyone who looks lustfully at a woman has already committed adultery with her in his thoughts" (Mt. 5:27-28 NAB). Thus, it is important in marriage to be faithful in all matters that count: one's sexual expression, thoughts, affections, inspirations, and aspirations.

Procreation   Finally, marriage is ordered by God for the continuation of the human race.

> God created man in his image; / in the divine image he created him; / and female he created them. / God blessed them, saying: "Be fertile and multiply; fill the earth and subdue it" (Gn. 1: 27-28 NAB).

This is the passage of the Old Testament Jesus alluded to when he instructed the Pharisees on marriage. From the beginning of time, the union of man and woman in marriage has been ordained by God for the continuation of the human race. Therefore, every Christian marriage must be open to procreation. Every spouse in Christian marriage must be willing to bring forth and rear children. We know that procreation, for biological or medical reasons, may not be possible for all married couples. God does not bless every marriage with children. Yet, it is necessary that every couple that enters into Christian marriage be *open* to children if that is God's will for them.

When considering the procreative norm of Christian marriage, we must not neglect the importance of family life. Jesus himself, when he willed to become man, willed to do so within the environment of family life. He did not arrive on earth fully mature, but was born of the Virgin Mary whose husband was St. Joseph. And by their life as a family, Jesus, Mary and Joseph together sanctified family life and modeled Christian perfection in family life.

The Church's procreative norm is not just ordered to childbirth. Rather, it includes education and formation of the children in the faith of the Church. The family is both the basic unit of society and the domestic Church, and as such is the image of the Blessed Trinity. It is in the family that children learn the knowledge, values and skills that will determine their quality of membership in society and the Church for fathers are the first and primary educators of their children, and their influence is essential, teaching by word *and* example. The home is the first school of Christian life, characterized "by the reception of the sacraments, prayer and thanksgiving, witness of a holy life, self-denial and active charity" [*Lumen Gentium,* 10].

In the passage to the Ephesians cited above, the apostle is writing to Christians. But marriage exists for those who are not Christians as well as for those who actively believe in Christ. Often Catholics are uncertain about the Church's attitude toward marriages which are celebrated between men and women who are not Catholic. Are such people truly married in the eyes of the Church? Is there a sacrament of marriage for those who are not Catholic? What if a Catholic marries a Protestant? What if a Christian weds a non-Christian? Does the Catholic Church recognize such marriages as valid?

Matter and form of marriage   In part, the answer to these questions will be given when one considers the *matter* and the *form* of the sacrament of matrimony. And in part, the answers will be given by reflecting on certain conclusions that flow from this knowledge. To begin, the *matter* of this sacrament is a mutual offering between a bride and groom of dominion over each other's body in those things that pertain to the begetting and rearing of children and in those matters that foster mutual love and affection. Notice that this is a mutual exchange, for marriage is an agreement between two people. Marriage is, consequently, a mutual offering of rights. This offering of himself by the groom to his bride and the offering of herself by the bride to her groom is the *matter* of the sacrament of matrimony.

From this it must follow that the *form* of the sacrament is the mutual acceptance of these rights by the bride and by the groom. Put another way, the giving of themselves to the other is the *matter,* the acceptance of this giving is the *form* of the sacrament.

Since the matter and the form of the sacrament can be provided only by the bride and groom, a number of conclusions follow immediately. First, it is incorrect, though we often speak in this way, to say that a couple "was married by" this or that priest, deacon, minister, or civil official. To be precise, a man and woman marry one another. The official who presides is only the public witness to the marriage which the bride and groom perform. Second, the giving and the receiving of marriage "vows" cannot be one-sided. Both partners in the marriage rite must express their offering and their acceptance. Of all the sacraments, marriage is the only one which needs a bilateral agreement between two human beings. Perhaps it is obvious that, if only one party actually expresses willingness to give and receive while the other does not, there is no marriage.

Although the Church customarily uses the terms "matter and form" to speak of the sacraments, the words can also be used of marriages which are not sacraments. What does this mean? Quite simply, the Church understands that true marriages occur between a man and a woman who are not baptized Christians. And, though such mutual agreements are true and valid marriages, binding the couple as long as both are alive, their marriage is not a sacrament. In studying the sacrament of baptism, we noted that one who is not baptized cannot receive any of the six other sacraments. Accordingly, those who are not baptized cannot receive the sacrament of matrimony. However, they marry truly if there are not obstacles to their marriage. The Church argues that marriage, whether it is a sacrament or not, is holy because God established this close and intimate arrangement for adult men and women. Moreover, Catholics firmly believe that such marriages are undertaken for life and that they cannot be dissolved except in very limited circumstances.

While it is obvious that Catholics who marry one another also receive the sacrament of marriage, the question can be asked: what if a Catholic marries someone who is not baptized? Indeed, the question should be slightly enlarged: what if a baptized Christian marries an unbaptized person? To be clear about these questions, one must acknowledge that the Protestant communions do not admit that marriage is a sacrament (since they do not acknowledge that there are such sacred rites called "sacraments"). But the Catholic, Orthodox, and Anglican communions believe that marriage is a sacrament as well as a binding agreement between a man and a woman. The Catholic Church, however, holds that the sacrament can be received only when both parties in a valid marriage are baptized, but both do not have to be Catholics. Even if only one of the spouses is a Catholic, or if neither is a Catholic, the sacrament of matrimony is received when both bride and groom have been validly baptized. We need to insist on this fact. When a baptized Lutheran marries a baptized Presbyterian, if their marriage is valid it is also a sacrament.

Note carefully that the law of the Catholic Church governing the ceremonies of a marriage bind only baptized Catholics who have not publicly foresworn or publicly abandoned the Church. Consequently, the man-made laws of the Church concerning marriage do not oblige those who are not Catholic. Of course, God's laws oblige everyone. The laws which the Church fashions for the public welfare of Catholics do not bind those who are not Catholic. This is particularly true regarding the celebration of marriages.

When, therefore, two baptized Christians who are not Catholic marry truly, their marriage is a sacrament. When two people who are not baptized marry truly, their marriage is not a sacrament. And when a baptized Christian (Catholic or otherwise) marries a non-baptized person, their marriage is not a sacrament.

The Catholic Church also believes that, when a baptized man and his baptized wife have sexual intercourse *following* their public marriage ceremony, they are bound by the sacrament of matrimony so firmly that no power on earth can dissolve their marriage. Under certain rare circumstances, however, the Church has the right to dissolve the marriage of a man and a woman who have contracted a sacramental marriage but who have not consummated their marriage by sexual intercourse. For example, a man once promised that he would not interfere with his Catholic fiancee's right to practice her Catholic religion and that he would allow children born of their marriage to be reared as Catholics. After the marriage rite, while still in the lobby of the Church, he affirmed that he had made these promises under duress and that he had no intention of abiding by his pledges. Then and there, the bride went with her parents to the rectory and informed the priest who had witnessed the marriage of this development. All agreed that the bride would totally avoid the company of the groom and that an appeal would be made to the local bishop for a dissolution of the marriage bond. Eventually this was obtained. Be careful to note that the bride and groom were united in marriage and that their marriage was a sacrament. But because it could be proven that they had not consummated their marriage with sexual relations, they were granted a "divorce" by the Church, more properly known as a "dissolution of the marriage bond." Both were then free to marry other spouses.

Pauline Privilege   At times, there are other incidents which allow the Church to grant divorces or
dissolutions of marriages. The most well-known of
these is the Pauline Privilege. Writing to one of the
early Christian communities which he had founded,
St. Paul has the following to say to the Christians of
Corinth, in Greece:

> If any brother has a wife who is an unbeliever but is willing to live
> with him, he must not divorce her. And if any woman has a hus-
> band who is an unbeliever but is willing to live with her, she must
> not divorce him. The unbelieving husband is consecrated by his
> believing wife; the unbelieving wife is consecrated by her believing
> husband. If it were otherwise, your children would be unclean; but
> as it is they are holy.
>
> If the unbeliever wishes to separate, however, let him do so. The
> believing husband or wife is not bound in such cases. God has
> called you to live in peace (I Cor. 7:12-15 NAB).

The Church's understanding of this passage,
known as "the Pauline Privilege," is the foundation for
the argument that the sacrament of matrimony is
received only by two baptized partners; and it is the
basis upon which the Church argues that only a sacramental marriage that is consummated after the rite of
marriage is forever unbreakable. According to the
Pauline Privilege the Church can dissolve a marriage
between two people neither of whom was baptized at
the time of their marriage. This can be done, however,
only when one party refuses to live with a spouse who
has become or who wants to become a practicing
Christian.

When the Pauline Privilege is invoked, it must be
clear that one member of the marriage has "departed,"
that is, will not live peaceably with the other spouse. If
this is shown, the believing partner may petition the
Church for a "divorce." When granted, the marriage
is dissolved at the time when the petitioner enters
a sacramental marriage, following that person's
baptism.

Petrine Privilege   An outgrowth of this ancient practice has come to be called the "Petrine Privilege." When two people, one of whom is baptized while the other is not, have been married, their marriage is a true marriage but it is not a sacramental union. Should their marriage dissolve, one or the other can become a Catholic and (in favor of a second marriage, this time to a Catholic), obtain from the Holy See a dissolution of the previous bond. The only difference between this privilege and the Pauline Privilege is that one of the partners in the original marriage was already baptized. Whether a petition is made for a Pauline or a Petrine Privilege, the petitioner must prove that the rights of the present spouse are not being violated.

Nullity   Apart from these privileges, the Church cannot annul an existing marriage bond (that is, it cannot grant a "divorce"). However, the Church often declares that what was thought to have been a marriage in fact is not a marriage. This pronouncement by the Church is called "a declaration of nullity," that is, a public pronouncement that, despite the marriage ceremony, no marriage in fact took place. When such a pronouncement is made, both parties to the invalid marriage are free, other conditions being fulfilled, to enter another marriage. Declarations of nullity can be given for any number of reasons. For example, if sexual intercourse is physically or psychologically impossible between this man and this woman–this is known as "impotency"–their marriage can be ruled as non-existing through a declaration of nullity. Sexual intercourse is one of the most important rights which are exchanged in the marriage ceremony. If sexual intercourse is impossible, whether for physical or psychological reasons, the Church will declare that no marriage exists. Of course, clear proof of impotency must be provided. Carefully to be noted is the difference between impotency and sterility. A man or woman who is sterile can have sexual relations but for any of a number of reasons is unable to beget a child. If either the husband or wife is sterile, the marriage is not prevented. No one can promise to have children at the time of marriage. What they do promise each other is the right to sexual intercourse suitably performed in the expectation that children will be conceived. Clearly, the Church has always rejoiced when a man lovingly marries a woman who is beyond the time of childbearing. To repeat, then, impotency renders a marriage null and void, despite the ceremony that was celebrated. Sterility does not render a marriage null and void.

Immaturity   In the contemporary world, many young people enter marriage without a full understanding of what they are doing. They lack that maturity without which one cannot be committed responsibly to another for life. With an increasing awareness of psychological obstacles to the full, mature consent that is necessary for true marriage, the Church has often granted declarations of nullity. In effect the Church says that there was no marriage between this man and woman because one or both could not maturely consent to an indissoluble marriage. Bishops of American dioceses and pastors of Catholic churches have, consequently, become more and more stringent about the requirements for Catholic weddings. A couple seeking to be married in a Catholic ceremony or in a ceremony which is approved by the Church, must demonstrate through a period of many months and with careful counseling from those who have experience in such matters, that they maturely seek to be married according to the Christian understanding of this sacrament.

Diriment impediments   The Church also acknowledges that there are many circumstances which make it impossible for a person to marry. Generally, these circumstances are called "diriment impediments"

(Latin: *dirimere,* "to destroy" or "to prevent"). These impediments are established by the law of the Church. For example, when a man is ordained to the diaconate, any attempt by him to marry is null and void. (Permanent deacons can be married before they are ordained to the diaconate. If a deacon's wife dies, he may not remarry.) A diriment impediment prevents the marriage of those in holy orders. When, as another example, a man or woman takes perpetual vows in a religious order or congregation that is approved by the Holy See, a diriment impediment to marriage is an effect of the profession of vows. Or when, as still another example, a man or woman brings about the death of a person's spouse in order to marry the surviving partner of that marriage, their attempted marriage is rendered null by a diriment impediment. Moreover, the Church has always taught that no one can marry a person who is related by blood (related by "consanguinity") in the direct line. For example, a son cannot marry his mother. Those related by blood in the indirect line can never marry in the first or second degree of that line. Therefore, you cannot marry your sister or brother because you are related to him or to her in the first degree of the indirect line. (The line of relationship is called "indirect" because one must find common ancestors who give rise to the relationship; you are, then, related to your brother or your sister through your parents and not by your brother or sister's direct descent from you.) And you cannot marry your first cousin because a first cousin is related in the second degree of the indirect line. In fact, the general law of the Church places a diriment impediment on second and third cousins. However, a dispensation from this impediment for third cousins will be granted when serious reasons are given in the petition for a dispensation. Even second cousins can be allowed by the Church to marry validly, but the reasons must be more serious still and proof must be offered that no second cousins from whom either of the parties descends have been married for several generations.

Affinity Another kind of relationship which bars the marriages of Catholics is *affinity*. Those related by affinity have an "in-law" relationship. Thus, an adopted daughter can never marry her stepfather. Stepbrothers, moreover, cannot marry their stepsisters if they are legally related by adoption. Nor can those who are first cousins by reason of adoption validly marry. Perhaps it goes without saying that a stepmother can never marry her stepson (since, as has been said, affinity is a diriment impediment to marriage in every degree of the direct line).

Many marital unions are called "mixed marriages" The description applies to marriages between two baptized Christians, one of whom is a practicing Catholic while the other is Orthodox, Anglican, or Protestant. When such marriages are contemplated, permission must be sought from the bishop of the diocese where the Catholic dwells. These permissions are readily given so long as the Catholic partner declares that he or she will continue in the practice of Catholicism and will strive to rear in the Catholic faith all of the children born to the marriage. The other partner to the forthcoming marriage must be informed that these promises have been made so that he or she is certain about the obligations which the Catholic has assumed. Mixed marriages may be celebrated in churches which are not Catholic, so long as permission has been granted by the bishop of the diocese. And the public witness to such mixed marriages may be a minister of religion who is not Catholic, again with the consent of the local bishop.

When a man and a woman marry in Christ, receiving the sacrament of matrimony or, more properly, bestowing it on one another, they receive special graces for the work which they set out to do. They commit themselves irrevocably to one another, and thereafter practice patience and forgiveness, gentleness and kindness, without selfishness or self-seeking; inevitably, they will grow in their love for one another and together they will grow in their love of God. Marriage is truly a mystery, that is, it is a work which two individuals accomplish because God is working with them secretly, intimately. Being generous to one another, being loving, they will achieve that happiness which, though never perfect in this life, engenders peace in their home and in their circle of friends. Growing older, they will naturally think more often about the end of this life and, if truly in love with each other, will support each other in the knowledge that they are preparing for a life of eternal happiness and joy with Almighty God—the Third and Silent Partner in their marriage.

Thinking it over • • •

1. Who were the priests in the Jewish religion? Why are there no longer Jewish priests?

2. Can we say correctly that Jesus is a human person? Explain your answer.

3. What did Martin Luther teach about the Mass or Eucharistic sacrifice?

4. The Council of Trent affirmed that there is a visible, external priesthood. What did it teach about this priesthood?

5. Since the sacrament of holy orders imprints a character on the soul of the man ordained, can he lose the power which this sacrament gives? Explain.

6. Give some examples of ways in which a man is attracted to the priesthood.

7. Why do some people hope that women will be ordained by the Catholic Church? Why does the Church teach that women cannot be ordained?

8. What four conditions must a candidate fulfill if he is licitly to receive the sacrament of holy orders?

9. Name five impediments which prohibit a man from being ordained.

10. Explain what Jesus did at the marriage feast of Cana.

11. To what does St. Paul compare the marriage of a man and woman?

12. Does the Catholic Church acknowledge that those who are not Catholic can truly marry? Explain.

13. What is the *matter* and what is the *form* of the sacrament of matrimony?

14. What if a Catholic marries someone who is not baptized? Do they receive the sacrament of matrimony? Does only the Catholic receive the sacrament? Why?

15. Do the man-made laws of the Church which oblige Catholics who are going to be married also obligate those who are not Catholic? Explain.

16. If a marriage can never be dissolved, what two conditions must be fulfilled?

17. What is a "declaration of nullity"? Give some examples.

18. What is the difference between impotency and sterility? How do these affect the validity of a marriage?

19. What is a diriment impediment? Give some examples.

20. What is a "mixed marriage"? What does the Church ask of those who are planning a mixed marriage?

Chapter 6

SACRAMENTALS

To complete our study of the sacramental life of the Church, we now consider *sacramentals*. Sacramentals resemble sacraments in that they use material objects and prayers to bring us God's grace. Sacramentals are instituted by the Church whereas the sacraments are instituted by Christ himself. Sacramentals are part of the Church's life of prayer, and they effect God's grace in us beyond the power of personal prayer. In general, there are two categories of sacramentals: *blessings* and *sacramental objects.*

Blessings   Blessings are first among the Church's sacramentals. We bless persons, meals, objects, and places. The purpose of all blessings is to praise God for his benefits to us and to pray for his gifts and grace. When blessing humans, the Church gives praise to God for that person or group and asks God to make them holy and fill them with his grace. When blessing objects or places, blessings are administered "with a view to the people who use the objects to be blessed and who frequent the places to be blessed" [*Book of Blessings,* #12]. Obviously, the purpose of all blessings is to sanctify God's people and bring them his grace.

The Church has published the *Book of Blessings* which contains the official blessings for a variety of persons and objects. A brief look at the six main parts of the book gives us an idea of the many kinds of blessings that the Church bestows. Part One contains blessings of persons in a variety of situations and circumstances, for example: families, engaged couples, married couples, students and teachers, even victims of crime. Part Two contains blessings of buildings and different human activities, for example: homes, automobiles, animals, tools, and athletic events. Part Three includes blessings of objects that are used in churches, such as: bells, baptismal fonts, lecterns, organs, and sacred vestments and vessels. Part Four has blessings for religious articles such as rosaries, prayer books, and medals. Part Five offers blessings related to seasons and feasts of the liturgical year, for example: Advent wreaths, nativity scenes, candles on Candlemas Day, throats on St. Blaise Day, and ashes on Ash Wednesday. Lastly, Part Six provides blessings of people who have special ministries in the Church such as lectors, cantors, altar servers, parish council members, etc. Thankfully, the Church blesses people and the many things people use with the intent of sanctifying their endeavors and bringing them closer to God.

Sacramental objects   People are sensate beings. We use our senses of sight, hearing, smell, taste, and touch to experience the world around us. Senses heighten our experiences and make them more memorable. Therefore, the Church uses sacred objects that appeal to one or more of our senses, helping us to elevate our minds and hearts toward God. The Church gives us these sacramentals in the hope of helping us become closer to God and to bring us his grace. Some examples of sacramental objects are: holy water, statues of Christ and the saints, incense, crucifixes, candles, scapulars, rosaries, holy cards or prayer cards, icons, medals, palms, ashes, and blessed foods.

When using blessings and sacramental objects, we must be careful not to view them as good luck charms or magical spells. Believers in these superstitions erroneously think that the charms and spells carry magical powers of their own. Rather, the efficacy of sacramentals comes from the grace of God working through the people who receive and use them in good faith. For the non-believer, blessings and sacred objects remain just what one sees on the surface. But for the believer, these blessings and objects lead one closer to God.

EPILOGUE
THE FOUR LAST THINGS

And at last there will be but four things:
death, judgment, heaven and hell.

DEATH

People seldom think about death, especially those who are young and healthy. The young rarely even participate in an experience of death unless an elderly grandparent dies or, on some occasions, a peer, another youth, is killed suddenly and accidentally. To think fearfully about death too often would be morbid, yet to ignore it would be foolish. For the most crucial time of life is its end. Death for each of us is an inevitable fact which we must face.

What is death? Negatively speaking, it is the termination of life. We should, then, ask: What is the meaning of life, when does it end, and what can we know of an afterlife?

We say that someone or something is animated. We mean lively or full of life. The word itself comes from a Latin word *anima,* meaning soul or spirit. "Psychology," the study of life, comes from the Greek *psyche,* meaning soul or life. This soul, or spirit, is the principle of all our vital functions. The human body is highly intricate, complex, and organized. A principle of organization is necessary to keep it going, just as a source of power is needed to keep a machine going. The difference between a living body and a dead body is obvious, especially to someone who has known a living person and then sees him dead and lying in a casket. The dead person looks similar to the one who lived, but something is missing. The principle of life has gone and soon, without that principle, the body will disintegrate, will come apart. Thus, it is silly to argue about the existence of the human soul or spirit as a vital principle. For it is either present or absent. As St. Ambrose in the fourth century very simply said, "Death is the separation of soul and body."

It is not always easy to determine precisely when this separation occurs, especially in a sudden death or the death of a young person who has been ill only a short time. The quick taking of a pulse, listening for a heartbeat, and looking for a sign of breathing are not sufficient for certitude. People may lie in a coma and show only weak life signs or none. The latter may have been the case when the synagogue leader called Jesus because his daughter was apparently dead, for when Jesus went to the ruler's house, he declared ". . . The girl is not dead, but sleeping!" And he lifted her up (Mt. 9:25). In the raising of Lazarus, there is surely a resurrection accomplished by Jesus, because Lazarus was already in the tomb, causing Martha, his sister, to say, "Lord, by this time there will be an odor, for he has been dead for four days" (Jn. 11:39). Jesus had already reminded her, "I am the resurrection and the life."

Often we read accounts of people who said they came back from the dead and who describe their passage graphically. They probably had been comatose; those who are very ill are subject to illusions, unable to distinguish fantasy or images from reality. For there are some definite indications of the fact of death which are more reliable than such accounts of "dying" and returning to life.

A prominent professor of medical ethics, Fr. Charles McFadden, O.S.A., describes a gradual progression in death: from loss of blood circulation and consciousness, to the dying of brain cells, to permanent cessation of brain function which is called "brain death." This progression takes approximately fifteen minutes. Even after such death, a priest may give conditional absolution (on the necessary condition that one is sorry for sin and desires union with God).

We instinctively consider an afterlife. We can imagine our eventual death and funeral, but not an end to our existence. Belief in an afterlife has been common throughout history. The Egyptians, for example, buried foodstuff and even slaves within the tomb to serve the deceased in the next life.

Death is an inherited punishment for original sin. Even without that legacy, Christ submitted to death to share more fully in our humanity. But he rose from death, and in his resurrection is the promise of ours. During his preaching of the kingdom he often spoke of life after death and warned us to be prepared for our judgment.

As Fr. Albert Nevins points out in his book *Life after Death:* "Death marks the end of our probation or trial. At the moment of death each one of us has already decided whether he or she belongs to Christ or Adam. Once death comes, we no longer have choices. Each one of us receives our recompense, as Paul tells us, 'according to his life in the body (2 Cor. 5:10 NAB).'" As the old expression goes, "As you live, so shall you die."

JUDGMENT

People often speak of "accountability," implying a responsibility for fulfilling obligations, either personal or corporate. We inevitably must face some judgment for that fulfillment, in our work and in our lives. A student is well aware of this when he receives his grades.

Each one of us is responsible for moral development—or corruption—because we have been given the gift of free choice. Your present character results from your deliberate choices in the past. Every person will be held accountable and will face an ultimate judgment after death which will determine his eternal life. That the good are rewarded and the evil punished is a fact of life and of afterlife. Do we finally accept Christ or reject him? St. Paul speaks simply and clearly on this point:

"We must all appear before the judgment seat of Christ so that each one may receive good or evil, according to what he has done in the body" (2 Cor. 5:10).

We recall the promise Jesus made to the repentant thief crucified with him (Luke 23:43), the desire of St. Paul to be "away from the body and at home with the Lord," (2 Cor. 5:8) the warning that Christ would come to us as unexpectedly as a thief (Mt. 24:43-44), and many of the parables about the sudden appearance of the master and how we should always be prepared for the coming of Our Lord. Again, St. Paul states bluntly, "It is appointed that men die once, and after death be judged" (Heb. 9:27 NAB).

We do not live our lives as isolated individuals. We live together in a society. We interact with others: with members of our family, with fellow students, with relatives and friends and companions, with classmates and teammates and co-workers. By nature, we are social, and just as we have personal responsibilities and obligations, we also have duties toward each other. We affect and influence one another. Our personal actions may have far-reaching effects. Every human action is like a stone dropped in water, causing rippling effects in ever-widening concentric circles, extending beyond the limits of our immediate surroundings and beyond a single point in time.

Jesus speaks to us not only of a personal accounting and judgment after our death, but also of a general judgment when he comes at the end of time:

The Church firmly believes and teaches that each person will be re-united, body and soul, and that he will appear before Christ in his body to be judged according to his own deeds.

> When the Son of man comes in his glory, and all the angels with him, then he will sit on his glorious throne. Before him will be gathered all the nations, and he will separate them one from another as a shepherd separates the sheep from the goats, and he

will place the sheep at his right hand, but the goats at the left. Then the king will say to those at his right hand, "Come, O blessed of my Father, inherit the kingdom prepared for you from the foundation of the world."

–Mt. 25:31-34

He then describes the works of a good person: feeding the hungry, giving drink to the thirsty, welcoming a stranger, clothing the naked, visiting the sick and those in prison. He identifies himself with such needy people, "As you did it to one of the least of my brethren, you did it to me." (Mt. 25:40) Those on his left he will accuse of not doing these acts of charity and neglecting those in need. Matthew concludes this passage, "And they will go away into eternal punishment, but the righteous into eternal life" (Mt. 25:46).

Christ, therefore, teaches that he will come again and will make a final judgment of both the living and the dead. We profess our belief in this teaching of Jesus every Sunday when we recite our profession of faith, saying, "He will come again in glory to judge the living and the dead." This is from the Nicene Creed, composed in the fourth century. In the Apostles Creed, composed much earlier, we also say, "He will come again to judge the living and the dead."

To sum up: we are responsible for what we freely choose to do, and we shall be held accountable at the end of our life and at the end of time.

HEAVEN

We become so absorbed in this world—with all its desires and pleasures, frustrations and sorrows, the struggle for temporary success and achievement—that we forget that this world is not all there is, that this life is temporary and limited, whereas our afterlife is eternal and forever. In reciting our creed we profess our belief in heaven and hell; yet, we seldom think of those states of life that are our inevitable options. Why is that so?

Part of the problem is the popular image of heaven: an ethereal atmosphere where winged creatures sit on clouds and play harps. Even the correct Catholic concept of the beatific vision gets awfully distorted. The imagination deceives us again as we vainly construct a huge theatre, brightly lighted, with God on the stage and the spectators staring at him. The problem is that we cannot *imagine* heaven, or hell, at all. We can only conceive these states or conditions as ideas developed from our personal experiences.

We have no experience of heaven, either directly or indirectly through a report from anyone there. St. Paul, usually so verbal about his belief, is speechless when he comes to a reference to our everlasting joy when we are united with Jesus in the life to come. He can only say, quoting Isaiah, "Eye has not seen, ear has not heard, / nor has it so much as dawned on man / what God has prepared for those who love him" (1 Cor. 2:9 NAB). St. John also acknowledges the limits of human description, saying, "Beloved, we are God's children now; it does not yet appear what we shall be, but we know that when he appears we shall be like him, for we shall see him as he is" (1 Jn. 3:2).

Notice that John, in referring to the glory we will experience in the kingdom of heaven, centers on the act of "seeing." St. Paul does too: "For now we see in a mirror dimly, but then face to face" (1 Cor. 13:12). Thus, we speak of the *beatific vision,* a seeing that makes us happy—seeing God as he is and being like him in that we share in his glory. Heaven, then, is a state or condition of supreme happiness, the ultimate goal desired by all mankind. We see God now as "in a mirror" because we see the reflection of God in nature or experience his workings in our soul, the created effects of his own beauty and goodness. But, in heaven, we see him immediately or intuitively and directly.

The central and primary joy of heaven is the ecstatic union with God, seeing God face to face, participating in his infinite and eternal joy. But with this joy will be a happy union with all those who have been saved and reunion with family and friends. Even our bodies, glorified and no longer subject to death and disease, will share in this beatitude. For, as Jesus Christ rose from the dead to a new and glorious life, so too shall we; his resurrection is the promise of our own. And, just as his resurrection was bodily, our bodies too will rise and be re-united with our souls. Our whole human nature, body and soul, will be bathed in the divine radiance and transfigured. And we shall see in our eternal bliss the fruition of all the good things of our life on earth: the sacraments, our listening to the word of God, all our good deeds carried out in God's grace. So heaven should be our goal and purpose even now; we should not think of heaven as something strange and remote and far away.

Perhaps our best approach to understanding the nature of heaven is to reflect on our own experience of happiness here on earth. Think back to the happiest times of your life. Everyone has had a few such moments, times of utter joy, no matter how briefly or how seldom. Then, magnify that moment infinitely, without the limitations of time or attendant circumstances. Enhance it, and extend it into everlasting bliss. That is the closest we can get to appreciate what heaven is like.

In concluding his own comments on heaven, Fr. Nevins writes:

> What each must understand is that earth is only a place of pilgrimage and that heaven is our native land, destined by God to those who serve him. We have no lasting cities on earth, but we do have a home that will endure for all eternity awaiting us at the end of this life. So we live now in hope and expectation, awaiting at the end of our days that invitation of Jesus: "Come, you have my Father's blessing! Inherit the kingdom prepared for you from the creation of the world" (Mt. 25:34).

> *–Life after Death,* pp. 56-57

HELL

Catholics who have no other problems with their belief will often say, "But I don't believe in hell." What they really do not believe in is their images of hell, and that is one of the difficulties here—imagination. The very word "hell" (*sheol* in Hebrew or *hades* in Greek) simply means "the abode of the dead." In the Apostles Creed, we express our belief that, after his resurrection, Christ "descended into hell." Here it does not mean a place for the damned, but where the saved awaited the opening of heaven after the redemptive sacrifice of Jesus was offered.

We cannot dismiss the word "hell" or what it means. Jesus often speaks of it (the word is used more than twenty times in the New Testament alone), and Our Lord does so in reference to a state of punishment. We do not even like the word "punishment," but if we accept the notion of rewarding good persons for their lives of virtue, why do we disregard the deserved punishment of bad people for lives of vice? But a good God, we may protest, would never reject or damn anyone. That is true. He does not. But some people may choose to reject *him,* and thus damn themselves. No one, no matter how often he has fallen into sin in this life, will be turned away by Christ as long as he ultimately turns to God, the source of all goodness and love. God is merciful, but he is also just. The balance of justice is never achieved in this life. That can only be accomplished in the life to come.

The nature of that punishment is not made explicit. The word "fire" is used in the Scriptures, even by Jesus himself. This is the most painful sensation known to mankind; yet, eternal punishment, like eternal reward, is the experience of the spirit. As the beatific vision is the source of our ultimate and everlasting joy, so the loss of this sight of God is the ultimate pain that a person can suffer.

We become ignorant victims of our own passive imagination and the creative imagination of poets and artists. Dante graphically described the fires of hell and tiers (or levels) of the damned. The artists of the period put his ugly scene on canvas and generations of the faithful, forever after, have been affected by these artistic extravagances.

The Church has never officially defined the nature of hell, except as separation from God. In fact, only two dogmas of the Church concern this subject. What has been clearly defined are two propositions:

1. The punishment of hell is unending (to correct an erroneous position held by Origen and a few other teachers);

2. The unconverted sinner faces the pains of hell immediately after death (not after the Last Judgment, as some had thought).

We can be sure that some people are in heaven: Jesus, Mary, the canonized saints, and many more, including we hope, our deceased loved ones. Whether anyone is in hell, or not, we do not know. For we do not know the spiritual condition of anyone who dies. Only God knows. Sometimes parents worry about their children, saying they have lost their faith. Usually they mean that a son or daughter is no longer practicing his or her faith in worship or in following the moral rules (and frequently these two defects go together). But a real loss of faith is a rejection of God, and even if such a profession is made, we cannot be sure that such an attitude is held internally by the person—and if so, does that disposition remain until death?

As for numbers of the saved or the damned, there is a disturbing passage recorded in the gospel of St. Matthew:

"Enter by the narrow gate," Jesus advises us, "for the gate is wide and the way is easy, that leads to destruction, and those who enter by it are many. For the gate is narrow and the way is hard, that leads to life, and those who find it are few."

–Mt. 7:13-14

That sounds as if there are few who are faithful and many who are not. Surely, that is true in life, but we never know what happens at the end of life. Consider the case of St. Dismas, "the good thief," who was promised a place in paradise with Jesus—and this was just before death because he was repentant. Perhaps, many others are so fortunate. But, as St. Antoninus once wrote, "God promises us his mercy, but he doesn't promise us tomorrow."

Ultimately we choose heaven or hell. The Church teaches, however, on the basis of scriptural texts, that if we die in God's friendship while still in need of further penance and purification, this is achieved in what is called "purgatory." Purgatory is a work of God's mercy, for no one stained with sin can enter God's presence. It is, so to speak, a chance to clean up so that we can be admitted to the eternal banquet.

The Church teaches also that by our prayers we can hasten the progress of souls through purgatory to everlasting happiness. Hence we should not be careless about praying for those who have died, especially those known and dear to us.

Angelo Roncalli (later Pope John XXIII) committed to memory during his youth a quatrain entitled *Four Future Things*. It remained a motto throughout his life:

Death, than which nothing is more certain.
Judgment, than which nothing is more strict.
Hell, than which nothing is more terrible.
Heaven, than which nothing is more delightful.

Everyone should keep these four lines in his memory as a motivation in living the Christian faith.

Thinking it over • • •

1. Can you think of some English words, often used, which are derived from the Latin and Greek words for "spirit" or "soul"?

2. How can we be sure that Lazarus was really raised from death by Jesus?

3. What is the final phase of biological death? How long may the death process take?

4. Why is there any need of a general judgment at the end of time when Jesus comes again?

5. In what two ancient creeds, or professions of faith, do Christians express their belief in the second coming of Christ and the general judgment?

6. Why do St. John and St. Paul have difficulties in describing the joy of heaven?

7. What is meant by the "beatific vision"?

8. How can we best approach an understanding of what heaven is like?

9. Does the Bible say anything about hell?

10. What is the source of the principal pain of hell?

11. Penance is a means of purifying, either in this life by accepting our hardships, or in the life to come. What do we call that state of purification still needed by those who die and are not deserving of an eternal punishment? How can we help such souls who can no longer help themselves?

12. Can you remember the quatrain called *Four Future Things*?

INDEX

tion, 244, of Eucharist, 255 FF., of reconciliation, 267, of anointing of sick, 279, of matrimony, 304 FF.

Galilee, 79, 81, 96, 155
Garden of Gethsemane, 28, 65
Genesis, 122, 172
Gentiles, 57
Gifts, 11, 51, 283
Glory (Exaltation) 58, 82-3, 85, 323-4
God, 2, 7, God-Man, 9, son of, 14, prescience, 16, love and mercy of, 53, dwelling among men, 167
Gospel, presentation, 104
Grace, 3, 28, 48, fullness of, 99
Gregory The Great, St., 272
Grievous (mortal) sin, 270

Harrington, Fr. Wilfred, 40, 49, 52
Hatred, world's, 63
Heaven, 324
Hell, 327
Heresy, 136
Herod, 69, 71, 155
Hierarchical, 130
Holy Communion, 259
Holy Orders, 285, three degrees, 288, bishops, 289, priests, 289, deacons, 289
Holy Spirit, 3, 11, 18, 56, 62, 63, 64, 82, 93, 96
Holy Spirit, role of, 209
Holy Trinity, 8, 10, 62, 98
Humanity of Jesus, 19
Human Nature, 9, human and divine natures, 9, defects of, 24
Hypostatic Union, 9

Image, or metaphors of the Church, 143, 144, Church in old and new covenants, 147, FF., metaphor and similar terms, 149, Church as Christ's spouse, 169
Imagery, of kingdom, 52, Matthew/body of Christ, 127
Immersion, 233
Impediments, 295 FF., 310 FF.

Impotency, 309
Incarnation, 8, 10, 11, 89
Indefectibility, 210
Indulgences, 276
Infallibility, 3, of the church, 205
Irenaeus, St., 116
Isaac, 149
Isaiah, 34

Jacob, 151
Jairus, 16, 32
Jeremiah, 5, 68, 189
Jerusalem, 78, 82, 106, 286, fall of, 66
Jesus Christ (see Christ)
Jews, 10, 46, 48, pious, 52, 57, 59, modern, 72, 104, 221
John, St. (Apostle), 8, 12, 62, 75
John The Baptist, 4, 12, 153, 154
Joseph, St., 27, 108
Joshua, 10, 150
Judaism, 124
Judas, 65, 68
Judgment, 46, last, 127, 322
Judgment, general, 322
Jurisdiction, 177
Justin, St., 253

Keys, to kingdom of heaven, 5
Kingdom, admittance, 38, parables of, 38, 46 FF., 47, at hand, 49, images, 52, Old Testament promises and prophecies, 150, development of the, 151, meanings of, 156, in summary, 162
Knowledge, 26 FF., kinds in/Christ, 26, infused, 26, acquired, 27, intuitive, 30, human, 107, divine, 107

Last Supper, 15, 55, 82
Lay People, 207 FF.
Lazarus, 16, 32, 321
Leaders, necessity of, 191
Leaven, 42, 160
Licitly, 226
Liturgy, The, 183, of Eucharist, 256 FF.
Liturgy, introduction to sacraments, 215, who celebrates, 216, how, when, where celebrated, 217, 218